From Queer to Eternity

From Queer to Eternity

Spirituality in the Lives of Lesbian, Gay and Bisexual People

Peter Sweasey

CASSELL

London and Washington

For a catalogue of related titles
in our Sexual Politics/Global Issues list
please write to us at an address below

Cassell
Wellington House
125 Strand
London WC2R 0BB

PO Box 605
Herndon
Virginia 20172

First published 1997

British Library Cataloguing in Publication Data

A catalogue record for this book is available from the British Library.

Library of Congress Cataloging-in-Publication Data

Sweasey, Peter.
   From queer to eternity : spirituality in the lives of lesbian, gay and
bisexual people / Peter Sweasey.
      p.   cm.
   Includes bibliographical references and index.
   ISBN 0–304–33551–7 (hardcover).—ISBN 0–304–33552–5 (pbk.)
   1. Gays—Religious life.   I. Title.
BL65.H64S94   1997
291.1'7835766—dc21   97–609
                                                                                   CIP

ISBN 0 304 33552 5 (paperback)

Designed and typeset by Ben Cracknell Studios
Printed and bound in Great Britain by Biddles Ltd, Guildford and
King's Lynn

Contents

For my parents, Diana and Denis,
and for Chris,
with love and gratitude

Acknowledgements

It's a genuine pleasure to thank the many people who have, in various ways, made this project possible.

The research that forms the basis of the book was generously funded by the Joseph Rowntree Charitable Trust. The Trustees are all Quakers, just as Joseph Rowntree himself was (although the Trust is not part of the Religious Society of Friends). At a time when many religions still view homosexuality as a sin, an irritant or an embarrassment, Quakers stand out in their genuine (and typically radical) concern for the spiritual needs of lesbian, gay and bisexual people. They are also, uniquely, prepared to put their money where their mouth is. This research would be thinner, and have taken far longer, without the grant the Joseph Rowntree Charitable Trust gave me. They have been consistently helpful, and, needless to say, made no stipulations as to what the results should be.

This book would not exist without the contributions of the hundred or so people who told me about the role of spirituality in their lives. Most of them can be found on the following pages. I am grateful to everyone who told a complete stranger intimate details of their lives, and then allowed me to share these with a reading public. Many people went way beyond the call of duty and showed me great hospitality as well. Unfortunately, in a book of this length, there is space to include only a mere fraction of the wise and wonderful stories and opinions that I collected; but *everything* that was contributed, by *everyone* who was involved, was of immense value in shaping the book, and has somehow been weaved into the overall tapestry.

I am indebted to Steve Cook, my commissioning editor at Cassell, who shared my vision for this project from the beginning, and took a chance on me being able to carry it out. His successor, Roz Hopkins, continued the admirable policy of leaving me to my own devices.

Chris Marsh brought his extraordinary mind to bear to the first draft, which led to considerable improvements. I love him dearly – and would any of this have been the same without 7 April 1995? Paul Keene, another much-loved friend, also challenged me into writing a better book, with his detailed scrutiny of the text – and his endless questioning. A number of other people took the time and effort to read through this book (or chapters of it) in its earlier incarnations, and came up with numerous valuable and constructive suggestions: Elizabeth Stuart, Catherine Hopper, Michael Seán Paterson, Fernando Guasch, Bruce Kinsey, Mark Solomon, Dirk de Klerk, Lee Adams and Glenn Palmer. Bernard Lynch managed to make some crucial amendments despite being on the other side of the Atlantic at the time. While he does not entirely agree with the book's style or conclusions, he has none the less allowed his words to appear in this context: I am grateful to his generous spirit.

When the book's theories were still in their formative stages I was stimulated by discussions with various groups: members of the Edward Carpenter Community, the 3F group, the CARA community, and students in Oxford and Cambridge. Many other people have helped by sharing ideas, alerting me to material, putting me in touch with other people, or being supportive friends (and often, all of the above). Some of them were thoroughly sceptical about the subject matter, but indulged me anyway. Acknowledging that there are bound to be some omissions, I'd still like to thank: Tim Robertson, Douglas Brown, Abigail Reynolds, Mark Miodownik, Matthew Beaumont, Matthew Sweet, Tory Fea, Hania Porucznik, David James, Nick Thorpe, David Bond, the Order of Perpetual Indulgence, John Dray, John Warner, Ann Peart, Mary Loudon and Alison Webster. I send my love to all members of the Millport family. I thank Stephen Lodge and Laurence Davis, with love and regret.

In the past, when I have read the acknowledgements in other people's books – those protestations about how other people had rescued them from countless errors – I've wondered how many mistakes it was possible to make in a single manuscript. I have found out the hard way: many of the people listed above are my saviours. And I now know why it is so important to conclude by saying: the mistakes and faults that remain are mine.

Introduction

Torment, secrecy, conflict, misery and shame. Wherever you look – a movie like *Priest*, or faggots and fundamentalists shouting each other down on *Oprah* and *Ricki* and the rest, or tabloid tales of pervert priests in sex scandals, or broadsheet pontification about outed bishops and the Church being torn apart, or patronizing documentaries – the message seems clear: homosexuality plus religion can only equal bad news. And yet, for a large number of lesbian, gay and bisexual people, both spirituality and sexuality are sources of joy and strength. The book that follows attempts to redress the imbalance, by letting their voices be heard.

Although all the people collected here identify as spiritual, none of them is unhappy about their sexuality. You will not find, amongst these pages, any bishops with grey areas, nor 'gin and sin' Anglo-Catholics who feel that homosexuality is their cross to bear. Nor will you find the fundamentalist Christian I heard about, who goes to gay nightclubs, but goes no further than cuddling. This isn't a book about 'religiosity', nor, except tangentially, about religious institutions or religious homophobia: it's about spirituality. This isn't a book about homosexuals, nor about what religions think of 'homosexual acts': it's about out and proud lesbians, gay men and bisexuals.

I do not offer any defence of homosexuality, because it needs no defence. My starting point is that homosexuality is as valid as heterosexuality. (If this isn't yours, there are other books you need to read.[1]) Most books published on homosexuality and religion (the vast majority of which are intended for Christian readers) are arguments against religious homophobia, and attempts to minimize the damage which has been inflicted by certain religions upon so many lesbian, gay and bisexual people. This is crucial work. But while, politically, we must never cease from attacking homophobia, we cannot spend all of our lives in opposition, reacting to criticism. We should be spending the majority of our time and energy on our own lives – including our own spirituality. This book moves off the defensive: in these pages, we are talking amongst ourselves, not justifying ourselves to hostile critics. *From Queer to Eternity* also aims to broaden the debate from the particular problems of the Christian Church which – for the majority of us, who are not Christian – are ultimately of limited interest: whereas spirituality, this book suggests, is a universal concern.

From Queer to Eternity is not a work of academic theory, still less of theology, and it is not an empirical, or statistically derived, study. Above all, it is a collection of lesbian, gay and bisexual people's experiences and opinions; a witness to *our* truth.

WHO'S IN THE BOOK?

Over one hundred people were involved in the research. Some of these responded to requests, in the lesbian and gay press, various newsletters, or on noticeboards. Others I contacted through organizations like the Jewish Gay and Lesbian Group, the Lesbian and Gay Christian Movement and Hoblink (a network for queer Pagans). The majority of the words quoted in the text have been extracted from taped interviews. Other people contributed by writing to me, sometimes at length. Though I have tried to represent some of the diversity of queer belief, a book this length cannot hope to be comprehensive: there are many more stories that could and should be told. The contributors were all living in the UK at the time of the research, and most of them were born in this country. I was particularly keen to allow British voices be heard: the wealth of excellent material about American experience depends upon a culture that is sometimes very different.

Except where I have quoted from previously published material, everyone in this book has approved their words being used here: contributors had complete power of veto. It does not necessarily follow that they would approve of my overall arguments. People's words inevitably appear out of context: out of the context of a discussion which lasted several hours, or a long correspondence; out of the context of a carefully formulated and expressed system of belief; out of the context of their lives. Spirituality and sexuality can both be, at times, beyond language, beyond quantification, even beyond human comprehension: the contributors to this book are remarkably articulate, but I am sure many of them would want to qualify their opinions by stressing how both words and concepts can falsify the reality they have attempted to address. I don't think anyone in this book would want the words that appear here to be taken as their conclusive position on the subject. For many lesbian, gay and bisexual people, religious belief is not a final destination but a journey: some of the people in this book would not express themselves in exactly the same way now as they did when they contributed, but that does not make the opinions collected here any less valid. These are snapshots of people's lives, not comprehensive biographies.

Most people appear in this book using their own names. A few have chosen to be identified by their first name (or in one case, by initials) only. Only the following are pseudonyms: Ben Stevens, David Allen, Carol,

Simon, Joseph, Dylan, Diana Reynolds, Dennis Fraser, Eric Bond, Jacqueline, Kauldip Singh, Rupi and Peter Wyles. Most, but not all, of the works cited in the text are by queer authors.

All the contributors self-identified as spiritual or religious. To define spirituality, let alone maintain that there is an 'essence' common to all religions, is way beyond my scope, and my capability (although some indication of how this book uses those terms will be given in the first chapter). Spirituality can be a very broad term indeed; not everything that may be called spiritual is included here. None the less, some very diverse understandings of the word rub shoulders in these pages. It would be impossible to maintain all of them at the same time. I haven't attempted to homogenize them, nor assess whether they make objective sense. The people in this book give very clear accounts of why they believe what they do, and how spirituality is a positive force in their lives, but I don't ask them to 'defend' their beliefs against every possible scientific and philosophical objection. Instead, they offer a defence against the criticisms that queer people are most likely to come up with. This book doesn't want to convert you to any particular belief: it might, perhaps, convince you that there is no incompatibility between spirituality and our sexual orientation, that there may even be reasons why spirituality is more likely to figure in our lives, and it's no bad thing for our sexual identity if it does.

I have not attempted to ensure 'proportional representation', nor equal space, for all the faiths that are included. There is sometimes a bias towards notions that come from the Judeo-Christian tradition: this reflects the fact that Christianity in particular has defined, for Western culture, what we think religion is and does, and it is often these dominant assumptions that are my starting point. Also, not surprisingly in a nominally Christian land, more contributors come from that background than any other.

WHO ISN'T IN THE BOOK?

Islam and the Baha'i faith are not represented in this study. Despite persistent attempts I failed to find anyone from those traditions who met my criteria of both accepting their sexuality unreservedly as a good thing – and as equal with heterosexuality – while continuing to practise their religion. There are many lesbians and gay men from Muslim and Baha'i families who left their faith behind when they came out. Other homosexual Muslims and Baha'is see their sexual orientation as a trial sent by God, and hope to be forgiven for their failing, or try to be celibate. There are fundamentalist Christians who follow the same line, and who are also excluded from this research. But the hard line taken by some of its sects

(Jehovah's Witnesses, Mormons, Christian Scientists and Baptists, for instance) does not prevent Christianity being well represented in this book; whereas, despite the fact that Islam and the Baha'i faith are major world religions, I have come across no branches sufficiently liberal to justify inclusion here.

The situation of homosexual Muslims and, to some extent, Baha'is in the UK is heavily intertwined with ethnic, cultural and racial issues. As a white observer I stand very much outside these, and would perhaps not be able to do necessary justice to their specific complexities. The pressure not to break rank with your ethnic community, which may be your chief defence in a racist nation, could have discouraged potential contributors from coming forward.

There is also a theological barrier imposed by these faiths: their scriptures claim to have been written down exactly as Muhammad and the Baha'u'llah commanded, and there is more historical 'proof' of this than can be mustered by other, older religions. To an outsider, at least, they appear to lack the re-interpretative leeway that queer Jews and Christians have made so much use of; whereas the latter can argue for mistranslation or turn to alternative traditions within their faiths, Muslims and Baha'is are stuck with scriptures that are pretty unambiguous. There has been some analysis of men who have sex with men in Muslim cultures,[2] but I have not found anything on the possibility of being both a practising Muslim and an out lesbian or gay man (perhaps because it is *not* a possibility). As publicly presented in the West, these faiths both tend towards fundamentalist and literalist interpretations of their scripture; which, as this book will argue, is exactly the sort of religion that is incompatible with being queer. Specific research from within these communities would seem to be urgently needed; at the moment, if the individuals I met are typical, homosexual Muslims and Baha'is can conceive of themselves only in ways that Jews and Christians began to deconstruct over three decades ago.

The Hindu and Sikh faiths seem less fundamentalist – and certainly have more potential for adaptation by their lesbian and gay followers. They are included in this book, although under-represented. Again, for Hindus and Sikhs in Britain it is very difficult to separate spiritual and sexual identity from cultural and racial issues, and this book limits its scope to the former.

LESBIAN, BISEXUAL AND QUEER

Many of the organizations that exist for religious queers are (nominally, at least) for both women and men; and the religions themselves (at least in the branches that queer people participate in) maintain visions of life that claim not to be separatist. Although I have regularly had to question the wisdom of attempting to write about the experience of lesbians and bisexual women, to have limited this book to the experience of gay men would, I think, have created an artificial and impoverished selection of viewpoints. I have no desire to obscure our differences: but in this book I have attempted to concentrate on what we share.

Unlike certain religions, this book does not claim that male experience and thinking is somehow 'universal', and simply assume that women will agree. However, there was a distinct male bias among those who responded to my research requests, and attempts to remedy this by targeting women-only organizations did not much improve the situation. There are sections which concentrate specifically on male experience; but, while there are many women who give direct accounts of their own experience, there are no corresponding sections by me on *specifically lesbian* life. I am confident that the relevant work has been and will be done elsewhere, by female authors.

I am acutely aware of how artificial it is to divide what is experienced as a result of sexuality from what is experienced as a result of gender. Lesbian understandings of spirituality are, of course, significantly influenced by the experience of being women in a patriarchal society and, specifically, in religions generally controlled by men. Most of the best critiques of institutional religion are written by women; one reason there is less gender-based analysis in this book is that I am taking for granted that these failings have already been established.

'Lesbian and gay' is always an uneasy alliance. 'Lesbian, gay and bisexual' is still more of a compromise. Some valuable contributions to this project have come from men and women who identify as bisexual. Again, while not wishing to suggest that bisexual experiences and identities are the same as gay and lesbian ones, I have concentrated on the similarities. Bisexuals are undoubtedly 'queer' in so far as they differ from heterosexuals; but, importantly for the argument that follows, they also differ from the majority of lesbian and gay people as well, seeming far less prone to constructing alternative (and ultimately limiting) sexual, social and spiritual orthodoxies of their own. If our understanding of sexuality and identity is to evolve – as I argue it must – then we will all need to learn from the fluidity of bisexuality, and from the (blessèd?) absence of a rigid bisexual 'lifestyle'.

Having said that I don't want to obscure the differences between lesbians, bisexuals and gay men, I do use 'queer' to refer to us other-than-heterosexual folk. In Britain 'queer' has never attained the same general acceptance as a catch-all as it has in the States. But I have used it partly through laziness (I get bored with writing 'lesbian, gay and bisexual', and it slows down sentences), and also because I like the implicit emphasis on difference (for reasons that will become clear). I am not, usually, invoking

Queer in its more specific sense of a particular sort of politics and culture, nor to be aggressive (I'm not a very 'in-yer-face' sort of person): and I want to state explicitly that some of contributors to this work would definitely not use the q-word themselves.

WHERE I'M COMING FROM

I do not belong to any religion, and never have done; my parents were (practically) agnostic, and the subject was rarely mentioned when I was growing up. I certainly never entertained the idea that religion had any authority with which to attack my sexuality. The absence of any religious trauma or guilt in my background undoubtedly makes it easier for me to be sympathetic towards spirituality. One reason I wrote this book is that I wanted to know if spiritual traditions had anything to offer a self-respecting gay man like myself. I was also aware that I wasn't finding my gay identity and lifestyle quite as fulfilling as queer theory and the gay media suggested I should do. As someone who grew up in the wake of Gay Liberation, and came out into an already well-established gay culture, here – Queer – can only be the starting point, rather than the end of the rainbow, or the promised land.

There is no consensus in queer thinking about spirituality, and I didn't get very far into writing before I realized that I had to give up the pretence that there was, along with the delusion that I could be an objective commentator. The end result is perhaps more an argument than an anthology. I would like to think of it as part of the continuing debate about who we are and what we want; and also as a work-in-progress. It is already a collaborative work, based as it is on the contributions of many lesbian, gay and bisexual people: readers are invited to continue this process. You can write to me, c/o the Contemporary Studies List, at Cassell, Wellington House, 125 Strand, London WC2R 0BB.

Peter Sweasey
Oxford
December 1996

Notes

1. If you are attempting to reconcile your same-sex feelings with the faith you grew up with, there are a number of books you can turn to, which prove that homosexuality is not incompatible with a Christian or Jewish life, and give you ammunition with which to fight those who say it is. Good places to start include: John J. McNeill's *The Church and the Homosexual* (Boston: Beacon Press, 1993); Michael Vasey, *Strangers and Friends: A New Exploration of Homosexuality and the Bible* (London: Hodder & Stoughton, 1995); Christie Balka and Andy Rose, *Twice Blessed: On Being Lesbian or Gay and Jewish* (Boston: Beacon Press, 1989); Letha Dawson Sanzoni and Virginia Ramey Mollenkott, *Is the Homosexual My Neighbor? Another Christian View* (New York: HarperCollins, 1994); and David Helminiak, *What the Bible Really Says About Homosexuality* (San Francisco: Alamo Square, 1994). In the UK, all of these (and many others) – along with information and counselling – are available from the Lesbian and Gay Christian Movement, Oxford House, Derbyshire Street, London E2 6HG, phone/fax 0171 739 1249.

2. Arlene Swidler, *Homosexuality and the World's Religions* (Valley Forge: Trinity Press International, 1993); *Sexuality and Eroticism among Males in Muslim Societies*, eds Arno Schmidtt and Jehoeda Sofer (New York: Harrington Park Press, 1992).

. . . he was not sure he had ever really stopped and quizzed himself. Who the fuck are you, instead of who are you fucking?

Somehow it didn't seem that he had ever been that interested before and now that it might have been interesting it was too dangerous. It was much easier to pretend there just wasn't enough time. No time to stop. No time for questions. Just sex, work, fun, life, in whatever order. They all sounded the same.

(Oscar Moore, A Matter of Life and Sex)

Our silence will not protect us. Our best protection is to speak the truths of our lives insofar as we can, with one another's presence and help, and cultivate carefully together those truths we cannot yet speak, truths that may be still very unformed and young. We are shaping history with our words.

(Carter Heyward, Touching Our Strength: The Erotic as Power and the Love of God)

If a man don't go his own way, he's nothing . . . A man should be what he can do.

(Said by Montgomery Clift, in From Here to Eternity)

PART I

From Queer . . .

1

Spirituality and Religion

My question is not: why should religions accept lesbian, gay and bisexual people? We know the answers to that by now, even if religious authorities refuse to hear them. My question is: why should queers want anything to do with religion?

Religion has not, traditionally, been very welcoming towards queer people, and continues to advertise its hostility. The Catholic Church calls homosexuality an 'intrinsic moral evil' and 'an objective moral disorder'.[1] Texts from the Qur'an are used to justify executing gay men in fundamentalist Islamic nations, and stir up hatred elsewhere. A former Chief Rabbi in Great Britain looked forward to the day when genetic engineering might rid the world of homosexuals.[2] The religious right in America claims homophobia is fundamental to its faith. Even the relatively liberal Church of England won't (officially) ordain practising homosexuals and declares that we 'fall short of the ideal'.[3] Heterosexuality is the eleventh commandment: followers of these and other faiths have experienced miserable inner torment, as well as prejudice and harassment, when they break it. People who do not hold religious beliefs – the majority, at least in Europe – are none the less hampered in their struggles against homophobia by the political power, and alleged moral authority, of religious institutions.

Given such treatment, it's hardly surprising if the self-respecting queer wants nothing to do with religion. They reject us, so we have to reject Them. Religion is not part of, or compatible with, lesbian or gay 'identity' – whether that's the image we hold of ourselves (in our media, our theorizing, our arts) or the image that is held of us (whether by friendly straights or by bigots). Religion is something of an unmentionable in many lesbian and gay contexts (in the UK, at least). When I first conceived of this book in 1994, Cassell's Sexual Politics list was already over forty titles long, and covered myriad aspects of queer life, including a whole slew of works on performing arts and the media: but religion didn't rate a mention, which seemed something of an omission for such a vast, and influential, area of human endeavour.[4] The gay media tends to cover religion solely in terms of political struggle: a fight for equal rights, much like the battle to serve in the military. As with the armed forces debate, many queers cannot comprehend why anyone would want to be part of institutions which seem to be contrary to everything 'we' stand for.

In short, religion is a *straight thing*. If you had it when you were younger, it's something to be left behind when you come out. You were brainwashed, but can be deprogrammed. Now you're out and proud, Heaven is a nightclub. Hell is a bad hair day. The only pilgrimage you should make is to Ikea. You can still kneel with adoration, but the objects of your worship should be human lovers and camp icons. Religion is all about guilt and sin – you reject the former, and embrace the latter willingly. Being lesbian, gay or bisexual is a way of life – who needs religion when you've got a lifestyle, the best nightclubs, lots of beautiful people to have sex with; or for the more earnestly inclined, when there's political campaigning to be done, a community to build, homoculture to be consumed, an identity to define, and a health crisis to survive?

Chief among the architects of post-Stonewall gay and lesbian identities have been political activists, whose hostility towards religion follows the general left-wing analysis (an antagonism that can be traced back to Marx). The feminist origins of the lesbian movement have bequeathed a similar suspicion of anything not strictly secular. Pink businesses, which have been so influential in shaping the collective image of gay men in particular, are even less likely to be motivated by spiritual concerns (or even, let's face it, by social concerns).

Losing religion is not confined to queers, of course: this century has seen the triumph of secularization, with religious thinking and practises becoming increasingly marginal to people's lives. Religion has seemed redundant in the light of scientific progress; irrational, superstitious and old-fashioned, with no place in well-educated and civilized societies like ours. Without the compulsion to believe, people don't. Lesbian, gay and bisexual people share all these reasons for rejecting religion, but have an additional motivation: it doesn't seem to want us anyway. If we accept that our sexuality is good, then we have to reject homophobic religions, on logical grounds: we know they are wrong, because what they say about our sexuality is so patently wrong. Because of this disjunction, lesbian, gay or bisexual people tend to be acutely aware of religious corruption – the hypocrisy of many of those who condemn us, the ways in which they can wield power to make our lives miserable and the joyless narrow-mindedness of their visions of life.

Why, then, are there some people who fail to understand this logic, and persist in identifying as spiritual while claiming to be self-respecting queers? How can anyone become involved in religion *after* coming out? Are they all in denial, or stupid, or sad? Why would any lesbian want to be involved in something so obviously patriarchal as religion? Why would an urban gay man do something that requires getting up early on a Sunday or Saturday morning?

To be both queer and religious is to face opposition from all sides. It means overcoming all the aforementioned problems with religion. It also means putting yourself on the margins of an already marginalized minority: as many lesbian and gay Christians have said, the one thing harder than coming out as queer in Church is coming out as religious to your fellow queers. The response is, at best, incomprehension, sometimes hostility: you are viewed as a traitor. There are all the usual problems of being 'doubly other', belonging to two minorities: but even less sympathy than usual, because these two identities are simply not supposed to exist in the same person – they should cancel each other out.

So what is it that people need so much they will court universal disapproval? What makes it worth it? Why can't these people be satisfied with our deeply fashionable queer identity? What can God give them that a good fuck can't?

The answers to these questions form the basis of this book. In spite of the apparent paradox – or assumed impossibility – there are many people who assert that you do not have to choose between being queer and being religious: you can be both. There are lesbian, gay and bisexual Christians – including Anglicans, Catholics and Methodists (many of whom are members of the Lesbian and Gay Christian Movement, the largest membership-based gay organization in the country). There is the Metropolitan Community Church, which was founded by a gay man the year before Stonewall and now has churches across the world, with predominantly lesbian and gay clergy and congregations. There are queer Quakers[5] and Unitarians. There are lesbian, gay and bisexual Jews, including several prominent out rabbis. There are openly gay and lesbian Buddhists, following various lineages. Queers are also Wiccans, Odinists and every variety of Neo-Pagan; Sikhs and Hindus; spiritualists, Sufis, Taoists, Tantrics, Hermetics and mystics. Not forgetting Transcendental Meditators and the many New Age queens and dykes who follow everything from 'A Course in Miracles' to the Celestine Prophecy; nor the many people who have been influenced by one or more of these paths but since fashioned an approach of their own, or who would identify as 'spiritual' but not with any particular organization.

The 'theory' – whether that's queer theory or theology – dictates that these sexual–spiritual hybrids should not exist, and so rarely admits that they do. To find out why queer believers are prepared to defy conventional wisdom, it is necessary to look at the details of individual lives. People's own reasons for becoming involved with religion, and understanding of it, generally contradict the assumptions that opened this chapter. For instance, one common fallacy is that religious queers are people who have yet to outgrow the religious indoctrination of their childhood; another is that they must be unhappy with their sexuality, and use religion to retreat from it (and real life). The stories that follow tell of people who were out and proud before – and after – they found their faith.

THREE LIFE STORIES

Victoria

Victoria Stagg-Elliott is a writer and photographer; her work can regularly be found in *Gay Times*. She was born in Sheffield, to a Church of England mother and Jewish father, and grew up in a Jewish neighbourhood in Chicago. 'I never rebelled against religion because there was nothing to rebel against. My parents were completely indifferent to religion. My Dad's idea of a Jewish education was Woody Allen films and *Jesus Christ Superstar* ("well, he is the most famous Jewish boy in the world," he would always say, "remember one of us made God"). In a way, it is easier for me to be religious than some of my friends who grew up in religious homes. They have huge amounts of baggage involving miserable experiences at Hebrew school and scary rabbis. I have none of that.

'It's clear to me now that, up till a few years ago, I had been starving my spiritual life. When I was twenty-three, I don't know why, but I started to search for God. A lot of people ask me if I was really depressed when I had this "religious re-awakening", but the truth of the matter is that my life was going great – good job, good apartment, great relationship with my family, good friends, a girlfriend – but I still wasn't happy. I went to the Catholic church of my stepmother and checked out other religious institutions. My first adult contact with Judaism was with a lesgay synagogue in Chicago. I went with a drag queen friend of mine (he's a nice Orthodox boy). At the time, I wanted to get in touch with my roots. I wanted to understand a bit better where my grandparents had come from – my great-grandfather was a very strict, ultra-Orthodox Hasid, and that is why my grandfather ran away from Poland. I was searching for God, but also a way of having a Jewish identity that was not exclusively based on Holocaust remembrance (it's very important, but it's not everything). What I found was something that really resonated for me.

'I find my belief in God to be very fulfilling. Believing in God does not make you weak. Sure, I am a self-respecting adult, as well as being a successful professional woman. But the world is a very lonely place without a support network. Friends and family are very valuable, but even they aren't for ever. An individual cannot survive by themselves in this world. God provides me with huge amounts of inner strength. We talk. I pray.'

Victoria now worships in London at progressive, Liberal synagogues. 'I speak to many Jews who talk about keeping tradition because it is their past. Being Jewish is my past, present and future. I refuse to keep ritual unless it means something, and I'm not interested in empty gestures. I enjoy going to the synagogue, but I'm not a regular shul goer. I bought my first yarmulke [the hat worn, traditionally by men, for services] about a year ago, a beautiful Yemenite one with burgundy satin and faux pearls. I don't keep kosher. I don't keep the Sabbath. I can't speak Hebrew, and I've never been to Israel. I use Jewish teachings as a guide for my life but they're not some kind of jail. I love Jewish learning. A lot of it makes sense. I'm very happy with my level of religious observance. This Rosh Hashanah (New Year) I went to North London Progressive synagogue and we threw bread on the water. The idea is that the bread takes this year's sins within. I felt great afterwards. It is important not to throw the baby out with the bathwater when you discard religion. Religion can be very comforting and there is nothing wrong with something just being symbolic.'

Nagaraja

Nagaraja is a thirty-five-year old gay man who manages a meditation centre in central London for the Friends of the Western Buddhist Order (FWBO). It's a long way from what he was doing ten years ago. For a start, he was called Gareth McMillan then. 'I wasn't looking for a spiritual path, I was looking to be an even sexier graphic designer. I had long ponytail, long white raincoat, portfolio. I had a *lifestyle*: I had places to go, coffee to drink, important briefs to fill. *Absolutely Fabulous* is a good send-up of all that busyness, how superficial it is. It's intoxicating, it makes you feel as if you're doing something, as if you *are* something. But I couldn't keep it going. I was the gay cliché, split between social and private life, the joker and the sad guy. I felt out of control.' On the surface things were looking good. As a young man he had met a 'stunning-looking boyfriend, very rich' who picked him up in a sports car and with whom he'd had a relationship for a couple of years. Like many gay men he regularly consumed large amounts of alcohol and other recreational drugs. He had ambitions; and dreams – 'I'll fall in love and it will be for ever, it will be just like the Hollywood musicals I watched as a kid, it will all work out.' But somehow it never did. 'When I got the things I thought I wanted, up would come my self-hatred. I hadn't really addressed what was happening in my life.' His mother had committed suicide when he was seventeen. 'I was trying to find the drug or the relationship which would fundamentally sort out death.'

Gareth felt no temptation to turn to the religion of his childhood for help with these feelings. He grew up in Glasgow, where Protestants and Catholics were in frequent, sometimes violent, conflict. Gareth was particularly aware of the futility of sectarianism, since he had been born to a Protestant family but adopted by Catholics: 'I changed sides at the stroke of a pen.' He gave up church-going at the age of twelve because he couldn't see anything he respected. What led him, in his twenties, to Buddhism was not any conscious quest for faith, nor a search for relief from his pain. 'I'd just read *Shogun*, which I now know has nothing to do with Buddhism at all, but somewhere I thought it was all quite sexy – all that talk of ascetic discipline to a higher ideal!' He saw an advertisement for a meditation course that appealed to his eye for graphic design, and to his 'self-improving side – I'd always been into lateral thinking and creative-thought stuff'. Although it sounded 'a bit spooky', he signed up for a four-week course, and instantly experienced what Buddhists term 'beginner's mind'. 'Sometimes people who come with no expectations get into really integrated states. Meditation is not about going somewhere else – it's about having a deeper experience of yourself. I had some really powerful meditations: intense, blissful. I had no intention of being a Buddhist – but I was interested in what the possibilities of it were.' Eventually Gareth went on a retreat in London. 'It was a profound experience. I didn't think I'd found "a path". All I was aware of was that on this retreat I met people who related in a way that I wasn't used to. I felt really innocent and naive again – I felt frightened – but it felt that there were grown-ups around. I mean, I'm a Glaswegian, I'm cynical, it wasn't like anyone was pulling the wool over my eyes. But when I was surrounded by people who were relaxed and positive, who were meditating and studying, who were talking about ideals, and who were sharing themselves – I was a completely different human being.'

This did not lead to instant conversion and enlightenment. Instead, as soon as the retreat finished, 'I went back to Glasgow for Hogmanay – all my mates were stoned, and I realized I'd been somewhere I couldn't explain to them. So I had a pint and fell behind the sofa.' The Buddhism was put on the back burner 'because it wasn't very sexy. It was slow progress after that. I kept trying to find the right combination of the right job, right drugs and right boyfriend. And meditation is a bit difficult when you're stoned all the time. As I got older, I'd get more and more into crisis – so I'd go to a meditation retreat, I'd get myself together, come out . . . and blow it. After several months I'd crawl back to meditation, go back to the Buddhist centre, they'd just go, yes, sit on your cushion.' Even when he began to work full-time for the FWBO and live in a Buddhist community, it was still a struggle at times. 'I thought everyone would be spiritual, lots of spiritual spiritualness everywhere – but it wasn't like that. It was like living with anyone who you don't necessarily get on with. All you share is your ideals.

'The spiritual life is about "know thyself". I had to start looking seriously at who I was and what I was doing. It was absolutely horrendous.

Becoming a Buddhist is basically saying that you want to change yourself, and the ideal that you use is the Buddha. You want to become a happy, healthy human being; you want to get a grip on life, and be more compassionate and generous. But you have to redefine what happiness is: it's not walking around with a huge grin on your face. You just feel a bit more *real* – you accept life. It brings meaning into your life, something to strive for. It's not enough for me and never has been enough for me to strive for a mortgage. People in the gay community see the spiritual life as a spooky thing. But it's no different to a man going to the gym and saying that's my goal, that's what's going to make me happy: that's his god. Buddhism is the same, except the ideal is less mundane. The muscle body will collapse at forty-five to fifty, no matter how strong your will is. You'll decay, grow old and die – that has nothing to do with being gay, it's the human condition. You have to find an answer. If you just sail along in a party you won't find an answer: then life meets you – you get ill, or someone dies.

'I came along to Buddhism thinking that it was a particular way of life, and you took on the way of life and something would happen. I thought it was passive. But it's not, you have to put effort in to make something happen. Although it was really difficult, I grew.' Eventually Gareth's deepening commitment led to him 'going for refuge', a process which involved spending four months living in primitive conditions on a Spanish mountain, at the end of which he received the name Nagaraja (it means 'the Dragon King' – a reflection of Gareth's fiery energy). 'It's about trying to make the centre of your life Buddhism – whereas other people make it relationship, job or whatever. It makes sense for me.'

Timothy

Timothy Spiers is well aware that gay Christians have an image problem. 'There is a stereotype of a gay Christian as a person who was brought up in a religious home, who as an adult discovered themselves to be gay, suffered great guilt because they thought themselves to be sinful and who spends their life on the fringes of Church life being rebutted by the Church establishment until they give up and become a militant humanist. I do not conform to any aspect of this. I grew up in a non-religious home, accepted my gay identity, and then as an adult became a Christian. I have received total support from my Church and see myself as part of the Church establishment.' This is possible because Timothy has always attended the Metropolitan Community Church (MCC). Religion has never rejected him; so he has less reason to reject religion.

Timothy realized he was gay at fourteen, and, in spite of the obvious prejudice, believed 'I was right and everyone else was wrong. I kept my sanity and my mouth shut'. Growing up in an era when the newspapers weren't full of clergy arguing about sexuality, 'I can honestly say that I do not remember ever hearing that the prejudice against homosexuality had any connection with religious belief or was justified by the Bible. It never occurred to me that homosexuality might ever be or could be written about in a book of any kind, or that the prejudice against it was associated with any particular group of people or might not be universal.

'In my teens and early twenties, my big question was whether or not God existed and whether the Christian faith was true. If God existed then God demanded to be taken seriously, and could not be ignored.' At a 1960s protest rally organized by a Christian group, Timothy had 'a conversion experience, what I would now understand to be a moving of the Holy Spirit: an inner feeling of love and excitement which somehow one realizes is shared by others present before you say anything about it' – this was not in response to what was being said or personal contact from anyone else there. In fact, 'nobody at these rallies befriended me or invited me to their church. In retrospect I am glad of this'; if they had, they almost certainly would not have tolerated Timothy's sexuality. It was through a Christian friend of a brief affair that Timothy heard about the early services of what was to become the first MCC in Britain. He went along to the Fellowship of Christ the Liberator, as it was then called, in 1973. It was only the second time he'd ever been to a church service of any sort. 'That evening I realized I had found what I was looking for, and I have never wavered from that opinion. MCC has made all the difference in my life. I might have found God in another body of faith – or I might never have dealt with my spirituality. The latter is a terrible thought. I would not know most of my friends, I would have spent so much of my free time differently and I would not have been to many of the places I have travelled to. I don't think I would have the same sense of self-worth or achievement or peace.'

Victoria, Nagaraja and Timothy are not religious through convention or through fear. Their faiths have not made it more difficult for them to be queer, and being out has not made it more difficult for them to follow their faith. This is not the case for every queer person, of course, although the fact that it is true for these three suggests that homophobia is not intrinsic to spirituality, but is specific to certain manifestations of religion.

The fact that it may be possible to combine being queer and being religious does not explain why people might want to do so. Even without threats of eternal damnation, people do not become Christians for the hell of it, or seek nirvana 'because it's there'. So if religion is not always the enemy that queers often imagine it to be, then what is it? And why do people want it in their lives? The trinity just quoted has begun to explain the why and the what: they feel that their lives are better for having acknowledged their 'spirituality'; and that this had been neglected before they found their faith. To ask why queer people have spiritual beliefs is to ask what spirituality is.

THE DIFFERENCE BETWEEN SPIRITUALITY AND RELIGION

'Spirituality is so difficult to describe. That is what religion tries to do, and in describing it makes an absolute balls of it'; such is the opinion of Bernard Lynch, a gay man who ought to know, having worked for many years as a Catholic priest. Although one of the buzzwords of the 1990s, spirituality is a slippery term, with connotations ranging from the traditionally theological to the substantially secular.

It is often used by people who feel uncomfortable with the word religion, sometimes as a deliberate contrast. Rabbi Elizabeth Sarah – an out lesbian – explains that 'when people think of religion they think of institutions, hierarchies, things that are fixed and try to control them. The word spirituality seems more autonomous, about where people are coming from in their own lives.' It is a concept she would once have disregarded, even when she first began training as a rabbi. Her background was politics – anti-racism, socialism, feminism – and she decided to become a rabbi 'mainly for political and tactical reasons – to take my struggle into the mainstream'. But during her training she began to discover 'what real spirituality is about, which is that it's rooted in your experience. I was beginning to pay attention in a deeper sense to who I am and the integration of all the parts of myself. I adore singing and music, I love writing, poetry – those elements had always been there. But they'd been in different places, they hadn't been gathered together. And as I brought myself more and more together as a being, what was (for want of a better word) my spirituality could be released. I found a new kind of language for understanding myself, and a feeling that there's more to life than the material. It's very difficult to find the adequate words for it, but it has certainly emerged out of paying attention to me as a whole, and myself as part of a whole. It's not just about having a political or social agenda, but about what it is to be human, what it is to be alive, what it is to be a part of creation. It's to do with a sense of community, humanity, something that's much bigger than all of us, that isn't above us but is more like a source of life – the "ground of our being" that supports us, that works through us, that we're in partnership with. All of that is not something I've read in a book and thought "well, those ideas are interesting, I'll take them on". It's come out of my own experience.'

Rabbi Sarah's understanding of spirituality contains elements that many others would agree with: having a deeper sense of oneself, addressing the whole of life, and a connection with something bigger. It is also far more than just a set of ideas: spirituality is rooted in life-as-lived, as well as affecting how life is lived. Rabbi Sarah uses another phrase which unites these elements, and is broad enough to include both traditionally religious and more secular understandings – spirituality refers to 'our sense of being'. By such a definition, everyone must have a spirituality, although not everyone will pay attention to it. The late Robert Crossman – the first openly gay mayor in Britain, and for many years both 'very anti-religion' and a Quaker – said 'we're all spiritual beings. Whether or not we express that in a religious way is a choice.'

Queer people from a variety of faiths are quick to distinguish spirituality from religion. The Reverend Elder Jean White has been a pastor for the Metropolitan Community Church in London for over twenty years, and has talked to many thousands of lesbian, gay and bisexual people about their spirituality. 'Most people say that they know there's something more than what they've got, but they don't know how to tap into it; they don't want organized religion, but they feel there's something else. That's what it's all about really, the "something else". It doesn't matter if you never come to Church, as long as you find who you are – a spiritual person.' Father Bill Kirkpatrick, who works in Earls Court,[6] has been alongside gay men living and dying with AIDS since the crisis began, and sees the love they show each other as spiritual – 'as they embrace each other into their unknown futures, they are involved in a spirituality that has nothing to do with religion, but everything to do with living one's life to the full'.[7] Chris Ferguson, a Buddhist, also talks about realizing the full potential of the individual's life: 'Religion's trying to make you what you're not. Spirituality is trying to make you who you are.'

Gordon Hunt lives on the south coast; he is a committed Pagan. He argues that a life lived to the full requires more than simply meeting basic needs – 'shelter, food, sex and all those things' – and sees spirituality as 'coming to terms with your humanness. The need for religion is caused by our spirituality. When you're talking about religion and deities, you can only talk in models. *There is no reality*. There is no truth. There are some nice working models, there are some crap working models.' He makes a distinction between spiritual Pagans and those who are merely religious. 'To undeveloped Pagans, it's about dressing up in unironed frocks, doing candle rituals and generally fucking about. To developed Pagans, the inner landscape is where they live. These are internal journeys rather than external journeys.'

Queer people have a particular incentive to make such distinctions: because the external forms of religion have so often been barred to us, we have been forced to emphasize the inner life. Religion is sometimes our enemy, but our spirituality cannot be colonized. Our 'sense of being' cannot be taken away from us. It may even be intensified by the experience of being queer – something that later chapters of this book explore in detail. Although the length of residence will vary for different individuals and different generations, all of us have, for a time, dwelt in the inner landscape, when we were in the closet.

Being queer can heighten awareness of the distinction between spirituality and religion; but it does not automatically lead gay people to reject traditional religious forms altogether; nor does it make one form of spiritual expression any more likely than another. It's not as if coming out leads inexorably to hanging up the dog-collar and joining the Sisters of Perpetual Indulgence. What does seem to be true is that, whatever path queers choose or continue to follow, they are more likely to respond to and emphasize the personal and spiritual, rather than the doctrinal and organizational. Just as Gordon Hunt separates 'internal' from 'external' Pagans, so Jacqueline – a lesbian priest – describes Christianity as 'a tool with which people can make sense of life, the world and their own place in it. It is for me. That is why I am a Christian and a priest. My desire is to get alongside people wherever they are and encourage/help them to explore their spirituality – their deepest belief about what, in the end, is ultimately important. For most people the established Church doesn't come anywhere near them. That's why I work in the secular world, as a chaplain, where I can mix and work alongside people, many of whom are deeply spiritual, and/or searching, and encourage/affirm them in their quest.'

THE BIG ISSUES

Jacqueline sees 'people searching for meaning and purpose in life' – a search which sometimes seems a bit of an embarrassment in the postmodern age, particularly in a gay culture that can raise superficiality to iconic status. Ignoring these issues, however, doesn't make them go away. 'It is the most crucial question in life: what am I? what am I doing? why am I here? but many people seem to pretend it isn't there,' says Dirk de Klerk, a gay man, originally from South Africa, who follows Tibetan Buddhism. 'For years I was hanging around not really knowing why I exist. People go around with utter self-confidence, so I thought they knew what they were doing. It's only while I was on retreat at Samyé Ling [a Buddhist monastery in Scotland] that it suddenly dawned on me – someone of little self-confidence

– that all of those people were building their self-confidence on fuck-all, they never knew what they were doing.'

Some gay men have had to address these questions sooner than most people would choose to. 'Being HIV positive brings up a lot of questions in your life of a spiritual nature,' says Chris Ferguson, a gay Scot. 'The questions have to be faced by every human being, but for a lot of people it's when they are older. If you're positive – perhaps with the additional problem of knowing a lot of other positive people and losing them along the way – the basic questions are: why is this happening? why are all these people I know dying? why am I going to die young?' Chris had come across Buddhism when he was younger, but returned to it with a new commitment following his positive diagnosis. He was inspired by Sogyal Rinpoche's bestselling *Tibetan Book of Living and Dying*. 'When my friend died, I read it from cover to cover. It was talking about questions I'd had – questions about life and death, and how we can live around those issues of death and suffering, which very few things I've found address. It was very relevant to what I was going through in my life. Because most people who are gay equate spirituality and religion, there is this situation where religions reject gay people and gay people reject religion – you get this vacuum with nowhere to turn.' In response to this predicament Chris and others have set up a support and discussion group at his local HIV drop-in centre. People come together to reflect, meditate, think and talk: 'calling it a spiritual group gives a sense that it's OK to bring up these questions'. And as Kauldip Singh, a gay Sikh who works in the HIV sector in London, points out, while HIV does raise important questions about 'who we are, what we are, why are we here, we can ask those questions irrespective of HIV status'.

Spiritual traditions do more than raise the questions; they allow them to be addressed in a systematic way. For Nagaraja 'the spiritual life has been about bringing me more into relationship with reality, and having a context with which to support it. Unless you've got a context, you can't make sense of what's going on in the world. In a sense, everyone's got their own religion, their gods, their morals', in so far as everyone has their ideas of what is and is not important, what their standards and values are, even if these are not articulated. Dr Elizabeth Stuart, a lesbian Catholic theologian, understands theology as 'reflecting what's going on in life from a perspective that's larger than the immediate situation'. Glenn Palmer, who at thirty-two has just been confirmed as an Anglican, feels his faith performs the same valuable function: 'I find Christianity very useful because it gives me a context in which to think things through.' Glenn is a social worker whose politics are left-wing; in the past he has drawn upon other analytical 'contexts', including Marxism.

Some may be surprised that a person fully capable of understanding secular theories is also able to find intellectual and philosophical depth in religious structures, but Glenn is not the only person to have come round to that opinion. Sheila Shulman became a rabbi in her late forties, after many years working in academia and the women's movement. Ultimately feminist theory wasn't enough: 'It wasn't hermeneutically adequate. It wasn't enough of a frame in which to think about either despair or evil. I don't know if this [Judaism] is either – but it's more adequate than most.' It is not only the major world religions that can provide such a framework. Richard Flynn is a gay man guided by the work of Alice Bailey, who wrote a large number of esoteric works in the first half of this century and has since become an influential figure in New Age thinking. 'Perhaps the most useful thing about Bailey is the considered approach her work brings to living. You end up with a far wider mental "structure" within which you exist.'

The questions posed by spiritual beliefs are not abstract philosophical speculations, irrelevant to everyday life. Peter Wyles, a bisexual Quaker, holds a physics degree: 'I love ideas, science, the rational mind. But the key question is how do I live on this world with five billion people – and how should they live with each other? Science doesn't tell us how to live.' Church of Scotland minister Dennis Fraser can find only one honest answer to the question, why are we here? 'No idea. What matters to me is that we are here, and being here we have to learn how to live with each other.' For another gay man, Maitreyabandhu, 'one of the reasons I got involved with Buddhism is that I wanted to find out what to do with life'.

THE EXPERIENCE OF BEING ALIVE

The late David Randall – the gay vicar who founded CARA (an organization which provides care, resources and spiritual support to people affected by HIV and AIDS) – opposed Christianity's frequent preoccupation with abstraction and the afterlife: he used to say 'dying is the easy part, it's my living I want some help with'. Spirituality is about life: 'each time we are present with someone who is asking ultimate questions, we minister spiritual support. The "spirit" is the life force in each of us which motivates us toward life and living.'

At their best, religious ethics and doctrine attempt to address this question of how best to live. Carl Jung, and later the American guru-figure Joseph Campbell, did much to popularize the notion of religion as a collection of myths which can be read as symbolic, psychological guides for getting through life. It was a phrase of Campbell's that first set me thinking there might be something to this spirituality stuff: 'people say that what we're all seeking is a meaning for life . . . I think that what we're seeking is an experience of being alive, so that our life experiences on the purely physical plane will have resonances within our own innermost being and reality, so that we actually feel the rapture of being alive.'⁸ Myths, Campbell maintained, teach you how to do this. And according to Craig O'Neill and Kathleen Ritter, in their book *Coming Out Within*, 'the shaping stories and themes from Judeo-Christian scripture and tradition can and do apply to lesbian and gay individuals if viewed from the vantage point of mythology or metaphor. If looked at literally, these stories of faith appear to be applicable only to heterosexual journeys toward the Divine.' Metaphorically, however, they are 'life maps and images that facilitate oneness with the abiding God'; the virgin birth, for example, 'may symbolise the opening up of the spiritual possibilities in the gay and lesbian heart where once there may have existed only sterile fear, bitterness, and closeted shame'.⁹ Guiding myths are not found only in religions: anthropologist Will Roscoe's collection of myths for gay men, *Queer Spirit,* draws on sources as diverse as nursery rhymes and pornography, as well as the stories of tribal cultures from around the world. Queer interpretations of various religious myths can be found in many of the following chapters.

Spirituality is more than conceptual: more than philosophy or ethics. 'People don't just believe in a cerebral, intellectual way,' says Catherine Hopper, a Buddhist (formerly known as Catherine Treasure, and for several years the religious correspondent of Britain's weekly *Pink Paper*). 'The heart has to be involved. You can't be ethical because you think you ought to be, or even just because you believe in it as a source of happiness. You have to have a strong attraction to the beauty of belief, and this is nurtured by ritual, and devotional worship. I find it extraordinary to watch my ex-radical-lesbian-feminist friends prostrating themselves on the floor, full length, in front of the Buddha. Something must have moved them *very* deeply to cause them to do something so extremely politically incorrect!' For the Reverend Jacqueline, ritual creates 'a forum through which ultimates can be expressed, and people can be helped to articulate and express what otherwise is very difficult, and be taken beyond words to a deeper reality'. Jason Oliver, a twenty-four-year-old Pagan from Birmingham, offers a simpler definition: 'a ritual is something that you do over and over again, that has a defined end and tunes you in to something'. There are, of course, many such rituals in the everyday life of queer folk. Catholic skinhead Mike Fox talks of how both pontifical mass and cruising are ritual acts. 'Humans are ritual beings. Ritual shapes and describes our relationships, to ourselves, others and the universe.' The Sisters of Perpetual Indulgence, a worldwide order of gay male nuns (and recently a few lesbian Fathers and Brothers) have, for over twenty years, worked in the interstices between queer rituals and religious rites. As well as taking the language and symbols of religion and making them shamelessly gay (they hold their own mass, for instance, and sing 'himms' such as 'Amazing Pride, how sweet the sound . . .'), they also solemnize the rituals that are already present in queer life (by blessing the Pride festival, or exorcizing cottages).[10]

TRANSCENDENCE

Spirituality includes areas of human experience that defy neat categorization. Most faiths suggest that people do not struggle with the how and why of life in isolation; humans can experience a sense of connection with 'something more', a reality greater than themselves – at the very least, something other than the conscious mind. Michael Seán Paterson, a former Benedictine monk who now works with CARA and at the London Lighthouse,[11] argues that in defining spirituality 'you have to include some element of transcendence. If you don't include some beyond-self experience or dimension, then it would be more honest to speak in terms of philosophy of life.' 'Beyond self' could indicate simply other people; maybe humanity as a whole; a sense of an underlying life force; or God. Although interpretations of transcendence will vary between different faiths and different individuals, a common characteristic seems to be a sense of connectedness. 'Spirituality is somehow our natural inclination to make connections between things and find meaning,' suggests Neil Whitehouse, a young gay man and Methodist minister working in Soho.[12] 'Some of the connections we make are about our own mortality. Within our lives there are experiences which question whether life begins and ends with physical existence: the emotion I'm feeling, the connections I'm making, suggest it doesn't stop, nor did it just begin with me, I'm part of something much bigger – yet, also, unique. The stirrings between people, or within you – that quality of being struck by one's connectedness with the rest of the universe – demand more. You can generate that in formal worship, or it can come up on you by surprise. No one's going to prove it to you, it's a felt thing; but those feelings are real feelings, and you have to make sense of them somehow. It's part of a bigger picture which we all need to belong to – I think there is an existential need there, which relates to the felt truth of human life, that we're not an island.'

Given that queers are more likely to talk of personalized, experiential spirituality than parrot a Papal encyclical, what they mean by 'God' usually bears little resemblance to the simple-minded storybook old man on a cloud that kids are presented with – or the philosophically 'proved' God beloved of theologians. Father Bernard Lynch, whose work for lesbian and gay rights and with people living with AIDS makes him a thorn in the side of the Roman Catholic authorities, no longer believes in 'the God I was indoctrinated with: the God of fear who deserves to be hated and exorcized. But I am open to the possibility that there is something more – the positive force of life, to put it in very secular terminology. Even science would be open to that. I would postulate that it's only when we are open to the transcendent that the transcendent comes into our lives.' Other people tend towards the 'non-realist' understanding that God is a representation of humanity's deepest longing and desires. The Reverend Diana Reynolds, a lesbian priest who works in the Midlands, explains that, horrified as some traditionalists would be by this sort of talk, 'there are lots of things we don't believe literally', and God can be one of those. Her understanding is that 'God is not an interventionary being but the energy that gives life. Those of us who say we have a faith are people who have acknowledged that life force, and try to live our lives in harmony with what that life force has already created around us, and bring the beauty that comes from that into the lives of other people.' Quaker Peter Wyles warns that the existence of God cannot be proved with logic: 'it is gut feeling. Anyone who argues for the existence of God through reason will be disappointed.'

Western concepts of God, even among atheists, are heavily pre-determined by Judeo-Christian monotheism, and consequently religion is sometimes reduced to whether or not one believes in God. This is an overly simplistic approach to the phenomenon of religion: Buddhists don't believe in any god, while other faiths have thousands. Growing up a Hindu, Siddharth Deva chose his favourite gods (Shiva and Ganesh) from a whole pantheon: 'It doesn't matter if they're real or an invention – Hindus don't have those debates, you can't talk realistically about this creature who wandered round with the body of a human being and the head of an elephant. They are mythological characters – they symbolize something. They tell you how to live, what one should strive to be. All these gods that you have statues of are vehicles of something that came before creation; it is impossible to know this being, it is so amorphous that I dare not put a name to it.' Jason Oliver is an Odinist – while some Pagans worship Greek or Roman deities, Jason prefers to invoke Norse gods and goddesses such as Odin, Thor, Loki and Hella. 'They're energy flows put into a form that is easier for humans to comprehend.' His version of Odin might differ from that of a straight person; 'but they're the same thing, just different parts of the same entity'. Like Siddharth, Jason believes there is an ultimate source 'from which everything came. I don't think there is a name for it. I know that it's there; my way of relating to that is through other gods.' An ultimate God that is beyond understanding is also beyond categories of male and female. 'God has very little to with gender,' says Vieta, a bisexual woman. 'It bugs me to have Him up there. Sometimes I'd like Her, and I'd like Her boobs in my face.'

The gods or goddesses that queers believe in are not the same as the God who is often invoked to condemn us. None the less, for some queers, the very idea of God remains too hostile to handle. Moira is a lesbian who has found spirituality through the twelve-step programme of Narcotics Anonymous. 'I have trouble with the word "God", because even though I can believe in something that is unconditional, if I call it "God", a judging, conventional image comes into my mind.' Instead she prefers the AA/NA concept of a 'Higher Power' (one of the twelve steps is belief in the power of God 'however we understand God'). Father Bill has worked with many gay men who have been traumatized and scarred by bigoted religion earlier in their lives. 'Mystery is a word many would rather use than "God", which some regard as unacceptable because it reminds them of the pain of rejection by their father or other parental figures. We can't escape this mystery, because we're caught up with it, I'm convinced of that.'

In addition to the painful associations the G-word (God, rather than Gay) can have, it can limit something which is, intrinsically, way beyond human comprehension. Rabbi Elizabeth Sarah explains that this is 'one of the things that has been most misunderstood about the feminist changes to language. We're not saying God is a she, but asking is God this one image? God is. Both nothing, ineffable, without end – and all these different things to all these different people, expressing ultimately the unity that unites all the diversity.'

ALTERED STATES OF CONSCIOUSNESS

Another important 'beyond self' component of spirituality, and another reason why people, including queers, may hold to a faith, is spiritual experience: intuitions or occurrences so far from the everyday, and so intense, that they feel incontrovertible, and leave the individual concerned with no choice but to believe.

At its most literal, for spiritualists, clairvoyants and some New Agers, spiritual experience means sensing the presence of 'spirits', of the dead and the yet to be born. For Christians, spiritual experience may include the 'gifts' of the Holy Spirit. 'I've had some weird experiences – that's the way most people would categorize them,' says Stewart Harrison, a gay man who, having lived for many years without any religious involvement at all, changed from his successful career as a planning surveyor to become an

MCC pastor. 'I have rested in the Spirit. I was very sceptical about these things. I'd seen one or two people doing it before and thought the person was maybe being a bit exhibitionist – or was he pushed? I went through all that sort of questioning until it actually happened to me.' The Methodism of Stewart's childhood had not prepared him for modern miracles; and even once he started going along to the MCC in Bournemouth, his return to Christianity was a gradual one. 'My pushes along the road have been these Holy Spirit experiences. Baptism in the Holy Spirit is committing your life to Christ and asking to be filled with the Holy Spirit, energized in a way to be of service. You get prayed over by the elders of the Church. I felt myself wobbling on my feet, I started resisting and a further prayer was said over me, and I just went back – I didn't feel anything, I didn't realize I was falling. I didn't hurt myself – which was amazing, I've got back trouble. Further prayer was said over me about speaking in tongues of the spirit. That happened – I just babbled along as though I was a baby. That really shocked me; afterwards I felt almost embarrassed about it.' He was also very impressed. 'I was on cloud nine, I was walking around as though I was on air for three or four days, I was worried I was going to step in front of a car or something. Healing things happen from time to time. I hang on to those in the darker times. Now I can see God working in particular ways, there's no point in swimming against the tide, trying to do my own thing. Letting the spirit work through you, and in you, and around you in your life is actually very challenging.'

Some experience which may be categorized as 'spiritual' does not require any particular faith, and is not necessarily given a religious interpretation. This is the 'numinous': feelings of bliss, euphoria, ecstasy, oneness and awe, which seem to stand out from everyday existence and point towards something greater. The numinous is important in religious mysticism – including the Gnostic tradition of Christianity, or kabbalist thought within Judaism – but, although altered states of consciousness can result from religious practice, they can also arise from the contemplation of art or nature, or from sex, the use of certain drugs – or sometimes, apparently at random, without any stimuli. Altered consciousness may lead people to a different perception of the everyday sensory world; or may take the form of hallucinatory 'visions'.

Chris Ferguson describes an altered-state experience. 'Early last year I'd been doing quite a lot of intense meditation practice, at least an hour a day – but not feeling I was getting anywhere. I had a shiatsu session; I was concentrating on my breathing very intensely for an hour. When I came out of the place, my whole perception of things was different. Everything was transformed. I remember sitting on the bus going through New Cross, which is a grotty area, and it seemed just amazing. Travelling in London people normally just ignore each other: but I felt a real closeness to everybody on the bus, I felt there was no difference between them and I. I remember going across Waterloo bridge, and I was transfixed by the beauty of the flag on the Shell building, it was so right and so perfect. The world burned with intensity. It felt like I was going to lose my breath. Veils had been taken away. It made me aware that there's more to our consciousness than our mundane awareness. Our normal state of mind is not the only one; it's actually quite a basic one, and there are higher states. It gave me a feeling of hope that there's much more to life than we normally experience, and in a positive way. I find it helpful to remember it, although Buddhism says that you shouldn't practise to gain that state – as soon as you try to catch something you lose it. But it feels less as if I'm wasting time.' While in this case the combination of massage and breath meditation may have been the trigger, similar experiences have been reported by many others in a variety of circumstances, not least by people on LSD. Although, as Henry Giles points out, 'this can happen on weak tea, I assure you.' Henry practises Transcendental Meditation, a technique based on the Vedanta, ancient texts concerning consciousness which are a source of both Hinduism and Buddhism. For Henry, 'the purpose of religion is the experience of transcendence and bringing it out into activity'. As a consequence of using the TM technique (a mantra meditation) he has had many experiences of what he calls 'refined' or 'celestial' perception, and 'seeing the divine unity in everything you look at'.

Whether altered states like this are just a particularly enjoyable biochemical reaction or a glimpse of eternity, they are not restricted to heterosexuals. On the contrary, some of the activities that lead to ecstatic epiphanies are disproportionately popular with queer people. 'I have met people at the Anvil, the Block, the LA,[13] who have come to follow a religious path simply because they got very heavily into sadomasochistic sex, and the only way they could feel that sense of tranquillity and inner peace which the sexual experience gave them was by following the spiritual path,' says Mike Fox. 'Most of our lives we live dissociated – we live in our heads. There are occasions when we become a unity – and when that happens, God goes "cooeee!" That can happen in sex, at mass, on E – whatever brings about that unity of being is spiritual or religious experience.'

While the objective nature of such experiences may be impossible to quantify, they are hugely important for the people who have them: they can change spirituality from theory into belief. 'Visions help you to conceive reality,' says a young gay New Ager known as Amneon – who has induced visions through breath and body work as well as dance and drugs. 'They remove fear. They give you confidence. They help you to see truths, therefore to conduct yourself in accordance with those truths – when you *realize* that you're an incarnate soul, not just because of reading and speculation but because of these experiences – you act in that way. You realize this life isn't the end, there's a long way to go.' Johnathon Andrew, whose background is Christian, had his first vision the year after he was diagnosed HIV-positive in 1984. 'Physically I was in church, after communion. The world darkened, closed in on me. I saw myself standing in a leather bar, in full butch drag, harness, cap, the lot. I was looking at my back. And beside me, but slightly back so that I was unaware, was this luminous white figure. My knees went. I was in tears all afternoon . . .' Whereas previously his faith had been 'heady and rather superior', after this experience 'I *knew* that there was something more than me. I'm not going to be ruled by "middle management" – the brain, all our theories. I knew that there was a huge difference between the dogma and all the theories about God – whether Christian or New Age or whatever, all the head trip stuff – and *this*. It's a living reality. It's extremely inconvenient: you try mentioning visions to your vicar. I think a lot of people have experiences like this, but they're embarrassed to talk about them because they're ashamed that they will be thought of as mad.' Johnathon's faith did at least give him 'spiritual back-up' – a framework with which to interpret and understand this experience. Many queer people are disenfranchised of any such context, because religion rejects them.

This book places more emphasis on transcendent experience than might be usual in more conventional religious works precisely because (unlike religion) these experiences are equally available to queer people. Mind-blowing as encounters with the numinous are, however, few would wish to limit the domain of spirituality to these rare, peak experiences. 'I think spiritual understanding is about the way we go about our daily life and the way we treat people rather than some high-sounding philosophy or deep, secret knowledge,' argues Eric Bond, a gay Christian from Bristol. If spirituality is anything more than a hopelessly vague intellectual concept, it has to be something that is felt and lived, for, as Bernard Lynch observes, 'it's not what we say about our God, our religion, our Goddess, or "it", or the force, or whatever, that matters: it's who we are as a result of our belief. Are we more free? Are we more human?'

BREAKING THE TABOO

Queers, who have to maintain their faith in the face of criticism from both religious organizations and their own community, are more likely than most believers to be aware of how multi-faceted and complex spirituality is – and why they want it. They develop a valuable ability to distinguish spirituality from its sometime vehicle, religion; to hold on to the baby while throwing out the bathwater. And it should be obvious, from the ways in which that baby has been defined in this chapter, why it is worth holding on to. If spirituality refers to our sense of being; if it grapples with the questions of why we are here and how we live, and seeks a context with which to approach those questions; if it fosters a sense of connection with other people, the universe we live in, and the force of creation; if it helps make sense of transcendent experiences – then it is surely something that belongs as much in the lives of lesbian, gay and bisexual people as in the lives of heterosexuals. We have a being to make sense of, the big questions are ours too, we experience connection and transcendence. We are neither excluded from nor exempt from spirituality.

If spirituality is so important, and so central to our lives, then it's worth talking about. One similarity between sexuality and spirituality is that both are, for the conservative mainstream, taboo subjects (although religion without spirituality, and heterosexuality which keeps quiet about sex, are the backbone of the Establishment). From the experience of being in the closet, queer people well know how destructive it is to be told to keep quiet about your deepest feelings. The no-go zones are established in childhood; Moira recalls that 'like sexuality, spirituality was not really talked about. I have the impression that my family are very uncomfortable with both subjects, and if I see my father praying in church – for example, at a funeral – he appears far too vulnerable to me, like I have seen him in the bath or on the toilet or something.' Mike Fox learned the same sorry lessons: 'as a child I was taught that spirituality and mysticism were "abnormal"; only the saints were mystic, only the saints were spiritual. I was also taught that being gay was abnormal.' Joseph, who would later become a Franciscan friar, remembers his schooling: 'Religious Instruction in my case was entirely Christian, Church of England. We were also given a class or two on sex, what physically happens. There was nothing about the emotions and feelings associated with sex or faith, the needs of one's mind or soul. Nothing about love, the word that connects sex and spirituality: love, and the need to be loved.'

Spirituality, like sexuality, is a bit embarrassing. It's not rational, it's too complex to be neatly categorized or even talked about, and often leads to people getting rather excited. It's also very serious, and has a power that can be revolutionary. These are all things that a conformist society – that is, a fundamentally frightened society – will hate. The consequence of these taboos is all too clear to David Allen, a Church of England vicar who has struggled with them both: 'Just as many have a stunted/limited view of sexuality – so too many have a narrow view of religion and spirituality.' Lesbian, gay and bisexual people have fought the stunting of sexuality; but this has not led us to break the taboo around spirituality. Heterosexuals cannot always be blamed for conformist pressures. In queer contexts, religion is generally mentioned only as a source of homophobia, a symbol of hetero-power. It is usually spoken of with the explicit or implicit message that queer life, free of the homophobia and hang-ups endemic in (some) religion, is unquestionably superior. But the needs and experiences which have been identified as spiritual are not automatically met by a queer lifestyle – however fab – nor by winning equal rights, however morally necessary.

Wouldn't it be a bitter irony if queers, who have fought so hard against the repression of sexuality, have colluded with our oppressors in keeping spirituality under wraps? Have we seen through one set of lies, only to believe another, which lead us to neglect an equally important part of ourselves? Steve Hope, a gay Quaker, thinks so. 'The attack that lesbian and gay people have to make against religion is in many ways necessary in order to survive. But one of the terrible disservices it does to them is that they can't sort out the wood from the trees. They feel the spiritual sensibility, which I think is essential to life, is something they have to reject, because it must be intrinsically hostile to them. Like the wizard of Oz, the patriarchs have been telling us the bullshit for so long, they're very good at making it seem like absolute truth. So even though we hate them, we believe it as well.'

Notes

1. Cardinal Ratzinger, *Pastoral Care of Homosexual People*, letter to American bishops, 1986.
2. Lord Jakobovits, who made these comments, was head of only one branch of Judaism – the (Orthodox) United Synagogues – and was criticized for his comments by many Jewish people, as well as many gay people.
3. A Statement by the House of Bishops, *Issues in Human Sexuality* (London: Church House Publishing, 1991).
4. Cassell now have a religious section in their contemporary studies catalogue; and the subject is generally less of a taboo, partly because of the increased media interest in gay people in the Church.
5. Throughout this book, the Quakers referred to are members of the Society of Friends in the UK, or attenders of their meetings – people who would be called 'liberal Quakers' in the USA. They should not be confused with the more Biblical/fundamentalist form of Quakerism found elsewhere in the world. The religious groupings used in this book reflect British society rather than worldwide trends.
6. One of London's gayest areas.
7. Many of the comments attributed to Bill in this book are taken from the texts of speeches he has given, which he kindly made available to me. These include his address to the 7th International Conference on Cancer Nursing in 1992 (*The Spirituality of Sexuality – with Particular Reference to People Living with HIV/AIDS*) and *The Gift of Homosexuality*, delivered to the Sheffield Diocesan Conference in 1995.
8. Joseph Campbell, *The Power of Myth* (New York: Doubleday, 1988), p. 3.

9. Craig O'Neill and Kathleen Ritter, *Coming Out Within* (San Francisco: HarperSanFransisco, 1992), p. 213.

10. Sisters of Perpetual Indulgence do not, necessarily, identify as spiritual or religious – although most of the ones who pop up in this book do. The Sisters are more than a parody of religion, although it is way beyond my abilities to sum up exactly what they are about. It is impossible to generalize about the Sisters' role or theory since they themselves resist all attempts at dogma (instead preferring their own, highly variable 'dingoma'). What can be said with certainty is that the Sisters often bring a valuable perspective to gay life.

11. A pioneering drop-in centre and hospice for people with HIV/AIDS.

12. Home of London's most prominent gay business district.

13. Clubs in London, popular with sadomasochists.

2

'The Truth Will Set You Free'

*He [the homosexual] would be forced to think.
His mind turned inward on himself would be
forced to tackle the problem of his own nature
and, afterward, the problem of the world
and of outer nature.*

(Edward Carpenter, *Intermediate Types Among Primitive Folk*)[1]

Against all expectations, and in the face of sometimes considerable resistance, it is possible to be spiritual as well as lesbian or gay. Some people – following the example of Edward Carpenter – argue that being both is more than a possibility: it is a likelihood. The experience of being queer in this society can give us insights which are spiritual, if we choose to see them as such. Our sexual orientation, and our sexuality, can be a starting point on the spiritual journey. And the fact that certain religions will wash their hands of us doesn't stop us making this journey; on the contrary, it's their rejection that can get us started.

QUESTIONING OURSELVES

Spirituality arises from (and is the process of asking, if not conclusively answering) the ultimate questions: why am I here, how do we live? To realize that you are other-than-heterosexual in this society is to initiate a process of self-analysis that can include, or eventually lead to, those same Big Questions. To be queer is an existential condition; it forces us to ask (even if only for a short while), who am I? If I am not like others that I see around me, what am I about? Elizabeth Stuart calls these 'deep spiritual questions which can be avoided or postponed by heterosexual people.'[2] Straight society purports to have all the answers: you do what everybody else does (it seems to work for them, after all). Actually, it could be argued that queer culture makes the same claims; but before it has the opportunity to do so – while we are coming out, at least – we have to look somewhere else for answers: inside.

'Because we're told that we're always wrong, that we're not meant to be here, gay people more than others go out of their way to find out what they *are* really here for,' argues Jason Oliver. 'They look inwards.' Adam James, a former fashion designer who is now an Aura-soma colour therapist, had to accept his sexuality when his marriage began to falter. 'I thought, not only why am I gay, but why am I a man? why am I anything? who am I? and where am I going? It is when we begin to ask these questions that we begin the spiritual quest.'

Nagaraja, from the perspective of Buddhism, reckons that 'once you've started asking questions, you can't stop.' As a result of this process, we 'fall out of innocence'; which is necessary for spiritual growth, as the Garden of Eden myth suggests. Because 'we are more compelled to wonder about our existence and our place in the world' as Dirk de Klerk puts it, we are (in Buddhist terms) more 'awake' to the truth. Michael Seán Paterson recognizes this potential for maturity: 'we've had to grow up – or we've been invited to grow up – much quicker than many. Some of the big existential questions were ours in our early teens; we didn't have to wait until someone died.' Realizing you are queer – or testing HIV positive – is 'an invitation to discover and articulate one's deepest desires for life. And if this is not spirituality, what is?'[3]

Philip Joyce, a gay complementary therapist, reasons that 'people who have opened up, and faced up to themselves in a deeper way, are more consciously exploring the spiritual path than people who haven't'. The Reverend Jean White agrees: 'I think every one of us comes to that spiritual crossroads – or crisis point – where we accept who we are, or reject or cover up who we are. Because we don't have the same resources to help us deal with the things that happen in our lives, you begin to seek a strength which you can't find in society around you. You fall back on your own resources, you have to turn to something inside of yourself (or outside of yourself) – and in doing that you discover your own spirituality.'

'When you're confronting your own sexuality, you're confronting yourself at the very deepest level of your being – and it's in that deepest level of your being that your spirituality dwells as well', explains Diana Reynolds. 'A lot of straight people never confront their sexuality. They're "normal" and they just get on with life; they never actually look at who they are because they don't think they need to. So because they don't go through that process of delving deep inside themselves, they never get to that level of looking at their spirituality either, or even realize that they have a spirituality.' Adam Sutcliffe, a Jewish gay man in his late twenties, comes to the same conclusion. 'In contrast with the unthinking, taken-for-granted way in which so many straight people seem to stumble catatonically through most of the key personal choices of life, the experience of confronting our sexuality initiates many lesbians and gay men into a much more self-aware, engaged way of thinking about our priorities and our identities. It seems a natural process, having carefully interrogated and re-defined our sexual feelings, for us to explore our spiritual concerns in a similarly penetrating and personal way.'

'Gay people often have a huge advantage because they have to lead examined lives, i.e. ask why this has happened to me,' says Johnathon Andrew. 'Thomas Merton said that you have to go to your cell, and your cell will teach you all that you have to know – which means you've got to go inside of yourself. Being gay has forced me to do that. AIDS has too.'

NOT FITTING IN

The catalyst for this crucial process of questioning and turning within is the feeling of not being able to identify fully with the surrounding world: our 'queerness'. Few things (other than being attracted to the same sex) can truly be said to be shared by all queers: but perhaps, if anything can, it is having had (at least for a time) a profound experience of not fitting in. David Philbedge recalls this from his childhood: 'I'd felt from a very early age an outsider, which I think is a common experience for gay men – as you grow up you feel somewhat out of synch from the other people around you. It shifted my perspective, my attitude to life in general, which basically manifested itself in me being incredibly discontented and difficult. If you have a sense that you're different from what's around you, you're not going to get sucked in without thinking, you're not going to accept received wisdom. All worthwhile spiritual paths involve asking questions: it's that sense of being an outsider that maybe begins that process. Spirituality is about realizing your place in the world: if you're lesbian or gay, your position in the world is going to be different from what other people tell you, and from their position in the world.'

Fernando Guasch, now, like David, practising Tibetan Buddhism, agrees that 'this radical form of dislocation is fundamentally the core of the gay experience. Not everybody makes it – people fuck up, kill themselves in various ways – but you can get some glimpses on the world from that situation that I think are fundamentally true, and deeply spiritual. The experience of the closet, of living as not-in-the-world because the world did not belong to you, of not finding your dreams and aspirations reflected in the culture around you: if gay people only dare wrestle with the freshness and the directness of the things that we can perceive about life, rather than inventing Disneyworlds, it's much more interesting. Jung says consciousness comes out of friction: where you clash with the rest of things. It makes you very aware. Being gay allows you to "read the world differently", as the American Indians say. Gay people can see through many of the "god-given truths" that so many straight people seem to believe are moral/ethical facts about the world – they're good myth busters. Gay people have always been able to point at the emperor and say he has no clothes.'

For another Buddhist, Maitreyabandhu, the enforced realization of isolation, although painful when he was younger ('I felt I had a secret, I didn't fit in. I felt wholly alone in a world I thought would never understand me'), was ultimately useful: what is most spiritually unhealthy is conformity. 'To the extent that we have not fully differentiated our thoughts and feelings from society's and not taken full responsibility for our actions, we will be group members. We will be characterized by unthinking prejudices and "moral" assumptions of the group rather than by our own individual awareness. It may never occur to us that we are conforming, that we think and feel just as the group does. However, when we come out we have that awareness thrust upon us. We realize that we do not fit in to the expectations of the group, whether it be the group of our immediate family, the Church, our peers or our work colleagues. For me this was a very frightening and isolating experience. I so wanted to fit in. I so wanted to conform to the group. But I couldn't. I was gay. Coming out can be the beginning of a realization that you're never going to fit into the group – you have to realize you're different. Only an individual can practise a spiritual life, a life devoted to developing our individual self-awareness.' Gary, a gay man in his thirties, remembers going through this process at a young age. 'I didn't identify with my parents or anything I saw around me. I couldn't identify with the group. So very early on I self-identified – I thought, I have to develop myself – and now I look at our culture without being part of it. I've been able to see things from a different perspective, as they really are; and I've had all sorts of experiences I wouldn't have had otherwise. Once you've gone beyond those traditional assumptions, anything is possible.' Maitreyabandhu enjoyed this same sense of greater potential. Being gay allowed him 'to experiment with ways of being which departed from the assumptions and expectations of my family, and the narrow-mindedness of the small town I grew up in.' For both Gary and Maitreyabandhu these experiments and experiences eventually led to spirituality.

Roberta Wedge, as a bisexual, is more acutely aware of being different than even the majority of lesbian and gay people, knowing both 'the experience of being not straight *and* the experience of not fitting into the old lesbian or gay organizations'. As a consequence of this, among bisexuals she sees 'more of an acceptance of other ways of doing things, other ways of looking at things', an acceptance that she also finds among fellow Pagans. That heterosexual convention is not the sole Way, Truth and Life – that there are other ways of being sexual, and of living – is the fundamental queer insight. As Sister Latex of the Order of Perpetual Indulgence says, 'heterosexuals don't have to "objectify", to see themselves from the outside. Their roles fit them. Gay people never fit in. We've got to live with cognitive dissonance all the time.' Part of the work of the Sisters is to symbolize and celebrate this queerness: there is nowhere that a group of gay male nuns will ever seem 'normal'. And it is our very queerness, the impossibility of fitting in, that sets us free. Niall Johnston, speaking from a position that at first sight seems very different to the Sisters – as a Church of England chaplain – feels the same: 'Being gay for me is about setting light to tradition; not feeling constrained by convention, but rather being free – liberated – to discover oneself, and to find out what it truly means for me to be human.' Religion ought to provide the same liberation, at least according to the Reverend Neil Thomas of the Metropolitan Community Church: 'true Christianity is about being free – it's about experiencing your own story, with no limitations. The Christian Church talks about freedom, yet it binds people up. Our spirituality doesn't need to be controlled.'

Catherine Hopper appreciates the liberty inherent in being lesbian. 'The slate is wiped completely clean. We can draw our own maps of our lives. There are no landmarks – no one expects me to get married, no one particularly expects me to have children or grandchildren.' Catherine maintains that, regardless of sexuality, 'anybody can leave the rails if they want to'. But whereas many heterosexuals never realize this, or choose not to – it is so much less effort to get on the marriage-mortgage-children route, and so much what is expected – things are not mapped out for us in the same way. This gives us the chance to search for what feels truthful, and good, instead of doing what we're told. We have the potential to create rather than inherit our lives, as Sister Latex, part of a growing and ever-adapting order, knows well: 'the thing about gay people is they can constantly reinvent themselves, and indeed must.'

Certainly, the pressure to have children is one burden that many queer people are glad to be relieved of.[4] Maitreyabandhu is aware of the advantages: 'Children are nice things to have I presume, it's perfectly valid – but it's not a spiritual thing to do, it's biological. Children are very time-consuming. The fact that you can avoid those sort of responsibilities means that you can – in principle – devote yourself more wholeheartedly to your spiritual life. Saying that because we don't have children we have no meaning in our life – that's just nonsense.' It is nonsense because, instead of having our life's meaning delivered automatically with a bawling bundle and buckets of goo, the majority of queers seek to find – or make – meaning in other ways. We are thrown back upon questions: 'You don't have kids –

what are you going to do with life? What's valuable? What are the priorities? Is it going clubbing? Having a steady partner? Is *that* it? Any step forward from there must be a spiritual one: to develop, to develop consciousness, to become a force for good in the world – to commit to a spiritual path.' Jason Oliver, a Pagan, takes a similar line. 'I think gay people are here to prove there's more to life than having kids and having a job. To procreate is pure animal instinct. There are enough people in this world to have children, so I'd rather get on with something more exciting. Gay people have more time to do other things. Gay people don't have set roles that are put down for them, we achieve our own roles – that's more spiritual. It's up to the individual to find out what their role is.'

Edward Carpenter, the remarkable socialist, feminist, environmentalist, poet, all-round good guy and gay rights pioneer writing at the start of this century, thought that queers (or Uranians, as he called us) were a people, and a people with a role: leading the spiritual revolution for humanity. This would be possible chiefly because we would not be spending time raising offspring. 'As the ordinary love [heterosexuality] has a special function in the propagation of the race, so the other has its special function in social and heroic work and in the generation not of bodily children but of those children of the mind – the philosophical conceptions and ideals which transform our lives and those of society.'[5] Although the post-Stonewall generations have failed to live up to Carpenter's vision, many queers have, in a more modest fashion, exemplified this understanding that our lives can be creative instead of procreative; that more can be birthed than children. As a young lesbian Christian said to me, 'I hate to think of myself as ending with myself. So my spirituality is a way of seeing myself as connected to everybody else; a channel through which things pass to other people.'

COMING OUT

Coming out is a refusal to be limited to how others define us, and an act of increased awareness. We become conscious of more of ourselves – and perhaps, as a consequence, more conscious. For this reason, coming out (especially its first stage, coming out to oneself) can be a road-to-Damascus revelation. It was for Philip Joyce. He was, at the time, a married father of three in his thirties, and priest to a higher education college. 'At a chaplains' conference, in a workshop on sexuality, I experienced a moment of profound insight and spiritual power, when I allowed in the "truth" that I am gay. It was an overwhelming insight, enabling me to make sense of so many of my previous feelings and experiences. It released an enormous amount of energy. I experienced a powerful sense of self, and a human warmth towards other people, which were new to me. I was illuminated and exhilarated, and it changed the course of my life. It was a new truth by which I had to live. It was so inspirational that I would say this was a major stage in my spiritual growth.'

For Diana Reynolds, now a priest, coming out was equally profound. 'I don't know how it happened really, but I was walking down the street one day and I suddenly saw a woman, and looked at her in a way that I'd never looked at anybody before. It wasn't just a physical lust that I'd never felt; it was like the sun rising in the morning, a whole new light came over me. I sensed this insight into who I was as a person. I was bowled over by it; it was almost like I was in a trance. There was a strong sense that *this was me*; I still couldn't name it, but I knew myself. I was living at the time in a lay community: we had daily contemplative prayer together, about half an hour's silence every evening. I'd been praying this way for ten years and had always felt there was some kind of barrier, I could never put my finger on what it was. That night the silence was different: it was like the wall had been taken away. There was nothing between me and God any more. Until then I'd managed to hide who I was from myself, and from the God I was meeting in that silence. I don't know if it was me that realized, or if God was telling me – it depends what kind of language you use about God – but I had an awareness then that I was gay, and that was the way I'd been made and that was the way God wanted me to live my life. It was a very liberating experience. I sat in the silence for three hours that night, and it felt like five minutes. I just soaked up energy from it; it was like I'd been a dry sponge that had been put in a bucket of water. I came out of that silence and said yes, I'm gay, that's fine, I'm going to tell everyone and celebrate it. And I did: I went to work the next morning and told everyone! It was a total transformation. It affected the way I saw everybody and everything.'

Because many people's experience of the closet is as a sort of living death – a life-denying restriction – coming out is sometimes compared with being born again. Another life begins, this time living according to the truth. Kate spent many years suppressing her sexuality, having been persuaded by years of Christian indoctrination that it was 'shameful'. 'When I finally stopped playing the game, I felt "born again", or rather that I had finally found who I really was. From being monochrome, life had become glorious Technicolor.' 'The empty tomb on Easter becomes the coming out experience,' says Eric Bond. 'One must always remember that Jesus was tortured and killed first and that this fate, metaphorically or literally, may await other pioneers in spirituality because they threaten the vested interests of the status quo and the hierarchy.' Jesus raises Lazarus from the dead with the words 'come out' (John 11:43). Lazarus is sometimes depicted as scared and reluctant, for the tomb (or the closet) has the comforts of a certain safety and security. But for those who break out, the new life is worth the risk. Christian terminology provides another useful concept: conversion. Life is turned around by a dramatic new insight into the way things are. Like conversion to a faith, coming out, although it may begin with a dramatic revelation, continues for the rest of one's life – its meaning is constantly revised, as new consequences arise.

This 'conversion' experience is not spoken of only by Christians. Buddhist Dirk de Klerk went through the same thing: 'When I came out, everything fell into place – I was so happy, it was a wonderful experience, like discovering meditation. It's a way of saying what you are.' Jewish tradition provides some important parallels to the coming out experience. 'The Hebrew word for "Egypt" comes from the verb that means to be in a tight place, in a narrow passage – and if that's not a description of being in the closet, I don't know what is,' says Rabbi Sheila Shulman. '"Coming out" is the most accurate translation of the Hebrew word *yitziat*, which in the phrase *zecher yitziat mitzraim* ("a remembrance of the coming out of Egypt") rings through our liturgy over and over again. That fundamental image of liberation is at the core of Judaism. It is the first of the commandments. It is how Jews understand our relation to God . . . a God who is passionate about the people's particularity, their uniqueness, and is engaged with them in their struggle for the freedom to realize their liberation.' Consequently, Passover – the festival which commemorates this coming out, and one of the holiest occasions in the Jewish calendar – has an added significance for lesbian and gay Jews. Another gay rabbi, Mark Solomon, has adapted lines from the Passover liturgy for the text that is used in regular worship by London's Jewish Gay and Lesbian Group – 'We have come out from darkness to light, from slavery to freedom, from anguish to great joy, from the closet to the world.'

I AM WHAT I AM

We can come out of the closet only having gone into the depth of ourselves; and in doing so we get closer to the 'ground of our being'. Harvey Gillman (a gay Quaker from a Jewish background) feels that 'exploration of the self, this journey to personal authenticity, is part of the journey towards God. In his *Seeds of Contemplation*, Thomas Merton wrote "the problem of sanctity is finding out who I am . . . if I never become what I am meant to be, but always remain what I am not, I shall spend my life contradicting myself by being at once something and nothing, a life that wants to live and is dead."'[6] What is coming out if not 'finding out who I am'? For Rabbi Elizabeth Sarah, spirituality is 'being as far as possible the whole of who I am'. The Reverend Jean White uses similar terms: 'for me it's being aware of ourselves, it's accepting who I am – I am gay, I am who I am – and living our lives within that context of saying, I am what I am.'

Jean invokes the classic gay statement of self, *I am what I am*; the same words are also the classic statement of spiritual truth. In the Old Testament they are how God is identified; when Moses asks the voice in the burning bush to identify itself, it replies 'I am what I am'. To be oneself, to be aware, to be conscious, to be; awareness, consciousness, being; these things have been the concerns of spiritual traditions throughout history, and they are signified by *I am what I am*. Queer posters, placards and T-shirts sometimes adapt Descartes, and proclaim 'I'm out therefore I am'. Descartes' original statement ('I think therefore I am') was interpreted as a spiritual intimation by Bede Griffiths – a Christian monk who founded an ashram in India. He wrote that 'to think is to reflect on oneself, to grasp oneself in the totality of one's being in the world'; and that human intelligence, with this capacity for self-reflection, 'gives knowledge not only of itself but also of its source in the universal, cosmic intelligence'.[7] 'I am out therefore I am' is thus more profound than it might, at first glance, seem – in so far as coming out can initiate the process of self-reflection, which leads to knowledge of the universal.

Obviously not every queer who has mouthed *I am what I am* is consciously articulating a profound spiritual discovery. All the same, by accepting more of who you are – by accepting that you are who you are – you inevitably undergo a degree of personal growth that can be the catalyst for further insights. 'I've kept coming up against the question of how to differentiate between spirituality and personal growth. For me they are the same thing,' says Nick Williams, who has spent years struggling with a repressive Christian upbringing and now looks to New Age writers for inspiration. 'The quest for connection to a life force (or the universe or whatever you call it) is about self-connection. In terms of energy, I see it as my duty and my greatest desire to channel the energy which is "me" and then I will know if there's anything else. More and more I am trusting the unconscious parts of myself and daring to believe my inner nature may be good and will lead me to my place (or even be my place).' Father Bernard Lynch, a therapist as well as a priest, sees the mark of existence as 'becoming myself in all the fullness of my person-hood'.[8] He asserts that 'the distinction between profound knowledge of oneself and insight into one's surrounds is artificial. We are examining questions of Being and our reason for being.'[9] Like several contributors to this book, Bernard is inspired by Irenaeus, the third-century saint who asserted that 'the glory of God is a person who is fully alive'. By being ourselves, we come closer to realizing our divine nature. This is something Roberta Wedge finds made explicit in the faith she follows: 'A common expression heard in Pagan circles is "Thou art Goddess"/"Thou art God".

Being divine doesn't mean that we all are (or even that any of us is) perfect, but it does mean that we each have a great, grave, joyous, holy responsibility for our lives, and to reach out to others too, to shake them and wake them into claiming the power of their own lives. The simplest way I look at it is to see each individual as a precious miracle, a unique being.'

THE TRUTH OF OUR EXPERIENCE

I am what I am is an incontrovertible proposition: it cannot be other than true. 'Coming out . . . is nothing more or less than a commitment to tell the truth, to live the truth, to "do the truth",' wrote the late Robert Williams, an openly gay man who was ordained (in the face of much protest) as an Episcopalian priest in San Francisco.[10] Telling the truth is a spiritual quality, and crucial to spirituality. It would be difficult to make spiritual progress if something was being hidden – as Diana Reynolds experienced before she came out, when her prayers were marked by a barrier between her and God. By contrast, Mike Fox can say 'because I am rooted in who and what I am, it is easier for me to honestly approach God': so 'being gay is an important way into spirituality', even though it might bring him into conflict with the hierarchy of the Roman Catholic faith he follows. A Zen teacher in America is reported to have said that 'anyone in the closet is not a Zen student'.[11] As Maitreyabandhu puts it, 'you have to be yourself to change yourself.'

Because we need to come out if we are to have the chance of a fulfilling emotional life, queer people experience a kind of gravitational pull towards truth-telling, an imperative to be honest (about sexual orientation, at least). A lot of religious groups are scared of truth, and will put pressure on their members to suppress it in order to keep up a façade of conventionality and conformity: this is how Christian denominations can criticize homosexuality despite a quarter of their clergy being gay (at a conservative estimate), and why marriage is promoted as an ideal despite all the divorce, adultery, abuse and everyday misery that accompanies it. Any religious group which uses 'niceness' as its badge of membership will produce hypocrites, because it will limit the ability of its followers to admit the truth about themselves. Father Bernard Lynch, who has worked with many people living with AIDS, says that if the virus 'is teaching us anything, it is teaching us that it is better to be whole than good. Being good is the stuff of religion – which is about control. Whereas being whole is the work of spirituality – which is about integrity, freedom and joy.'

Being queer leads us not into the temptation to 'keep up appearances'. 'What was then the most fundamental part of my life became absolutely public a few years ago,' Catherine Hopper asserts. 'I've got nothing to lose. I don't think I've really got much to withhold from people any more. We have this saying in the FWBO: there are no secrets in the spiritual life.' Although there are losses involved in coming out, these are endured in the promise of future gains. For Bernard Lynch, although the 'conversion' of coming out 'may involve an Exodus as personal and political as Moses and the people of Israel from Egypt – "leave your family, your country and your father's house, for the land that I will show you" – here the soul grows by a process of subtraction. For all spirituality is based on truth: the truth of our experience.'

Our experience cannot be denied, although certain religions may try, for they would like to have the monopoly on truth. As Rabbi Lionel Blue puts it, 'more truth has been revealed in our time than is officially allowed. The labels have been unfamiliar, but all truth is holy . . . Our problem today is not the lack of truth, but its abundance and variety. It is so various that our religions cannot contain it. It overflows our traditional compartments and categories. Saintliness can be found in a disco, and a blessing in a bar. This is no esoteric truth. We know it, straight and gay alike, from our own experience.'[12]

To come out as lesbian, gay or bisexual is to assert the importance of the truth of our experience, even though this risks our security. Having done so, we are unlikely to surrender our hard-won insight into the way things are. If the existential questions provoked by being queer cause us to look to religion for answers, we have a yardstick with which to judge what they tell us. If we're told that we should not exist, or that our sexuality is wrong, we have reason to doubt the veracity of anything else they may say. We are sceptical of anything that will not acknowledge or allow the truth of our experience. We have a built-in – some might say God-given – bullshit detector. This is a necessary tool for any encounter with religion which attracts more than its fair share of charlatans as well as bullies. Any spirituality worth its salt survives our scepticism; a lot of conventional religion does not.

THE AUTHORITY OF OUR EXPERIENCE

From the scrutiny and self-questioning of coming out comes the strength of self-knowledge, and the realization that we need to value our internal life, rather than simply conform to the external world. This confidence in the authority of personal experience is a marked trait of spiritual queers, and is important whether the individual concerned is following an orthodox tradition (such as most forms of Christianity) or a looser, more individualistic path (for instance, a 'New Age' approach).

The Reverend Jacqueline has first-hand experience of the conflict between inner spirituality and external religion. 'I have always been a quester, a searcher – and torn between what I was told I ought to believe and what I actually did believe. There has been a lot of internal struggle and angst, but I have always valued highly my own experience, and sought to shape my understanding of the Christian faith in the light of that, rather than interpreting my experience in the light of my received understanding of the Christian faith.'

To people with a paternalistic concept of religion (God commands, we obey) it may sound heretical to value personal experience over the supposed authority of religious institutions and scriptures. But for queer people who follow religions that embrace this paternalistic model (which, not coincidentally, are the religions whose leaders are most likely to attack queer people), there can ultimately be no choice about where the power should lie. In order to survive, they *must* value their own experience, even if this means rejecting their religion. Gay people learn the hard way that 'the root of happiness, the only happiness possible, is to be oneself', in the words of Father Bernard Lynch. He often says that 'if it comes to a choice between God and self, one must always choose self'. Alienation from self, for Bernard, means alienation from God. 'My true self is God. As Meister Eckhardt put it, "Between God and Us there is no between." God is for the heart. When you know your heart then you'll know God.' In so far as religion prevents queer people knowing their hearts – and encourages them to deny their true selves – 'all religion is about the denial of God'.

Rabbi Lionel Blue argues that religion is valid only if it acknowledges the reality of people's experience. 'The traditional scriptures in isolation are not sufficient, and indeed never have been. That is because they are external to us. Books stand still, experience does not. Books can only speak of God's redemption to other people at other times. We have to supplement them with our own experience, which tells us how the same God redeemed us from our own Egypt in our own time. . . . the text that needs most examination is the fabric of people's lives.'[13] This is the text queer people are forced to examine. In doing so, the external scriptures may assume less importance. Although a priest, Diana Reynolds freely admits she is very rarely guided by what the Church says. 'I don't think Jesus was either, and I'm quite happy to follow his example.' Diana began her theological training shortly after the 'revelation' of her sexuality described earlier. She was aware of a wide gap between her religion and her reality: 'What we were taught at theological college was too simple: my life hasn't been like that.' Now she argues that instead of blindly obeying the rules (which in her case would mean that she should not have been ordained), we should 'listen to ourselves and what's going on inside. I think whatever we do must be motivated by love, real love for our humanity. If that's not our primary reason for doing things, then we shouldn't be doing them.' The Reverend Richard Kirker, general secretary of Britain's Lesbian and Gay Christian Movement, also wrestled with this split between what the Church taught and what was going on in his life, when he was coming out (and falling in love) at theological college in the early 1970s. 'Just as my relationship was formed without the benefit of positive role models, the Church has not given us any assistance in creating a spirituality which is appropriate to the people we are, and that's made me much more doubtful about simply using old formulas. I don't see lesbian and gay people trusting a spirituality predicated upon a notion of what constitutes authority, truth and integrity which simply doesn't fully acknowledge their own authority, their own truth and their own integrity.'

The need for his experience to be validated, rather than ignored or condemned, is one of the main reasons Peter Wyles is a Quaker. 'Quakerism is a religion of experience. We go every week, and indeed between meetings, back to that source, to reconnect ourselves with the world and our fellow people. Ultimately it does come down to the sovereignty of personal experience, thereby allowing people with an extraordinary range of views about God, Jesus, the spirit, the afterlife' – and, in some meetings, sexuality – 'to come together each week and to be a community'. Buddhism also emphazises the sovereignty of personal experience. 'The Buddha urged his followers to not just take his word for it but to test everything for themselves,' explains Maitreyabandhu. 'I wasn't asked to believe anything I couldn't check out for myself, or couldn't eventually experience.' This suck-it-and-see approach appealed to Dirk de Klerk: 'Meditation was an incredible discovery: it meant I could find out for myself, nobody was going to tell me what to believe (as the Church was doing all the time then). Concepts are not important, ideas are not important; it's not what you believe, it's what you *know*. All of the philosophy, all of the teachings of Buddhism are simply for you to take out of that whatever seems reasonable to you, whatever you might find useful in order to widen your understanding. But if there's anything you find useful in the Bible then use it, because *you* are the person who wants to get wisdom, *you* are the person who wants understanding. Take out what's useful, and don't worry about the rest.'

Trusting internal experience even
when it contradicts cultural norms

SPIRITUAL MATURITY

Buddhism and Quakerism are paths that have traditionally placed great importance on the individual's experience and development. But queer people are likely to favour this experience-centred approach *whichever* faith they follow, not least because they are often forced to, for the sake of their survival. To understand faith in this way is more than a defensive necessity, however; it is psychologically healthy, and spiritually mature. Spiritual maturity is marked by the shift from external religion to internal spirituality; as with psychological maturity, it can be characterized as the movement from childish dependence to adult independence (or interdependence). A useful model of spiritual maturity is the simplification of James Fowler's work made popular by M. Scott Peck.[14] Queer people are likely to leave behind, or be forced out of, the 'formal/institutional' understanding of faith: this is Peck's second stage, where believers are dependent on the outward forms of religion (institutions, rules, clergy), look to religion for discipline, and generally understand God as external, male and punitive. Lesbian, gay and bisexual people are far more inclined to stage three, the 'sceptic/individual', which Peck depicts as spiritually more advanced even though it may involve rejecting religion altogether. Stage three people pay far more attention to their inner life: they acknowledge doubt, are more inclined to be critical of what they are told and take responsibility for themselves. Peck identifies a fourth stage which he terms 'mystic/communal'. Fourth-stage people find God within as well as around them, perceive the connectedness of life, and are open to a degree of ultimate 'mystery'. Unlike second-stage people, they do not need everything to be explained and legislated.

This psychological approach to spiritual growth has been conceptualized in slightly different terms by various other people – including some gay and lesbian psychologists. John J. McNeill – a gay psychotherapist and priest, who was expelled from the Society of Jesus for his public support of queer people – makes a distinction between pathological and healthy religion. Pathological religion resembles the sort of family background that leads to pathological behaviour: it represses feeling, discourages individual independence and ensures obedience through fear of punishment or rejection. Healthy faiths – and healthy families – value individual choice but recognize human vulnerability and limitations. 'Whatever is psychologically destructive must be bad theology,' McNeill reasons. 'We must ask ourselves which of the church's values we continue to want, respect, and love; in other words, which values are compatible with who we are and are not destructive of our dignity as persons.'[15] Craig O'Neill and Kathleen Ritter, in *Coming Out Within*, describe the movement from pathological to healthy religion as a journey from external authority to personal integrity, from rigidity to openness and from literal understandings of the world to symbolic ones.[16]

The clearest example of 'formal/institutional' spirituality – i.e. pathological or 'rigid' religion – is fundamentalist Christianity. Drew Payne spent his teens involved with a group of fundamentalist Christians who eventually attempted to cast out the 'demon' of his homosexuality. He describes their thinking: 'It's a religion of answers, not questions and exploration. It's very safe. You don't have the worry and trouble of working out what you believe, someone else has done that and all you have to do is believe what you are told . . . in a world of uncertainty, that's very attractive. As a very troubled adolescent, introverted and almost self-hating, very afraid of my sexuality, it was certainly attractive to me.' Drew eventually let go of the 'harsh and judgmental God'; he realized 'God was love not hate'. With that image of God, he also lost the easy certainty of fundamentalist belief, and for many years longed for it to return; however, 'I've come to realize that I can never refind that unmoving and unchanging faith because emotionally and intellectually I have changed and moved so far from my teenage years. Spirituality, for me, is something changing and evolving, growing with time and experience.' Since coming out is a process of asking questions, a religion of easy answers will not suffice.

Dennis, a minister with the Church of Scotland, once found himself 'in a study group where someone said that two men can't love each other, because love is defined by the Christian faith, and so had to involve a man and a woman'. The ludicrousness of this 'logic' is a good example of how pathological religion can elevate its own doctrine over any evidence to the contrary (like the Catholic Church insisting that Galileo could not be right about the earth revolving around the sun); and how it assumes it has a monopoly over experience. Dennis is clear that you can minister to people's spiritual needs only if you start where they are, not where authority says they should be. 'What I try to do in my work is to listen to what people are saying, to acknowledge the reality of people's lives, to be honest, and not come in with a big moral sawn-off shotgun.' The moral firearms are not wielded just by institutional religion; many individuals, in their attempts to understand their spirituality, are hampered by an internal shotgun of their own, implanted in childhood, and ready to shoot their own reality to pieces.

The gun can be disarmed by the introspection and self-affirmation of coming out – and by the rearticulation of religious belief that is often necessary for those people who follow a faith before coming out. As people move from the 'formal/institutional' stage to the open understanding of the 'individual/sceptic', religion is seen less as a threat and more as an ally. 'I've always looked on Buddhism as a tool, something to actively make me feel better – rather than a prop, which is something one leans on for support, something I see as static,' says Peter Ashby-Saracen, a gay man from Cumbria. In the past he too been tempted by fundamentalism. 'Christianity was something I wanted to protect me from the hurts of life and to take away certain things I couldn't handle at the time, like my sexuality. Nowadays I look on life as a voyage of discovery, and a "prop" would only tie me down to one point.' What attracted Peter to the Buddhism of Nichiren Daishonin was its 'emphasis on the practice serving the individual, rather than the individual serving the religion. It is a liberating experience to know that there is a non-restrictive practice aimed primarily at encouraging you to be what you are. Being able to become the real me is of immense importance. If I ever felt that Buddhism wasn't serving my purposes any longer I would reject it without hesitation.' He believes because he chooses to; because it is useful for him to do so. He is not disempowered by his faith. In this, he is typical of queer believers.

'The process that every human being has to undergo in order to become fully healthy includes the identification of, and detachment from, the socially conditioned values, concepts, attitudes and behavioural patterns which, beginning as children, we adopt uncritically,' writes Richard Woods, another therapist-priest.[17] Everyone has to do this if they want greater psychological well-being – or spiritual maturity. Many people can avoid the process: but queer people cannot. The very sense of not fitting in that was identified earlier requires us to be critical; coming out involves detaching ourselves from the dominant social conditioning. Thus what other people strive for – or may sometimes not even realize they need to strive for – is our birthright, or rather, our coming-out-right. Whether or not we followed a faith before we came out, we've already laid the groundwork for a healthy, open spirituality.

OUT OF ORTHODOXIES

My initial question – why do queers get involved with spirituality, when they appear to have good reasons for rejecting it? – is beginning to be answered. Chapter one argued that spirituality consists of much more than those religious institutions which condemn us. Now there is another answer: spirituality is a useful tool. Queers are involved because they want to be, not because they feel they ought to be. Religion is assessed according to its utility rather than its claim to authority.

Even a religious professional like Rabbi Mark Solomon refers to himself as 'a religious utilitarian'. This has not always been the case. Mark had been educated at an ultra-Orthodox Lubavitch college, and became the rabbi of an Orthodox congregation. He saw religion as 'fitting into patterns that are already established'. He knew he was sexually attracted to men, knew that Judaism condemned this, and consequently every occasion he prayed or tried to relate to God became 'a spiritual beating up': 'I felt I was so evil, how dare I?' Slowly, he came to value his sexuality, aided by some eclectic guides – Lionel Blue, *Torch Song Trilogy*, *The Color Purple* and the work of lesbian Jewish theologian Judith Plaskow. 'They helped me to realize that the quite rigid categories in which my Judaism had existed were not the only categories possible. In place of the rigid, patriarchal, hierarchical way I'd always thought of God was a new concept of God – gentler, more immanent, more loving – which made it possible for me to come out. I couldn't have done so without that realization that God was beyond all the narrow concepts and systems to which we confine God and confine religion. God broke out of all of that.' Now, instead of rule-based Orthodoxy, he believes that 'there are no answers that are identically suitable for everybody . . . each person has a personal relationship with God which is different, because no two people are precisely the same, no two relationships are precisely the same'. His sexual life obviously improved when he felt it was not sinful; but so did his spiritual life. 'When I didn't have to keep apologizing to God for existing, our relationship improved immeasurably. I became a much nicer person as well: in order to accept oneself, it's important to feel that you are acceptable to God.'

Mark's rejection of rule-based religion meant challenging the authority of scripture – which, in Orthodox Judaism, is a very powerful authority indeed. A particular problem was Leviticus 18:22, often used to justify religious homophobia ('Thou shalt not lie with mankind, as with womankind: it is abomination'). Many have argued for its re-interpretation; Rabbi Solomon took a more radical step. 'Sustained reflection on my situation led me, for the sake of religious and sexual survival, to reject the commandment altogether. Such a prohibition, resulting in centuries of needless deaths and ruined lives, is utterly incompatible with the nature of the God whom I love and worship.' This line of reasoning 'led me to revise my whole conception of the Torah, which I have come to regard not as the unmeditated revelation of God's immutable will, but as an earthly record of the sustained encounter of our people with God, at times expressing the highest wisdom, beauty and goodness of which inspired humanity is capable, at others reflecting the prejudices and fallacies of a primitive and patriarchal society.'[18] Mark now works within the Liberal branch of Judaism.

For people who had some sort of religious life before they came out, this shift from an orthodox, law-based faith to a more liberal, personal understanding is very common. What starts as a defensive renegotiation ends up as a far better deal. Rosie is another person whose spirituality has been transformed in this way: 'I began life as a Catholic but married at eighteen, to the boy next door from the Anglican Church. My faith changed as I grew older, and I suppose the more questions I had (or admitted to myself) about my selfhood, my sexuality and my happiness, the more I also questioned the Church and its constructs. I realized with the death of my sister nine years ago that I didn't have to be "mainstream" anything, I didn't have to suffer or acquiesce on any grounds. I discovered that life could be short and it should be lived to our individual plan and potential. I began to see prayer and meditation as part of my personal survival plan. I found God dwelled in often unusual places, in nonconformity and being true to yourself.' God was less obvious in 'the "Sunday face" of worship at the middle-class high Anglican (very pretty!) village church I went to with my husband and sons. We looked the perfect family . . . husband Church Warden, sons both choirboys, myself sidesperson, reader of prayers and lessons.' Rosie and her husband divorced; she recently celebrated a ceremony of commitment with the woman she loves, Chris. She no longer views religion 'as being about buildings, Church councils and organizational dictates. Religion, for me, is an offering and receiving of something that transcends the everyday. My faith is in my love, in Chris, in friends; in God, which is in all of these. My shaking off of "blind faith", of "blind, unhappy, heterosexuality", and much more, led me to really reach within myself (to find God, to find me), and discover new ways of being. It was a big wrench, but if you don't change, you don't move forward and so you "die". It was exciting and liberating to say "I won't be what people want me to be any more". When I read the Bible now, with my deconstructionist, humanist, liberationist, gender-aware eyes, I am excited because I see the spiritual message of love, acceptance and value. Anglican Sunday services have a place/part for some, but to me they stifle, they are about static modes and constancy that is disrespectful to others, or harmful. They don't offer "magic"; they offer fuel for exclusion, bigotry and mistrust. Hardly what God is about.'

Eric Bond began to revise his faith when, having spoken the sin of his 'homosexuality' in confessional, he was told by the priest that the Church had got it wrong and he should find someone nice to settle down with. 'I realized there are two sorts of Christianities: one was a smug judgemental religion, such as the Pharisees were criticized for in the Gospels; the other is a religion of grace, which states that God accepts us without ifs and buts, just as we are. Other scripture . . . began to make sense to me too: the Exodus experience of the Israelites from bondage through desert to freedom, is mirrored in my leaving rule-bound religion, to feeling a lack of spiritual support, into discovering nurturing relationships. As Ezekiel prophesies that God will replace our hearts of stone with hearts of flesh, I find I become decreasingly hard and critical, even with homophobic people, and increasingly vulnerable and youthfully playful. I still value church membership and attendance, but find more "help" in setting aside at least an hour a day for private prayer and meditation.'

An increased sense of spirituality, awakened by coming out, may actually lead people further away from organized religion, rather than towards it, just as Scott Peck's model suggests. Philip Joyce, having realized he was gay, also realized that his former faith was no longer appropriate. 'Unhappy with the professed attitude of the Church towards gay people and feeling vulnerable in the Chaplaincy where I then worked, I resigned from my appointment and have had a distant relationship with the Church ever since. The reality is that I am growing spiritually. My personal faith has grown through my experience and is open to truth from wherever it may appear. That, I think, is a position of humility not pride. It feels as if there is no undisputed way forward, I have to discover my own path. It feels as though true spirituality is about just such private pursuit of truth (not the application of hard and fast rules), and that real spiritual fellowship involves sharing and being with others in their own spiritual quests.'

AGAINST LITERALISM AND FUNDAMENTALISM

The test that queer people apply to the pronouncements of modern religious institutions – does what they say correspond with what I know from my experience? – is also applied to religious scriptures. I have yet to meet a lesbian or gay fundamentalist, although I have no doubt that some of them are homosexual (by fundamentalist, I mean someone who thinks they believe in the literal truth of every word of the Bible). Fundamentalist Christians and Orthodox Jews argue that homosexuality is wrong because it says so in the Bible. Lesbian and gay Christians and Jews have had to learn how to argue with this: by proving that the Bible has been mistranslated, by arguing that it needs to be understood according to the context of the time that produced it (and times have changed), by emphasizing other teachings in the Bible, by appealing to a history of alternative and suppressed traditions, and by relativizing the usefulness of the Bible when compared with subsequent knowledge and lived experience. In short they have read and interpreted the Bible according to their own needs and experience; and, doing so, argue that all Christians and Jews do the same. Scripture, like religion in general, is transformed from a weapon used against us into a tool that we can use.

Peter Wyles exemplifies this approach: 'Of course large chunks of the Bible aren't literally true and large chunks of it are no more divinely inspired than the Criminal Justice Act. It is not like a car manual – look up the reference, that's what you need to know. There is a power in these stories, though, that still achieves a purpose.' Rabbi Elizabeth Sarah contends that her faith, throughout its history, has always presented – and valued – a number of alternative interpretations of its central events. 'Literalism is totally alien to any form of Judaism. In the great commentaries on the Torah you find two lines of text, and around them eight, nine, ten comments, talking to each other across the centuries; they're all different, and they're not coherent, they contradict one another. It's part of the Jewish reality: everything is not given and set. The whole notion of God's role in history suggests movement, change, journeying – you have a past, but are discovering new things. We have to bring our own experience and understanding into dialogue with the tradition.'

This understanding of religion as a process which is ever changing is one that at least gives lesbian, gay and bisexual people a chance to participate; unlike fundamentalist belief which claims to be static (because the rules were all set long ago). Adam Sutcliffe sees his relationship with his faith as dynamic: 'By embracing spirituality and engaging with tradition, it seems to me that gay people face up to the difficult but exciting realities of modern life in a particularly direct and intense way. Like all gay people I have to figure things out for myself: social conventions offer no straightforward model. I find great strength in my connection with an ethical tradition that stretches back more than three thousand years. Spirituality, for me, isn't about an escape into the eternal, but about finding bridges between the eternal, the traditional, and the inescapable modernity of my life as a gay man. Dynamic spiritual life today surely has to be about searching for such new connections – rather than blindly denying or condemning the complexities of the modern world, as so many religious leaders do. Because lesbians and gay men cannot but confront some of these complexities in our everyday lives, we should be amongst those taking the lead in liberating religion and spirituality from the false certainties and easy answers that degenerate so easily into bigotry.'

SPIRITUAL FREEDOM

Above all, queer people are free to realize that our life is lived for ourselves, not for society or religion; that we must not deny our experience of life in order to please someone else; and we must oppose any orthodoxy – whether social or religious – that encourages us to do so. 'Ultimately you have to answer your own questions,' says Pam Mears, who follows a Shamanic path. 'I believe I'm guided; but nobody is telling me the answers, they come from inside of me. That's why I believe it more.' Seamus is a gay man who has drawn on both Paganism and Buddhism in the past, and was raised as a Christian: 'the only place I can be is where I am now. There's a Pagan invocation that ends along the lines of "you who seek me, if you don't find it within yourself, you won't find it outside yourself." Spirituality is not something that happens "out there", it's something that happens here, inside of us, now.'

'To be *told* is to put the person off, that's why I don't like religion,' says Basho, who spent many years as a *sanyassin* – a follower of the controversial guru Bhagwan Shree Rajneesh (known, by the end of his life, as Osho). 'Change has to come from the individual desire and need for God or spirituality: any transformation that comes out of that will have integrity. I truly believe that each individual is a unique and intrinsic whole – although we're all part of the whole thing, in each manifestation of that we're complete. Therefore if I have a question, I must have the answer to that question. It's my belief that our life is our individual journey for our own growth. The Buddha and Jesus don't have a monopoly on enlightenment – if it's possible for them, why not me? Why not you? Osho was my ultimate master, not because of what he said as a doctrine or philosophy – a lot of the time I think he was talking nonsense – but because of what he did in me, to create a way of re-evaluating things, so it became *my* truth, not handed down from somebody else.'

Freed from the conventionality, or the conformist demands, of the Church, queers are better able to concentrate on their own spirituality – and perhaps more receptive to spiritual experience. Peter Cooper points out why this may be so. When two gay Christians make love 'they know that in the eyes of the majority they are performing a forbidden and sinful act. They have to break free from taboos and conventions to do so. Perhaps because of this, some gay Christians have a capacity for awe and wonder, for transcendence and ecstatic experience (sexual and spiritual), for experiencing God as Liberator and Life-Giver rather than Law-Giver and Enforcer.' Research into transcendent experiences supports this connection. According to scientific studies, they are most likely to occur when cultural censorship loses its power: when people have broken free of social taboos (which discourage 'spirituality' because it is embarrassing, subversive and overly individual), and when it is acceptable for people to do things that may trigger them (including intense sex, or drug taking).[19] Queer people score on both counts.

Perhaps this explains Jung's famous observation that queers have 'a wealth of religious feelings, which help bring the *ecclesia spirtualis* into reality, and a spiritual receptivity which makes them responsive to revelation'.[20] Because we are not imprisoned by the false consciousness and constructs of religion, we are better able to sense what religion is supposedly referring to. 'I think being gay means that you are very open to the transcendental,' says Sister Latex. 'It's just that my transcendental experiences don't fit together into a mosaic of belief.' Whereas straight worshippers may feel obliged to keep quiet about their spiritual experiences, for fear of embarrassing the well-behaved world of conventional religion, queer people are already an embarrassment to that world – and so have no incentive to deny the transcendent, or any of their beliefs. 'One of the huge gifts that I've been given by my sexuality, and by HIV and AIDS, is that I've been given the opportunity to go and explore all this stuff,' says Johnathon Andrew. 'And I've also had the cheek to allow people to think that I'm mad, and to follow the spirit, wherever it might lead me, no matter how doctrinally absurd it might seem to be.' Dr Elizabeth Stuart, a lesbian Catholic, has found that 'recognizing the hetero-patriarchal view of the world for what it is – a sham – means that I am prepared to believe more, not less. I am quite prepared to believe that the witches on Beachy Head do prevent rain from falling on Pride each year, and that it is possible for us to have relationships with those who have gone before us, because these are part of queer experience – which hegemonic theology wants to deprive us of, through the tyranny of reason.'

REAL FAITH, REALISTIC FAITH

It might be imagined – certainly by fundamentalists, and other people who complain about falling moral standards – that the individualistic and utilitarian approach of lesbian, gay and bisexual people creates weak and watered-down faith. On the contrary: queer faith is strong because it has been so fiercely tested – and survived. Since queers are not encouraged (by our own community, nor by most religions) to acknowledge their spirituality, those who none the less persist, and overcome all the hurdles in their way, must genuinely want to.

Richard Kirker believes that faith needs to be tested and scrutinized. 'Unless you can make a convincing case for going to church, which can withstand rigorous criticism from the most virulent atheist or humanist, then you've not done what all Christians ought to do.' He says the Lesbian and Gay Christian Movement he works for consists of people who 'are not just pew fodder – they don't just go there, sing a hymn or two, and retreat into a little holy huddle amongst their friends and family. They don't leave their brain at the church door. They are not preoccupied with conservatism, political or moral. They feel compelled to engage with the world, they are realists, and are profoundly compassionate.' Damian Entwistle has spent half his life in what he calls an 'exhaustive dialogue between life and faith' – a dialogue that never stops, though it has led him to be a Quaker rather than the Franciscan friar he once was. The same scrutiny is applied by queers on other paths; Jason Oliver testifies that 'gay people tend to have a stronger vision of Paganism, because they've had to redefine it for themselves'.

Queer faith has been born out of struggle. Rabbi Sheila Shulman strongly identifies with the story of Jacob wrestling with an angel ('I will not let you go unless you bless me' – Genesis 32:26). 'What's been enormously useful to me is the Jewish tradition of arguing with God, which runs all the way through. I could not imagine a God with whom I could not be angry and struggle against.' Many queers can tell of the good that emerges from the turmoil of coming out; 'an awful lot of gay people have been through fire and come out the other side', as Catherine Hopper puts it. Jim Cotter uses the same metaphor: 'in the imagery of the Exodus, we have felt the fire of the burning bush, searing and warming at the same time, pruning us of the dross . . . We have been burned but not consumed.'[21]

We benefit from the struggle. Greg, a follower of Vaishnavism (a Hindu faith), recalls a proverb: 'If Krishna likes you, he'll give you everything – riches, fame, whatever. If Krishna loves you, he'll take it all away.' This is not to suggest for a moment that homosexuality is our 'cross to bear', that we should welcome oppression and bigotry as somehow ennobling; it is simply to say that insight has been born from our current experience, and that being barred from the conventional 'riches' of cosy, conservative, unthinking religion is no great loss. Any sense of spirituality that we have is, as Rabbi Lionel Blue points out, 'earned.' Although he says being gay has made his life more difficult, 'precisely because the price has been high spiritually, it has been more valuable'. To try to unite one's religious and sexual identity 'is painstaking work, fitting two pieces of creation together. It requires devotion, patience and discipline, the faithfulness to the truth and precision that religion has to learn from science; but it is honest work, not rhetoric. It does not avoid or evade. Such do-it-yourself religion cuts away the frills. In a packaged society, such plain and simple truth is rare and valuable.'[22]

Steve Hope, as a Quaker, insists upon 'plain and simple truth'. 'It's a bleak, minimal vision of reality and experience – but it's also where true freedom lies, and true responsibility lies. As soon as you begin articulating any belief you are imposing a structure on reality that's completely false. I've come to believe that any kind of religious formulation is an attempt to find supernatural justification for the particular view of the world one wants to maintain, and that is infantalizing – it prevents human beings from growing up. To me, being grown up means accepting that there is no rational way of claiming one's values represent the ultimately real, but that one has to take absolute responsibility for them, as the way one has chosen to make sense of one's life. It's never a finished process – the freedom lies in being as open as possible to ever more realities and experiences, and to share and be enriched by other people's experience; to look beyond however the world seems to be organized at the moment. A lot of religious belief is idolatry, the worship of one's own concepts. The former Bishop of Durham, David Jenkins, once told me that being open to God is being open to more and more reality.'

Not everyone would be comfortable with the comparatively minimal framework of beliefs that Quakerism offers; but what virtually all queer believers do share – even at the 'frillier', more ritual and traditional end of the spectrum – is a firm rejection of sentimentality and escapism. 'I don't think by having a spiritual practice you can exclude yourself from the hard reality,' says Johnathon Andrew. 'What the spiritual practice is about is coming to terms with the reality. And transforming it, somehow.' Michael Seán Paterson takes the same view from his work at CARA: 'Here there is no room for bullshit or fig leaves or pretence.' When Michael was training for the priesthood, 'I believed that theology had the answers to life's mysteries. The Roman Catholic perspective is that nothing is provisional. If everything's so definite, it doesn't leave any space for people who are exploring – what's the role of coming out (spiritually or sexually) in a world where everything has been found?' For this, among other reasons, Michael could no longer be a priest. 'I could never have things pinned down under any scheme that's normative. I don't give scripture or authority that place. I've a hunch that there's more truth to be found in the not knowing than there was when I was very clear. I can't say *this is*.'

Uncertainty is truthful, and preferable to certainties that were false and restricting. At their healthiest, religions admit their limitations and question their own orthodoxies. 'You find in Hinduism statements that admit certain things are unknowable,' says Siddharth Deva, citing a passage from the Rig Veda which reads 'who knows and who can say whence it all came and how creation happened? The gods themselves are later than creation.' Dirk de Klerk explains that in Tibetan Buddhism 'if there's a rule, it may need to be broken, because Buddhism is not about rules, it is about insight. There's a delight in unconventionality; conventionality might be another trap.'

PARADOX AND HUMOUR

Conventional truths can become dogma; unconventionality more often takes the form of paradox, which is central to various spiritual traditions, particularly more mystical forms, like the Kabbalah or Zen. According to psychologist James Fowler, faith at its most mature values 'richness, ambiguity and multidimensionality'; it 'comes to cherish paradox, and the apparent contradictions of perspectives on truth as intrinsic to that truth'.[23] Paradox is something that queer people can take in their stride: we are used to there being alternative truths, and to there being more to things than their surface alone.

Nowhere is queer appreciation of paradox more obvious than in our humour: camp depends on it. Humour does not spring to mind on hearing the word religion. No less an authority than the Dalai Lama, however, has said jokes are a good thing: 'your brain becomes a little more open. It's helpful to get new ideas. If you think with too much seriousness, your brain somehow is closed.'[24] Being open to experience is the quality that this chapter has argued is intrinsic in being queer – and to queer understandings of spirituality. Something that comes fairly naturally to us – a humorous attitude to life, and above all the ability to take the piss out of anything that takes itself too seriously, not least the grand institutions of Heterosoc – turns out, again, to be to our spiritual advantage. And, once again, this advantage is related to our unique perspective – which is itself due to our difference from the norm, our 'queerness'.

'I find humour to be central to my own spirituality,' says Elizabeth Stuart. 'Being a proud, out lesbian is like being let in on a vast joke. The joke is that life does not have to be like this, ultimate reality is not heterosexual, marriage is not God's ideal, the very categorizing of people according to their sexuality is artificial and ephemeral. Not taking the "Establishment" seriously is actually extremely threatening to it. Laughing at life is also, of course, a strategy for survival. I often think that if we cannot laugh at something we are not taking it seriously enough. The Sisters of Perpetual Indulgence are perfect examples of people who, by laughing at aspects of religion, actually perform a religious act, in releasing people from the burden of guilt that the Church has placed upon them – and also relieving the Church of some of its power, by bursting its bubble of pomposity and arrogance.'

'What the nuns are into is promulgating universal joy and expiating stigmatic guilt,' according to the late Mother Kiss My Arse Goodbye (so named following his colostomy). 'If my mission in life is to leave people with a smile on their faces or to have a good time in my company, then there's no harm in that at all. And it's part of being a Quaker' – which Mother Kiss also was – 'spreading the light, not in a serious way, but in a determined way. We're God's fools.' One of the original San Francisco nuns claimed that 'humour and sexuality are at the roots of spirituality . . . They are the transcendental experiences that take us beyond mortality. Through humour and sexuality we can realize visions and feelings beyond everyday life . . . Being nuns is a practical application of our spiritual feelings as gay men.'[25]

SCEPTICISM IS THE BEGINNING OF FAITH

'Originally I was looking for answers, and on a quest for salvation,' says David Donlan, recalling what religion meant to him before he came out. 'Later it became a quest to find myself and relate to others. As for the answers to life: I realize I know less than I did at first, although my knowledge now is more than before.' Being queer forces us to ask questions about ourselves and our place in the world. The great spiritual gift of being queer is that we will not be satisfied with easy answers to those questions, whether they are offered by society or by religion. We cannot accept either social or religious orthodoxies: and this is to our immense advantage. The spiritual journey is an inner one: our head start is that we can understand it as such, because we are guided by internal, rather than external, authority. We are freed from pathological, rigid, fearful, literalist religion; we are freed to look honestly at ourselves and the world. What emerges from this scrutiny may not take the form of conventional religious belief, but will at least have the virtue of being truthful – even when that truth may be uncomfortable, or paradoxical. Such committed realism is spiritual: for, while it acknowledges that there are no definitive answers, it also refuses to let us off asking the questions. Sheila Shulman recalls when she first considered becoming a rabbi: 'my friends kept asking me had I lost my marbles, was I hearing voices, what was going on – *had I found the answer?* I said no, all I'm doing is committing to engaging with the question. It's made me more trouble rather than less, I would say.' Oscar Wilde, whose conversion to Catholicism is rather less well known than his sexual orientation, predicted as much. 'Scepticism', he wrote, 'is the beginning of faith.'[26]

Notes

1. Edward Carpenter, *Selected Writings, Volume 1: Sex* (London: Gay Men's Press, 1984), p. 274.
2. Elizabeth Stuart, *Chosen,* (London: Geoffrey Chapman, 1993), p. 3.
3. This point can also be found in Michael's passionate and highly recommended exploration of Christianity, sexuality and AIDS, *Singing For Our Lives: Positively Gay and Christian* (Sheffield: Cairns Publications, 1997).
4. While many of us choose not to have children, it should, of course, be a choice: I would not want to suggest for a moment that we have any less right or ability to be parents, nor to suggest that we are less queer if we do.
5. Edward Carpenter, The Intermediate Sex in Carpenter, *Selected Writings, Volume 1*, p. 215.
6. Harvey Gillman, *A Minority of One: A Journey With Friends* (London: Quaker Home Service, 1988), p. 5.

7. Bede Griffiths, *Universal Wisdom* (London: Fount, 1994), p. 17.

8. Bernard uses this phrase in 'A Land Beyond Tears', an essay included in Ide O'Carroll and Eoin Collins (eds), *Lesbian and Gay Visions of Ireland* (London: Cassell, 1995), p. 214.

9. From Bernard's essay on 'Religious and Spirituality Conflicts' in Dominic Davies and Charles Neal, *Pink Therapy: A Guide for Counsellors and Therapists Working with Lesbian, Gay and Bisexual Clients* (Buckingham: Open University Press, 1996), p. 206.

10. The Rev. Robert Williams, *Just as I Am: A Practical Guide to Being Out, Proud, and Christian* (New York: Crown Publishers, 1992), p. 171.

11. Recounted in Bert Herrman, *Being, Being Happy, Being Gay* (San Francisco: Alamo Square Press, 1990).

12. Rabbi Lionel Blue, *Godly and Gay* (London: Gay Christian Movement, 1981), p. 4. The text of this brilliant lecture (the Fourth Michael Harding Memorial Address, to the Gay Christian Movement), which over fifteen years ago outlined many issues that have yet to be fully addressed, is also printed, in a revised form, in Jonathan Magonet (ed.), *Jewish Explorations of Sexuality* (Oxford: Berghahn Books, 1995).

13. Blue, *Godly and Gay*, pp. 5–6.

14. M. Scott Peck, *Further Along the Road Less Travelled* (London: Simon & Schuster, 1993), chapter seven. Stage one is chaotic/antisocial. See also James W. Fowler, *Stages of Faith: The Psychology of Human Development and the Quest for Meaning* (San Francisco: Harper & Row, 1981) and *Becoming Adult, Becoming Christian: Adult Development and Christian Faith* (San Francisco: Harper & Row, 1984).

15. John J. McNeill, *Taking a Chance on God: Liberating Theology for Gays, Lesbians, and Their Lovers, Families and Friends* (Boston: Beacon Press, 1988), pp. 22–30.

16. Craig O'Neill and Kathleen Ritter, *Coming Out Within: Stages of Spiritual Awakening for Lesbians and Gay Men* (San Francisco: HarperSanFransisco, 1992).

17. Richard Woods, *Another Kind of Love: Homosexuality and Spirituality* (Fort Wayne: Knoll Publishing Co., 1988), p. 124.

18. Recalled in Mark's essay 'A Strange Conjunction', in Magonet, *Jewish Explorations of Sexuality*, p. 82.

19. A useful survey of scientific research into 'transcendent' experience can be found in David Hay, *Religious Experience Today: Studying the Facts* (London: Mowbray, 1990).

20. C. J. Jung, *Collected Works*, translated by R. F. C. Hull (New York: Pantheon, 1959), Vol. 9, p. 87.

21. LGCM, *Order of Service* for Southwark Cathedral, 16 November 1996, p. 6.

22. Lionel Blue, *A Backdoor to Heaven* (London: Fount Paperbacks, 1994), p. 143; *Godly and Gay*, p. 3.

23. Fowler, *Becoming Adult, Becoming Christian*, p. 65.

24. Quoted in Robin Skynner and John Cleese, *Life and How to Survive It* (London: Mandarin, 1994), p. 78.

25. Mark Thompson, *Gay Spirit: Myth and Meaning* (New York: St Martin's Press, 1987), p. 61.

26. Oscar Wilde, *The Picture of Dorian Gray*. A Bishop of London called Oscar 'the most Christian man I've ever met'.

3

Off the Straight and Narrow:
Structures for Spirituality

Queer questioning may lead to a sense of spirituality – scepticism may be the beginning of faith – but what's the next step? Being sceptical and individual is better than being credulous and conformist, but, if queers are to capitalize on the headstart they have been given on the spiritual journey, they need a few signposts, and to find fellow travellers. The valuable ability to distinguish spirituality from religion does not mean that religion becomes redundant. Simply being unorthodox and challenging conventionality is not enough: although it might well be a good thing politically, and valuable for whoever is being challenged, it has no inherent spiritual value.

Spirituality, according to Sheila Shulman, 'needs forms, needs structure. The reason I object to the word is that it so often seems to refer to something terribly inchoate, and people keep wanting to reinvent the wheel.' For Rabbi Sheila 'the Jewish forms and structures are as good as any, if not better than some'. Peter Wyles turns to Quakerism for his structure: 'At one level, I believe that all religious groups are merely forms, and the true reality can be reached in many different ways. What works for me may not work for someone else. Some people need pomp and circumstance to find the divine, some find concepts helpful that are a definite barrier for me. I also believe that completely free-floating belief is somehow not enough, you do need a tradition to struggle against, to give you some purchase. We each have our own spiritual path, but the journey is one we need to make with friends, with a background, with the insights of others and the past.'

Since self-affirming queers do not believe out of a sense of fear or duty, there is a welcome and unusual sense of choice about how they can address their spirituality. If you feel God is pointing a gun at your head, you probably won't feel that you have much choice. But if you are looking for a tool to develop your inherent sense of spirituality, then it becomes a question of assessing which best suits your needs. You might use the one you were given when you were younger; or you might have to throw it away, as no longer able to do the job.

ROADS WE CANNOT TRAVEL:
THE NECESSARY EXILE OF HERETICS

One of the lies that we have taken on, without question, from the mouths of our oppressors, is the proposition that, since *some* religion is very vocal in its homophobia, it somehow follows that *all* religion is inevitably homophobic. Admittedly there are a few paths – fewer than you may think – that queer people genuinely cannot follow. Personally, I'm not too upset that I can't become a fundamentalist Christian. By refusing to have me in the same room as them they are doing me a favour. They are saving me from a narrow-minded literalism that would retard, rather than develop, my spirituality. 'I think I could have bought into the whole fundamentalist culture,' says Simon, a gay man who was involved with a charismatic evangelical group in his early twenties. 'I'd probably have been right-wing, intolerant and oppressive. Being gay has enabled me to move out of that. I feel my life experiences have made me a much better person.' It's a point that people from various backgrounds make; being gay prevents us from over-identifying with 'pathological' or 'rigid' religion. 'My gayness saved me from self-righteousness,' says Lionel Blue.[1] Boy George, who has explored Hare Krishna and Nichiren Buddhist spirituality, has referred to his homosexuality as his 'saving grace'. Although Richard Kirker feels that his spiritual life has been 'compromised' by being queer, he says it has also been 'very stimulated by a desire not to turn myself into a conventional Anglo-Catholic clergyman'. Being queer makes certain choices for us. Providing we are out – and not prepared to go back in the closet – our sexuality protects us from becoming involved with some of the more authoritarian or deluded religious organizations.

Distancing yourself from religious authority – or challenging it directly – has a long and noble history: Jesus was in continuous conflict with the religious leaders of first-century Judaea. Arthur Evans, in *Witchcraft and the Gay Counterculture*, argues that gay people in particular have, since the rise of Christianity, consistently rejected religious authority, and that this was our defining characteristic during the past. One of the earthier English words for us, 'bugger', was originally synonymous with 'Bulgar' – i.e. someone from Bulgaria, a country notorious, in the Middle Ages, for its refusal to accept Christian orthodoxies. Because Pagan religions did not share Christian prohibitions against sex, Christian heresy trials often used evidence of extra-marital sexual practices as proof that their practitioners were not good God-fearing folk. As a consequence, according to Evans, 'Heresy and homosexuality became so interchangeable that those accused of heresy attempted to prove their innocence by claiming heterosexuality. A thirteenth-century weaver accused of heresy replied: "Gentlemen! Listen to me! I am not a heretic, for I have a wife and I sleep with her. I have sons . . ."[2]

Hoblink, a network of queer Pagans, deliberately places itself in this historical tradition. It asserts that 'the rise of both the Pagan movement and overt homosexuality (it was always present, but knew when to lie low) is confronting the monopoly of religious orthodoxy. From now on we will fix our own moral and spiritual reference points. We have become the heretics and challengers of vindictive orthodoxy.' Hoblink member Gordon Hunt points out that the Latin root of Pagan is not *pagus* (meaning countryside, which modern Pagans often claim) but *Paganus*, which means civilian. The *Paganus* were the opposite of the *milites*, who in the Christian Roman Empire were 'the people who fought as soldiers of the lord, the army of salvation'. It is the difference, once again, between 'those who followed orders and marched; and those who did their own "thang". Paganism is about doing your own "thang". Pagans don't march – they're out of step. Which is a good definition of poofs, isn't it? If you ask why you're out of step, why aren't I what my Daddy wanted me to be, then you are creating a space for spirituality – because spirituality will give you the answer from within you.'

The *Oxford English Dictionary* defines heresy broadly as 'maintaining theological or religious opinions at variance with the "catholic" or orthodox doctrine of the Christian Church'. The Greek root for heresy (*hairesis*) means choice, which I have argued is the great spiritual gift of queerness – we are free not to conform, able to choose alternatives to dominant orthodoxies. But it is not just queer Neo-Pagans who are heretics; in a sense *all* religious queers are heretics. This is true of even the Christians in this book. We are all out of step: we don't want to march to the beat of the orthodox drum.

CHOOSING MY RELIGION

So some roads, leading to places we don't want to go, are closed: we'll just have to get over it. There are many other paths available. With their heretical ability to choose, what choices are queers making?

I suggest that there are three main ways in which queers seek spirituality in their lives. The first falls outside of any formalized framework: it may be generated by nature, art, physical experience or drugs. The second broad category that I use is traditions in which (in their Western incarnations, at least) a substantial amount of freedom and authority is retained by their practitioners. Included in this grouping are Buddhism, Neo-Paganism and New Age beliefs, Quakers and Unitarians. In this second category the chief authority is internal; in the third of my groupings, authority is supposedly external. So the third category consists of more 'orthodox' incarnations of religion, where power is claimed by the governing institution and clergy, and the individuals' needs and experience are given less credence than the 'official' interpretation of scripture and tradition. In Britain most 'mainstream' religion would fall into this category: certainly Roman Catholicism, the Church of England, and Orthodox Judaism. Belonging to one of these 'exterior' religions will probably cause more conflict for a queer person than following an 'interior' path; but there are queers who testify to the benefits they derive from these traditions, and who survive reasonably unscathed. This path is not absolutely out of bounds, unlike fundamentalist belief.

These approaches can be very different: there's not necessarily very much in common between someone who swallows LSD on their spiritual quest, and someone who swallows a communion wafer every Sunday in church. But I want to emphasize that there is none the less something common in the queer approach to all of them: we test all of them against the truth of our individual experience. Whatever the path, we do not confuse the journey with our reasons for taking it: we do not mistake religion for spirituality, bathwater for baby. Even within an 'orthodox' religion the queer approach is unorthodox.

Before looking at each of these three categories, and the many alternative traditions within them, it is worth remembering that since queers assess a religion's worth according to its usefulness, and are less likely to take every detail of its claims literally – and because of this are not troubled by the way in which most religions contradict themselves and other religions – then they are less likely to feel restricted to just the one faith. There's no authority to keep us from wandering. We can be shamelessly, spiritually promiscuous – free of the fear or convention that would keep us religiously monogamous. Being faith-full doesn't necessarily make you faithful. Lionel Blue is a rabbi who hangs out in Christian monasteries; he has no qualms about his mix-and-match technique. 'I had to find bits here, bits there, wherever I found people who'd teach me something. I couldn't give a damn about the label, I needed the content.' Clive Barker, the prolific fantasy author and film-maker (of *Hellraiser* and *Weaveworld* fame), has described himself as 'loosely Christian' but with 'a magpie approach' to religion. 'I don't see anything wrong in finding – constructing – one's own jigsaw of faiths. Finding wisdom anywhere. Because we stand outside conventional systems, gay men have a view of faiths and dogmas which is particularly useful. "What can I use?" we ask. "How can I grow?" "How can I be wiser?" "How can I be healthier?" How can I be more loving?"'[3]

Henry Giles is sixty-one, an artist and a retired teacher of design. When it comes to his spiritual life, he is guided by a dictum of Oscar Wilde: 'I have the simplest of tastes – I only want the best.' For Henry this means his chief practice is Transcendental Meditation; but he has also found a number of other things useful, including Tai Chi, 'past-life' readings, the Edward Carpenter Community and personal growth seminars (including those run by Landmark Education, an offshoot of 'est' encounter groups). He believes that 'all the great systems of spirituality say the same things, but with different emphases'. Though only in his thirties, Gary has explored (amongst others) theosophy, Zen, Paganism, Buddhism, 'channelling' spirits, astrology and tarot: 'If something in some tradition felt right – seemed applicable or relevant – then I'd identify with it, and use it. These things are only contradictory on an intellectual level – not an energy level. I've always had an open mind, I'm not ruled by shoulds. I like the metaphor that we're all God's bees, and we all collect nectar. The nectar is the experience of life. We collect experience. We have God within us – God isn't out there, or in scriptures – so anything can guide you.'

'In my experience being a lesbian has led me to cut through all the crap that keeps Christians and other faiths apart from one another,' says Elizabeth Stuart. 'When some people will not break bread with you – or wouldn't if they knew who you were – you become willing to eat bread with whoever will eat bread with you.' She does not believe that 'anything goes, or that all spiritualities are as truthful as each other'; but maintains that 'one of the most important insights emerging from queer, feminist, black, Asian, disabled and Hispanic theologies is that diversity is not incompatible with truth, and that truth is multi-coloured and multi-dimensional.'

Again, this sort of approach is possible only if religion is serving you, rather than demanding that you serve religion. Lev is a gay man grateful for the spiritual tools he was given by a Jewish childhood ('a language of prayer, rituals and ceremonies'), who has since explored the Havurah movement (sometimes dubbed New Age Judaism) as well as the Radical Faeries,[4] and is currently attending an ashram. He is clear that 'the world's religions are vehicles for us to find our core, for us to find our true purpose. It doesn't matter which vehicle we use – you may as well use the one you're given, but if you don't want to that's fine. They're not an end in themselves.'

SPIRITUALITY WITHOUT RELIGION

The sorts of experiences that are sometimes labelled 'spiritual', and the insights that can come from these experiences, are not the exclusive preserve of religion. Religions might aspire to guide us towards such experiences, and help us interpret them – but, in a society as rightly suspicious of religion as ours, the church, synagogue or temple might well be the last place you'll find them.

The natural world could be a better place to start. Moira finds her 'higher power' there: 'I can relate to her in a very tangible way, particularly through the earth, the sea, rivers, trees, and other aspects of nature. It is something I can feel with my whole body. I have a memory from childhood, of lying in a field, being extremely aware of the feel of the ground under me, the sounds of the insects, the heat of the sun – but also there was another feeling, a sort of tingling going from the ground into my body. It was a moment of feeling totally OK, at peace with myself, of complete acceptance, also thrilling ecstasy. I feel this often in recent years. The less "man-made" stuff around me, the more I feel it.' Christian beliefs do not prevent Diana Reynolds, a priest in the Midlands, from responding in a similar way: 'I've always been strongly drawn by creation around me, never doubted that God could exist because there was all this beauty, so powerful.' Roberta Wedge understands her chosen faith, Paganism, is 'in essence a worship of Nature (though there's a lot more to it than that)' and has a deep and sensual relationship with the land. She has written of rising for dawn one vernal equinox in terms that blend the sexual with the spiritual. 'The north east line of hills slowly appeared as the smooth soft shapes of supple bodies, sinuous backs, strong thighs, sloping shoulders. And I loved it all and I was part of this land, beyond my own fragile human body, breathing the breeze, opening myself to the Sun like the tiny flowers at my feet. And the breeze stroked the hairs of the back of my neck like a lover, and as I scrambled down the rocks into the unexplored valley, the bushes held on to me, hugging my legs, saying slow down, watch your step, not so fast, enjoy our company, be here now.' She makes an effort to spend time outdoors alone, whether in the country or in city parks. 'That connection is for me a connection with the divine, which I choose to call goddess. It's the life force.' Although people feel embarrassed about saying it, many value the feeling of being 'at one with the earth'. And where there are no other people around, you won't find homophobia.

The depth of relationship which queers, from opera queens to techno babes, can have with music is another indication of (often latent) spirituality. 'One reason', believes Bernard Lynch, 'that music is universally accepted across class, culture and sexuality is that it is a language of the spirit rather than of reason'.[5] For many people music, is one of the few ways which they are regularly 'taken out of themselves' – that is, achieve transcendence. Christopher, a schoolteacher in the Midlands, has recently become a Buddhist, but explains that 'music has always been a central part of my experience of "depth" in life. Music can alert us to a world beyond the material.' From an early age he found 'spiritual connectedness' through classical composers, and a sense of 'stillness'. He 'felt loved' – it helped him feel secure during his adolescent uncertainty about his sexuality. It was 'a private garden of rapturous experience for me. Through music I could experience passion – the heights and depths. I remember being rendered breathless and almost hysterical through listening to the surging tides of Elgar's Second Symphony, for example. It was a quickening of my being more than equal to anything wanking could achieve . . . I was somehow aware of the "truth" of Elgar's music as it expressed my searching for love and meaning, and naturally conflated sexuality and spirituality together.'

Gay male culture's obsession with fitness may also have unexpected spiritual side effects. 'Running, for me is a form of prayer,' says Bernard Lynch. 'I run (religiously) every day. I realize that strenuous physical exercise releases the same endorphins in the blood stream that heroin does, and so there is a "natural" high that is addictively attractive. But for me there is also – I would say primarily – the attraction of a kind of heightened consciousness that accompanies the physical high. I would call it the Zen of running – a space within which I gather "all of me" in the presence of the great spirit, Christ, and remember my name and my nature is love. It is also the time, in this age of AIDS, where I meet the angels – my gay brothers who have gone before me.'

Consciousness-altering substances have been found on the gay scene since the days when homosexuality was as illegal as most drugs still are. Altered states of consciousness have – in other cultures – traditionally been understood as insights into a higher reality: hallucinogenics were consumed ritually by everyone from the native Americans to Siberian shamen. Given their widespread acceptance, particularly among gay men, it might be expected that for some queers this is another route to spirituality. Gary is an ambient techno musician and masseur, who for a long time avoided any form of drug – including alcohol and caffeine. During the last couple of years he has taken LSD at regular intervals, 'as a deliberate spiritual practice. I have had what I'd regard as very spiritual feelings on acid, more intense than at any other time in my life – in the realm of bliss, active bliss. Crying with the joy of being alive in the world. On acid you can experience heaven and hell. That's what I would take acid for.' He sees drugs as tools which can be used creatively, to 'go beyond'. Their stigmatization by mainstream society is a senseless – but significant – taboo. 'There's good and bad with drugs just like there is in the gay world – or the Church. Because sex and drugs are put into the dark side of our culture, they're not treated rationally, with intelligence and application.' Gary does not use drugs to get off his face: he uses them consciously. 'Different drugs have different spirits. It's like you're evoking different gods.' Ecstasy can open 'the heart chakra – it clears the bullshit away, you focus on what's true, it's centring. It's good I find to use as a sacrament, for celebration.' He has used it ceremonially with his partner: alone in a candlelit room, 'to say I really love you and these are the things I love about you. A lot of the time people in ordinary consciousness are too inhibited.' By contrast, 'my preference for LSD is taking it outside in nature. I particularly like Hampstead Heath in the daytime. On acid it feels like it's meant to be.'

Gary has little time for sceptical objections that a chemically induced experience is not 'real', or that you can't get any genuine insight from such unnatural methods – 'If you fast for three days, you'll feel different – is that real? If you jump out of a plane you'll have certain feelings – are they real? Natural is a funny word in such an artificial world.' He would not claim, however, that drugs bring instant enlightenment, or that everyone who necks a pill becomes shamanic. 'They are doors to perception. They open – and they close again, they don't stay. You think, well how can that inform my everyday state of consciousness – how can I bring some of that spirituality into my everyday life?'

Gary has a thorough grounding in a variety of spiritual traditions, stemming from his involvement in the alternative and green movements in the 1980s, and this may explain why Gary finds his drug experiences spiritually useful whereas the vast majority of gay men appear not to. It is obvious that there is no *automatic* link between drugs and spirituality when you look at the statistical evidence: many thousands of gay men are taking all sorts of mind-altering substances every weekend, but there has not been a consequent spiritual revolution bursting out of the scene: rave-new-world idealism has apparently been satisfied by nightclubs that stay open until lunchtime. The conditions may look the same – as well as taking drugs, shamen (famously described by Mircea Eliade as 'technicians of ecstasy') would dance with increasing frenzy to a fast, repetitive beat, in an environment that was intensely different from the everyday, 'profane' world. But what differs is the context and intent: shamen performed their rites within a well-established framework of beliefs, in order to achieve a spiritual end. Gay men (and a small number of lesbians) take drugs to get off their faces, in environments which are focused entirely on sexual hedonism. There is no explicit or shared belief system with which they can interpret any transcendent intimations; on the contrary, anything other than toeing the party-party line is discouraged, so talk of spiritual experience could have you quickly written off as just another drugs casualty. The people whose lives have been changed by their ecstasy insights – and who are consciously working with what they have learned – have generally come from the free-rave and New Age traveller scenes, which have philosophies of life much more conducive to looking for the significance of chemically enabled experience. These people are mostly heterosexual – or, at the very least, don't take their drugs out on the gay scene.[6]

Nor would any of the gay men I have spoken to suggest that all you need is drugs. Seamus started taking mushrooms and acid in his early teens. 'I did get a sense of spiritual awakening as a result of drugs, but always in combination with being in nature, and it only took me so far. Then I got lost in it. I felt like I'd connected – that's what I was trying to get to subsequently in my spiritual quest, that sense of connection. I'm not seeking the same level of high now, expecting to have visions. A lot of Taoist practices warn against it – you can achieve altered states of consciousness through spiritual practice, but it's a branch off the main tree, it is an illusion. You get diverted from who you really are. I was taking the drugs more and more for that good feeling and never really got it again; actually it took me further away from that path.' Seamus suffered from the potential side effect of drug use – moving on from mushrooms and LSD to other substances, he developed a serious dependency problem. Others, who avoided addiction, none the less warn of limitations. For the Venerable K-N, a gay man who is now a Buddhist monk, the drug culture of the 1960s broke through the 'sterile' atheism he subscribed to at the time – 'spirituality crept through the back door. Acid can open your mind to wider horizons and perspectives: I was incredibly stubborn and I needed a sledgehammer to crack open my fixed ideas.' But the drug scene 'got boring. The best acid trip can be extraordinary, but it's illusory.' His spiritual practice leads to far more interesting results: 'acid's nothing by comparison.'

Drugs, physical activity, music and nature, along with other inspirations, like visual art, can be important sources for spiritual experience – and form the whole of some people's spiritual lives. But the meanings of such experiences are difficult to articulate; and their impact on the rest of the person's life may well be somewhat nebulous, given that the experience is generally not supported by a group, or ritualized or translated into ethics for behaviour. This, then, is where more traditional structures can be useful. 'Religions are a way of talking about spirituality, of articulating and formulating beliefs about what otherwise is mysterious and beyond understanding,' suggests Philip Joyce. 'They are, in a sense, languages, they make communication about spiritual things possible, by sharing concepts, vocabulary and mythology.' Tradition can help you build on your intuition.

'INTERIOR' TRADITIONS

The paths described in this section offer the benefits of religion – the shared structure and language, community and guidance – without the considerable disadvantage of making a big deal about our sexuality. The relative absence of homophobia seems to be related to the way these traditions are propagated (in the West, at least): they tend not to rely on hierarchical institutions, and, because they are all relatively small-scale (compared to the orthodox mainstream), they are less intertwined with the established social order. Above all, they, like queer people, emphasize the inner life – spirituality – rather than obedience to external conventions. Although mostly they believe in some sort of external God, they are also less likely to order people about using divine authority as an excuse.[7] Ethics, in this group of traditions, 'are likely to be born of experience of that which makes us and others happy and unhappy', rather than being 'commands from On High which we have to obey even if they make no sense, or make us unhappy' (in Catherine Hopper's words). 'Interior' traditions perhaps correspond more readily to the individual/sceptical/open stage of spiritual maturity than the formal/pathological/rigid stage (which is more at home with the 'exterior' traditions) – although any tradition can be understood in a literalistic and unhealthy way (for instance, there are people who are basically New Age fundamentalists).

Neo-Paganism

Paganism is an umbrella term for the various religions that existed in pre-Christian Europe. Its association in the popular imagination with everything from orgies to ritual sacrifice is, for modern Pagans, proof of how effective Christian propaganda was in stamping out the competition from the Jesus-cult's older rivals. Arthur Evans, among others, has argued that Pagan cultures valued women as well as men, understood and sought to live harmoniously with nature, empowered the people who lived in them, and were sexually liberated (sometimes treating homosexuality with particular reverence). All this behaviour was irritating to the early Christians – Evans takes the line that Christianity is *intrinsically* patriarchal and authoritarian – so they crushed such 'barbaric' practices and imposed their own instead. Because queers have fewer sexual hang-ups, and have more reason to be aware of and oppose patriarchal and authoritarian social structures, Evans argues that we are all Pagans. Regardless of whether we identify as spiritual, we are a valuable remnant of ancient counter-Christian opposition.[8]

Some queers are Pagans by more than default, however. Neo-Paganism is a loose term for the twentieth century revival of ancient Pagan practices and traditions. Some forms of Neo-Paganism resemble any other religion – Wicca is perhaps the most formalized, with membership, set rituals and scriptures. Other Neo-Pagans work more individually, but draw upon the vast range of material that has been published on the subject, particularly in the last fifty years. The Christians' ancient rivals are flourishing, and still give a warm welcome to queer folk.

'Goddess' spirituality, particularly popular with feminists in the 1980s, is most commonly connected with Paganism (although it can be found in liberal forms of Christianity and Judaism as well). In contrast to the patriarchy manifest in most Judaeo-Christian institutions (from which lesbians are, of course, doubly excluded, by gender and sexual orientation), Paganism is a tradition described (by Roberta Wedge, a bisexual) as 'revelling in womanhood instead of ignoring it – and revelling in the physical body in general'. Some women meet in Dianic groups, worshipping only the Goddess (rather than other Pagan gods); others, including Wiccans, are reclaiming witchcraft from centuries of slander. 'Witchcraft is the empowerment of womanhood', according to one lesbian witch. 'Women have been put down by men for years, but we are the creators and we need to get back the power. It's something we can all do through witchcraft, if we really want to.'[9]

Homophobic Pagans do exist; they do not, however, have much power, or tradition, on their side. Roberta Wedge describes the Pagan world as 'diffuse and mostly anti-hierarchical. There is no Pagan Pope, thank Goddess! And so there is no one to say, here is the official Pagan doctrine about bisexuality.' Gordon Hunt supports this analysis: 'this is the joy of Paganism, there are no rule books, no scriptures. There is no authority in Paganism except your own authority.' Gordon can, however, draw some support from scholarship which proves the presence (and often acceptance) of queer people in the Pagan past – 'Somebody has been there before. Being a poof, you do need some sort of validation.' He also emphasizes that the modern revival of Paganism was in part motivated by the need for sexual liberation. 'For most of the original Wiccans, and certainly the Alexandrians, who reinvented it as a religion for the twentieth century (with lots of nice ritual and amateur theatricals built in), it was aiming to release the restrictions that the monotheistic churches still put on sexuality. So to a certain extent Paganism is *about* sexuality.' Aleister Crowley (strictly an occultist rather than a Pagan, but another figure who led the revival of non-Christian practices earlier in the twentieth century) had sex with men. The law which banned the practice of witchcraft in Britain was repealed only in the decade before male homosexuality was partially decriminalized.

These days there are queer covens, and various networks for lesbian, gay and bisexual Pagans; although the tabloid image is still something of a millstone for them. Mike Shankland, from the Hoblink organization, protests that 'It's not like the high priests of Wicca that you read about in the *News of the World* that have slept with everybody in the coven. If only!' Jason Oliver, who meets regularly with other Pagans in a London gay pub, also quashes the popular image – 'to look at us you'd just think we were a load of queens out on the piss'. It does seem appropriate, however, that one of the synonyms for Pagan – heathen – means heath dweller, a term that could freely be used of gay men who frequent the open spaces of Hampstead . . .

Buddhism

'Buddhism does not see homosexuality as a problem either spiritually, ethically, or psychologically,' according to Maitreyabandhu from the Friends of the Western Buddhist Order. 'At least, no more of a problem than heterosexuality! It sees craving as a problem, yes, but whether that craving is expressed in sexual relationships with the opposite sex or the same sex is neither here nor there. I'd been brought up in the Church of England, where it definitely is an issue. Discovering that my sexuality wasn't an obstacle was the first bonus of Buddhism.' Against the background of queer suspicion, Maitreyabandhu was keen to make this explicit, and set up very popular meditation courses and retreats for gay men, 'to say simply: this includes you. Lesbians and gay men have long been aware that the major spiritual traditions of the West *say* they are for everyone, but that when it comes to homosexuality and the vexed issue of gay sex, they are not.' Promoting this message is what motivated Catherine Hopper, who is preparing for ordination into the Western Buddhist Order, to help run meditation classes for lesbians: 'lesbians and gay men wanting to learn meditation have no reason to expect that we're going to be any different from all the homophobic religions'. Catherine testifies that the London Buddhist Centre is 'very popular with dykes'; but, as involvement in the Order deepens, sexual orientation ceases to be an issue at all. Nagaraja agrees – 'You come out in the FWBO and they say "huh, is that interesting?"' For gay Christians, who often face the choice of suffocating closetry or rejection by their Church, this is all rather startling. Whereas those ordained to Christian ministry are mostly forced to keep silent if they're queer, Maitreyabandhu asserts that hiding his sexuality would be 'spiritually unhelpful. Buddhism gives me a context in which to practice a spiritual life without having to deny my sexuality, either publicly or privately.'

The various lineages of Tibetan Buddhism that have established themselves in the West are equally unconcerned about sexual orientation. The Dalai Lama is unique among religious leaders in having been interviewed by a gay magazine.[10] Not all Buddhist cultures accept homosexuality; but Dirk de Klerk has never heard of a lama condemning it. When Dirk came out to 'a rather traditional' Tibetan lama, 'he smiled and said "if you are a Buddhist it does not matter whether you like boys or girls"'. Fernando Guasch has a background in radical queer activism; he attends a meditation centre ('full of queers') set up by one of the lamas who did most to popularize the Tibetan tradition, Chogyam Trungpa. Fernando has never found any homophobia – 'and I've looked for it. It's infuriating in a way – it's so much against every single intuition I developed in OutRage!' Trungpa's successor as head of the lineage was a gay man. Ancient Buddhist texts rarely mention homosexuality, except to say it is wrong for monks (as is any sexual conduct – they take a vow of celibacy). Japanese Buddhism had a tradition of celebrating male love (*nanshoku*): a book attributed to the founder of esoteric 'True Word' Buddhism in Japan, Kobo Daishi, instructs the layman on the 'mysteries' of loving boys and helpfully includes hints on seven different positions for anal intercourse (like keeping 'cut plums' on hand in case you want to attempt insertion without saliva).[11]

The Buddhism of Nichiren Daishonin (sometimes known as Nichiren Shoshu Buddhism) is another variant popular with modern queers. It originated in twelfth-century Korea, but owes its current prominence to Sokka Gakkai International, a Japanese organization which ceaselessly promotes itself using all the tools of modern marketing.[12] Other Buddhists consider Nichirens somewhat heretical for their belief that instead of transcending craving, you should satisfy your desires by chanting for what you want. (This is no doubt what appeals to Edina in *Absolutely Fabulous*, whose chanting 'as she speaks' is a parody of the central Nichiren mantra.) Peter Ashby-Saracen has been practising for a couple of years: 'so far I haven't personally encountered any homophobia towards myself or others in the movement, though I don't doubts that there are some who are homophobic. I have come across no prohibitions against any sexual practice, the emphasis being on do whatever you like as long as you harm nobody' (an ethic also adhered to by Neo-Pagans – showing how, in both paths, authority lies with the individual, rather than an institution). 'There's enough in the philosophy of the religion,' says Robert Bristow, 'to be able to see there's no discrimination between any people – whatever their race, sexuality, social background – everyone is equal. That includes whether they are practising Buddhists or not. What had worried me in Christianity was that I myself could repent for the things that *I'd* done – whether taking drugs or sleeping with men – and save *my* soul, but what happened to those people I loved and cherished who didn't repent?' SGI UK's monthly magazine has carried a number of articles by out gay members; in America Nichiren Buddhists have started holding gay weddings.[13] (Incidentally: contrary to the popular image, Buddhists – in Britain, at least – aren't required to shave their heads. Although given the number of gay skinheads and Sineàd-alike dykes, they wouldn't stand out much if they did.)

New Age

In theory, the New Age is that of Aquarius, an astrological shift into a new era which will witness a global spiritual revolution; in practice, what's on offer under the broad New Age banner ranges from trance-channelling, creative visualization, numerology and tarot to healing with colours, aromas, crystals and the ubiquitous 'energy'. What these diverse practices generally have in common is an emphasis on the power the individual has in their own lives, the benefits of emotional positivity, and an openness to whatever seems to work (which can sometimes lead to credulity and charlatanism). The New Age frequently castigates traditional religion for being corrupt, power-hungry and spiritually dead – failings lesbian and gay people have experienced first-hand, which is one explanation for the homo-appeal of the Aquarian approach. [14] Many New Age practices are revivals of much older folk-based traditions: again, lesbian, gay and bisexual people can readily relate to this anti-authoritarian emphasis on reclaiming what has long been oppressed.

Rupi is a television researcher in his twenties, from a Sikh background. He recently discovered the work of New Age guru Louise Hay and was 'blown away' by her ideas. His explanations for her appeal make clear why many queer people find New Age beliefs easier to cope with than traditional religion. 'You don't have to change your life. I've found it really helpful – it's given me a focus. I don't think I could have reached it through Sikhism because it's a very proscriptive religion, and it has certain rituals that I wouldn't fee comfortable with. I'm not one to follow a party line.' The style is very 'Californian' – full of cute phrases and upbeat observations – but for Rupi, this is part of the attraction. 'It is packaged in terms that I understand very readily. Before, I've been into bookshops thinking I want to learn about Buddhism. You see these huge tomes and you think, "I haven't got time for this" – I suppose I'm typical of the consumer generation – "I want this in a nutshell".' He has found her philosophy empowering – something queer people often need. 'One of her phrases is "the point of power is always in the present" – she would say you are completely in control of every action, and you are completely responsible for everything that happens to you. I know this is where arguments begin, and where I start to get a bit hazy. But each book is prefaced by a statement which says, pretty much, if you don't agree with something I say, don't take it on board. When I read that I thought, this is perfect.' (Hay has a big following among gay men; her controversial theory that all illness is a result of self-hatred and other negative feelings – and can therefore be healed with sufficient love – gains her both enemies and converts among the HIV-positive and those who work with them.)[15]

Quakers and Unitarians

Followers of the preceding paths have laid the blame for religious homophobia firmly at the well-washed feet of Christianity, which does undoubtedly have a shameful record of holy queer-bashing, and is still showing only sporadic signs of penitence. Among the hundreds of branches of Christian faith, and among the sects that have emerged from two thousand years of schism, however, are some which are distinctly homo-friendly. Most prominent are the Society of Friends (or Quakers), and the Unitarians, both organizations which place emphasis on the authority of individual conscience and divine worth of humanity, rather than dogma. Neither has a formal creed; Quakers do not even have clergy, preferring to minister to each other. Both have long histories of radical social action. No doubt attracted by this, and by the absence of any scriptural or human authority that can exclude them from worshipping, lesbian, gay and bisexual people have long felt more at home in these denominations than most Churches. Their collective policies have consequently been considerably more progressive than any other Christian organizations.

'In general I have found Quakers welcoming on sexuality, with out gay people in many positions of responsibility throughout the Society,' reports Peter Wyles, a bisexual. 'It is recognized that Quakerism probably has a higher proportion of gays in its membership than the population as a whole, as one would expect from an organization which tries so hard to be accepting and tolerant. The new *Quaker Faith and Practice* (revised 1994) includes a chapter on personal relationships which is extremely positive about gays, lesbians and bisexuals. Some meetings have officially conducted ceremonies of commitment for gay couples – although this remains something of a grey area, with the Society nationally not adopting a clear position.' It is true that, as is probably the case with any collection of people 'some Quakers are homophobic, just as some are racist or sexist. People don't become saints when they join.' Although Steve Hope, another Quaker, has experienced homophobia among Friends in the past, the meeting he now attends (in Oxford) has had a lesbian clerk and now has a gay one, staged an exhibition for the twentieth anniversary of Pride, and includes among its members a straight woman in her eighties who 'would regularly stay up past her eight o'clock bedtime to watch *Out*, and would buttonhole me or my partner Jon on Sunday to ask us questions about it. How many eighty-six-year-olds try to find a new understanding about the world? How many forty-year-olds or twenty-year-olds do?' Steve and Jon's partnership was celebrated at a Quaker 'meeting for commitment' in 1995. *Towards a Quaker View of Sex*, which created considerably controversy when it was published in the early 1960s, was perhaps the first Christian publication to take a positive view of homosexuality – and helped to decriminalize male homosexual behaviour in Britain.[16]

Being a prisoner of war in Singapore gave Dudley Cave a lot of time to think. He came to terms with both his sexuality (helped by an eminent sexologist who was imprisoned in the same camp) and his spirituality. Attending confirmation classes, he began to question the tenets of the Anglican creed; 'I thought, I can't believe this, it really is rubbish', and realized that the minimal things he did subscribe to meant he was a Unitarian. Dudley, now in his seventies, describes the essence of Unitarian belief as 'freedom to think. I felt theologically at home with the Unitarians – the gay thing was a bonus.' In the 1970s the Unitarians set up gay/straight integration groups, 'people who'd meet on the basis of mutual esteem'. When a local paper ran a campaign against cottaging, the local Unitarian minister took issue with it. Unitarians encouraged the founding of the much-treasured Lesbian and Gay Bereavement Project, and contributed to the funding. The Unitarian general assembly voted by a substantial majority to open the ministry to lesbians and gay men. When Dudley's partner of forty years died, the minister at the funeral was a lesbian; the funeral director and coffin bearers were gay; and Dudley himself was chief mourner.

'EXTERIOR' TRADITIONS

Traditions which emphasize the interior life give queers enough space to be themselves. It is the 'exterior' religions – the public, established orthodox faiths, the ones that issue reports and pronouncements about our 'condition', the ones who see us as a 'problem' that might split their precious unity – that really pose a challenge to queer belief. They are the ones that people have in mind when they say it's impossible to be out and devout. What's a nice gay like you doing in a place like *this*?

That question can be answered in a number of ways. The degree to which you experience orthodox religion as homophobic will depend on where you find yourself within it. Judaism and Christianity are both enormously diverse. Quakers and Unitarians represent only the most liberal of hundreds of possible Christian sects, some of which would be accepting.

The New Age movement and feminism have made some impact on the Jewish and Christian worlds: queers can be found thriving in women's spirituality networks, the Jewish Havurah movement, or among the 'alternative' Christian worshippers of the Iona Community or St James's, Piccadilly (a national centre for 'creation' spirituality, which emphasizes 'original blessing' rather than original sin). The Metropolitan Community Church is, naturally, entirely welcoming to gay and lesbian people – while remaining fairly orthodox in its theology and evangelical in its style of worship. Bournemouth's pastor Neil Thomas explains MCC's role as an alternative to the established churches: 'MCC was founded by people who were tired of waiting for "them" to change and instead established a new church that was already changing.'

The oft-quoted Chief Rabbi only speaks for his particular branch of Judaism – one of many. Openly lesbian and gay rabbis can be found in the Liberal tradition and the Reform Synagogues of Great Britain; they include Lionel Blue, perhaps the best-known rabbi in Britain, and certainly a national treasure. Leo Baeck College – which trains people for the rabbinate – has accepted a number of 'out' applicants in recent years. Rabbi Elizabeth Sarah holds an important position in the Reform Synagogue movement, and is also deputy director of the Sternberg Centre, the largest Jewish cultural institution in Europe; previously, she led a congregation: 'I was completely out to my community, I wouldn't go to one that wouldn't accept me and my partner of the time. I didn't lecture on homosexual issues but my lifestyle was open and accepted. I left at Simchat Torah, when we celebrate the end of the Torah reading cycle and its beginning; we were honoured as the two brides of the ending and the beginning, given speeches and presents – which is a measure of the degree of acceptance.'

Although there has sometimes been controversy about lesbian and gay issues in the Reform Jewish movement, and winning their current level of acceptance has not been easy, these rabbis are given a level of official support that is still denied most Christian clergy. A few clergy are publicly out – particularly those who do not have congregations, for instance hospital and college chaplains, or directors of retreat centres. There are many more whose sexuality is known to a select group of people. Gay people have found a friendly space even in the Jesuits, who might be feared as the most Catholic of Catholics (although all people training for the Catholic priesthood are expected to be celibate, regardless of sexual orientation). There is a Gay Jesuit Group, and a Jesuit retreat centre runs weekends for lesbian and gay people to explore their spirituality.

There are Anglican, Catholic, and Orthodox Jewish congregations who support their lesbian, gay and bisexual members – even if their leaders do not. Catholic Mike Fox argues: 'there is a big difference between the Church as community and the Church as institution. The church as an institution obviously has an enormous hang-up about sex – it comes as no surprise considering it consists of mostly older men who are not supposed to have sexual relations, and a culture that reinforces that. But the community is very different.' For Quaker Harvey Gillman, it is with the Christian community, rather than those who profess to lead it, that spiritual power resides: 'The Church is the people. Jesus taught that the divine realm was among his disciples. He didn't tell them to consult the priests or the rabbis, but to change their lives. Life could be lived abundantly and the new realm was beginning amongst them there and then.'[17] Catholic Elizabeth Stuart sees this as a major reason for continuing to struggle against the homophobes who wield power: 'They cannot be allowed to win because they do not own the Church. The Church as the people of God is larger than buildings, larger than institutions, larger than hierarchies and denominations, larger than any religion. Where two or three are gathered together in God's name there is the Church. Most of the Church exists outside the structured institutions, and rightly so, for Christ came and worked in the world – not in temples or ivory towers. He taught people to find God in the daily round of their ordinary lives, in places where the religious establishment believed God to be absent.'[18]

'I have found the average Roman Catholic congregation to contain a large cross-section of the community,' says Jenny Bullen, a thirty-year-old school teacher who has recently converted to Catholicism. 'There are some very intolerant people and there are brilliant philosophers and they all come together for the mass. I love the diversity. I have met a number of people in the Catholic Church who are quietly working for gay Christians'. Her approval for these aspects does not stop her noticing what is wrong with the Catholic Church – its being 'very undemocratic and totally male-dominated' for instance. There are, however, things she dislikes about other places she might choose to worship; and so she chooses the place that she finds spiritually helpful, because she recognizes that the external forms are not of ultimate importance. 'I really love Jesuit spirituality. I love the liturgy and I love the Eucharist. The Church has a bloody history and definitely does not have all the answers. God's spirit does have answers but you need to look inside for them, not outside.' For Jenny Catholicism is the external form that best helps her do this internal work. The same is true for Father Bernard Lynch: 'I love the Church for so much that it does represent, and for the many good people in it . . . through it I too received "the deposit of the faith", for which I am eternally grateful. I love the mass, the sacraments, the sacred music, art and culture.'[19]

Neither Bernard or Jenny believe for a moment, that the Catholic Church line on homosexuality is remotely defensible. (Bernard has written that 'to identify with the present Roman hegemony of sexual oppression is like trying to be Christian in the Third Reich . . . I choose to be an outcast with the outcasts'.)[20] They are, however, able to draw on the spiritual tools and tradition of Catholicism, while maintaining their faith that their sexuality is God-given.

As a vicar David Allen works for an institution he doesn't entirely agree with: but then, so do many employees. 'Maybe there is a need for the Church in spite of some degree of compromise. Life is more than sexuality, even though sexuality is an important part of it. One can belong to a political party, or vote for it, without having to agree lock-stock-and-barrel. Party X is the one that most approximates. In looking for a life-partner one often forgoes the Ideal and settles for a practical alternative. The Church is always on the way to becoming. It's a matter of balance, compromise, which I maintain is basic to most aspects of human living. This is not a perfect world – no matter how much we strive to make it so/pretend it is. Perfectionism can be a tyranny.'

WHY STAY?

In her book about women's experience of Christianity, *Found Wanting*, Alison Webster points out, that it is naive to ask Christians 'why don't you just leave?', as if, simply by leaving the Church, people would never again experience patriarchy or homophobia.[21] In a society thoroughly warped by both, there is no escape. As one recently ordained gay priest said to me, 'if we rejected everything that's been oppressive, there wouldn't be much to work with'. The fact that left-wing political groups condemned homosexuality as a bourgeois perversion for many years did not prevent queer people from becoming socialists.

For people who would claim their belief is – at some level – objectively true, there may not be a choice. Certainly, few people wear their faith lightly: although some queers might be described as spiritually promiscuous, this does not mean that everyone can simply give up a lifelong faith and have a go at crystal-healing instead. Kate's lesbian and feminist friends expected her to give God up – but 'it is as close to me as breathing. It is like living life without seeing the colour red. I know that red is red and God is God. I cannot "unknow" it. I cannot decide that I will no longer believe.' She remains a Christian, although now 'the difference is that I do not believe in religion, but in God'. For many people who were raised in a religion, it is such an integral part of who they are – deeply entwined with their personality, values and beliefs, as well as family and social network – that they cannot contemplate living entirely without it. For Dennis, who realized he was gay having been ordained as a minister with the Church of Scotland, to choose between his religion and his sexuality would be like having to choose 'which arm do you cut off'.

People also remain for political reasons – political in the widest sense, including a concern for the fate of other people in the same situation. 'Until we have a real cross section of society represented, the Church will never be the body of unity that it's supposed to be,' argues Diana Reynolds, an Anglican priest. 'So we have to stay: if we don't, it will never change.' Many queer people are passionately committed to change, having experienced what is wrong with the status quo. Since we know that religions have got it wrong about sexuality, we have to teach them the truth, not simply to improve life within such institutions for queer people and for the many others who have yet to come out, not just because there is a moral imperative to counter injustice, but because homophobes suffer from a diminished vision of creation, and hence of their God: they need us to help them see the glory of the full picture.

Not everyone has the strength or the will to do this work, which requires sacrificing time and energy that could be spent on our own spiritual life for the development of other people's. Nevertheless, for many lesbian, gay and bisexual people there is a sense that to leave their organization would be conceding defeat, and acknowledging that a minority of powerful men have the right to judge our sexuality. It would be abandoning others to homophobia. 'If you don't stay within the institution then what happens to those who do?' asks Mike Fox. 'If people like me desert the Church and don't try and change it through our example, then the people who are coming up after us who face the same problems will have no one to turn to, and we will be making the misery worse. Part of my love for my neighbour is staying in there, helping others fight their battles and being the shoulder to cry on.'

The political dilemma – how best to agitate for change – is as relevant in this context as in the secular world. 'I constantly asked myself whether I could bring about change more effectively kicking from the outside in or the inside out,' says Diana Reynolds. She chose to be ordained. 'I know that I change more as a priest. I see my ministry as a revolution in the Church.' Neil Whitehouse is a Methodist minister who is involved in Kairos, a social and spiritual project in London's Soho. 'A lot of what I stay in the Church for is to make religion good not bad. Religion is a terribly powerful thing which can be awfully destructive as well as very good. Jesus didn't attack religion so much as seek to reform it – to make God the true God, the loving God.'

WE HAVE EQUAL RIGHTS TO OUR RELIGIOUS HERITAGE

Adam Sutcliffe is another queer who takes a political stance on his faith. 'It is politically extremely important that Jewish lesbians and gay men claim our place within the wider Jewish community. At stake is our right to full access to and participation in our own ancient and precious culture and tradition, over which patriarchal conservative cliques cannot be allowed to claim exclusive stewardship. Our history, our myths, our festivals, our accumulated wisdom, are as much a part of queer Jews as they are of any Jew. If we abandon all this to our enemies, we are delivering a great treasure into the hands of bigots.' Adam attends Beit Klal Yisrael, a synagogue in London that has a largely lesbian and gay membership. Although it has a mission to include those who feel disenfranchised by mainstream Judaism, it still considers itself firmly within Jewish tradition. 'What's most exciting is not so much the radicalism of the rituals, but the opposite – a sense of deep continuity, as a community, with the traditions of worship, meditation, mourning, remembering and celebration of Jewish communities across the world and through time. One of the most joyous occasions for me is the autumn festival of Simchat Torah – "rejoicing in the Law". On this day the annual cycle of Torah readings is completed and then immediately re-started – and then we celebrate the gift of the Torah, in dancing, song and general frenzied partying. As is traditional, members of the community take turns to carry the Torah scrolls around the synagogue, giving everyone in the congregation a chance to touch and kiss them. In few other shuls, though, are the scrolls carried by same-sex couples, perhaps with one prayer-shawl draped over both of them, and feeling just as free to kiss each other as to kiss the Torah. After the scrolls are put away, we eat, drink, and dance manically to the music of a Klezmer band – very much, I imagine, as my great-great-grandparents did in their impoverished, Yiddish-speaking *shtetl* in rural Latvia. Not nearly such a high proportion of my great-great-grandparents community were queer, I'm sure – but that's a minor detail. I just hope that they experienced as strong a sense of joy in being part of a loving, caring, intimate and riotous community before God as I do on Simchat Torah.'

Sue Vickermann, a Methodist, is another person who sees both political and spiritual value in reclaiming her religious heritage. 'It seems to me that we have a right to draw on the cultural and religious tradition that we were brought up in and gain spiritual strength from it. It's familiar, we know it, and it's ours. Just because current social mores might dictate that this or that social sub-group is unacceptable, we shouldn't allow our connection to a long and profoundly meaningful tradition to be cut off. It always seems a shame when people are compelled to throw the baby out with the bathwater, that is, reject their entire religious tradition wholesale. This leaves us with an enormous hole in our background. The irony is that the possibility of reclaiming my "birthright" tradition (I use the term with tongue slightly in cheek) arose *because* I described myself as a lesbian, not in spite of this.'

Sue's story is a not untypical example of how queer people renegotiate the terms of their relationship with institutional religion. 'There was a time when I was so distraught about the patriarchy of the Church that I was permanently angry and outraged. Sitting in a pew and being witness to a service could bring me to choking point. I discussed, I fought, I despaired, and I left, with a big wound that I couldn't heal, so that I couldn't find peace wherever I went.' She explored many other ways of expressing the spiritual dimension – notably the women's movement and peace movement – 'yet I was drawn back into the realms of the Christian community via, of all things, the Lesbian and Gay Christian Movement.' When friends first invited her along to LGCM she had no inclination to attend any kind of worship; she went along to a 'housegroup'. 'I don't think we even prayed together, we just shared experiences and discussed.' Through LGCM Sue heard about, and visited, a Metropolitan Community Church. 'The familiarity and the sheer un-coolness of singing choruses together and holding hands was great. It struck me as starkly obvious that belonging to a community and being active in building it up (and reaching out of it) is very, very important.

'There was a sense in which I had sidled into the back seat of the church again. Having found a peaceful niche to reflect on my Christian heritage, well out of the way of the battlefields of sexism and homophobia, I re-found what was fundamental and underlying it all. The sexist rubbish, not to mention the homophobic rubbish – that isn't the essence of the faith is it? What I've come to realize is that the core of Christian faith is an awareness of God's love. God is the precious essence of all loving, caring relationships, I think'.[22] Within the Church that had once made Sue so furious 'changes were happening, there was an openness'; besides which 'I was only mixing with reasonable liberal Christians. The fact that there were other Christians out there who I would certainly have disagreements with stopped being a stumbling block. Feeling at home and accepted instead of "on the outside" I was, and continue to be, able to involve myself ever more deeply with my re-found spiritual home. With the passage of time the tables have turned, so that now, the Church does not affect me as it always used to. Rather, I feel myself to have the upper hand: *I* can affect *it*. My presence as an out lesbian who is accepted unconditionally speaks for itself.

'It's only a matter of time before the Methodist Church's homophobic policies at the international level "get real". In the meantime the full participation of as wide a spectrum of people as there exists in this world, at the grassroots of the Church, can only increase the groundswell of tolerance until it bursts through the ranks of the committees, panels and forums. Of course I know that the corner of the Christian community that I've come to rest in, which is the Methodist Church, can be, and has been, lambasted for patriarchalism, misogynism, heterosexism, homophobia and the rest (I might as well add racism to the list of sins), just as those words can be thrown at every nook and cranny of the institutional Church worldwide. Those charges are indefensible and when I hear them I certainly don't rise to the defence of the Church that I belong to. But I can say that the Church is represented by me too, and many others who are striving against the aforementioned isms. It's not right to make blanket accusations. I certainly would not "belong" if any one of those isms predominated in the Christian community as I know it. Just like society at large, the Church has to deal with these issues of injustice. As a member I am part of that impetus for ongoing development towards enlightenment.'

TURNING TABLES: PARTICIPATION ON OUR OWN TERMS

Sue found a way to draw once again on the spiritual tradition she was raised in, while not compromising her political integrity. She can do so because, as far as she is concerned, belonging to a religious institution does not mean automatically giving that institution – or the religion as a whole – her full or uncritical support. The same is true for many queer believers. It is another sign of mature faith. Johnathan Andrew is clear about what he wants: 'I'm not interested in a relationship with the Church. The purpose of the Church is to facilitate my relationship with God. The problem is the Church thinks that it's God. It doesn't see itself as the servant any more.'

'There's been a sea change in my relationship with the Church,' says Father Peter O'Driscoll. The catalyst for this change was not one that he would wish upon anyone; he was outed as a 'pervert priest' in a grubby *News of the World* exposé (simply for going to a gay club). This had shattering consequences, psychologically as well as professionally; Peter credits his survival 'to some unseen nurturing and holding, and drawing through all of that to a deeper experience of me and therefore a deeper experience of God, and a greater maturity of relationship, *vis à vis* God – and *vis à vis* the Church.' There was a time when Father Peter would become very defensive if anyone raised the slightest criticism of the Church. Not any more: 'I suppose one of the gifts of the experience is that I've grown up, and I'm not dependent on the institution for my validation.' He remembers getting up in the small hours of the morning to see the Pope at Galway racecourse on his visit to Ireland: 'I'd cross the road to avoid him now.' Peter agrees with his colleague Bernard Lynch, who told him 'God shits on those She loves'; he is convinced that, through the outing, God was guiding him out of an unhealthy dependency on the institution. 'I've been led into a new relationship with the Church, in terms of my own perceptions of that relationship – it's totally different to what it was when I was ordained, that's for sure.' Whereas in the past he felt 'abused by the Church' and 'constrained from being myself', now 'the real me has been liberated'. Father Peter has set up the English version of the Rain Trust, an HIV/AIDS support organization that draws on congregational resources to deliver intensive care. It is an organization he passionately believes in, so much so he managed to enlist his Bishop's support for the project. His sexuality has thus led him to a radical, empowering form of Christian action – miles away from the stereotype of the servile Catholic priest.

ON THE FRONTIERS OF BELIEF

Although these queers are worshipping within orthodox religions, they are not taking orthodox positions. They are not following orders, nor turning a blind eye. Their presence does not validate the mistakes and prejudice of those in power. Instead, queers are a thorn in their side – and a catalyst for change. Queers are reforming them from the inside; or maybe even detonating from within. 'Lesbians and gay men, together with feminists, liberation and black theologians, are reclaiming the Christian tradition "from the underside",' believes Eric Bond, an Anglican. 'I believe the outcome will be inyigorating. It may lead to the death of the Church as we know it and that may be no bad thing. What will replace it will be exciting, nurturing and subversive.' Where religious authority claims its theology is objective, queer heretics point out that, in fact, subjective choices can and have been made – religious 'orthodoxy' is merely the consequence of choices that were made, perhaps incorrectly, in the past, and present experience can change our thinking about God and religion. Robert Goss was for many years a Jesuit priest; he mixes queer direct-action politics with 'liberation theology' in his book *Jesus Acted Up*. He explains: 'Liberation theologies challenge dominant Christian political regimes of universal truth with the concrete, lived situation of oppressed peoples and their liberative practices.'[23]

Lesbian, gay and bisexual Christians and Jews are not people who can't pluck up the courage to leave their religious 'home'; they are pioneers. They are living on the 'frontiers of belief'.[24] Simon Bailey, an Anglican priest who died of an AIDS-related illness in 1995, wrote that to be gay and Christian was to be 'a pioneer on a lonely journey. Not many other people are going to join us here. We have the hard task of thinking what cannot be thought and praying what cannot be prayed – not so much because it is thought to be horribly wrong, though it is, but simply because none of us have ever been allowed to think like this – we are pioneering outside of the very minds – and spirits – our culture has given us.'[25] Although Simon felt there were 'no landmarks, milestones, not even any oases – not marked anyway, only unexpected ones', increasingly there is a religious culture in which people from these traditions can begin to consolidate their experience. 'Though our journey through the wilderness is not yet over,' wrote Jim Cotter, in celebration of the Lesbian and Gay Christian Movement's twentieth anniversary, 'we have travelled enough to know that we are no longer slaves in Egypt. If at times we still trudge across barren hills and plains, we have also recognised a climatic shift: the rain has begun to fall and the desert has bloomed in unexpected ways.'[26]

Part of LGCM's function is to guide people through the frontier territories, according to Richard Kirker. 'What we're doing is giving permission to people to accept, rejoice in and explore their spirituality as well as to admit to doubts and difficulties. The spiritual is never an easy path to explore – there are no easy answers which you can pick off a shelf, or even out of any book. It's about pioneering, and if we do nothing else I hope we do provide people with the opportunity to take risks when it comes to defining and extending the parameters of spirituality. We have no way of knowing where its going to lead, but it's worth the risk of making mistakes; that's the only way we might enrich our experience. That's the way spirituality has always evolved. Out of that process, an authentic reflection of truth can rise to the surface and be a model for future generations. People are certainly saying things with a far greater degree of candour and honesty, and saying that there are no taboos, that we must talk about our experience. The more people tell their stories, the more they find others with whom they can share those experiences, and the more opportunity they have to listen, the more wonderfully diverse the whole community is as a result of people not needing to put up façades, or resort to conventional definitions and traditional explanations.'

According to Dr Elizabeth Stuart, a sign of the confidence of lesbian and gay Christians – and the threat they pose to the current orthodoxies of the religion they worship in – is that they have begun 'to articulate our spirituality, our understanding of reality in terms of our relationships and faith, in liturgical form'. When Elizabeth compiled a book of this liturgy, *Daring to Speak Love's Name*, the Archbishop of Canterbury forced the church publishing house, SPCK, to cancel publication. In her preface to the book (eventually published by a secular company) Elizabeth writes that the idea of gay liturgy is 'threatening to those with power in the churches because it is an acknowledgement that we do not need them to help us makes sense of our lives. It is also threatening because it cannot be argued with. One can enter into a debate over an academic thesis, but one cannot argue with a person's articulation of their experience . . . By daring to speak love's name we expose the extent to which Church teaching and liturgy can have very little grounding in reality and become irrelevant.'[27]

As well as this pioneering work, queer Christians and Jews have also been uncovering their buried history. 'There is a great deal in the tradition which is rich, subversive and deeply empowering,' says St Elizabeth the Positively Revolting (a title conferred on Dr Stuart by the Order of Perpetual Indulgence, in recognition of her miraculous work). 'Most of this has been silenced or "forgotten", but it is gradually being uncovered. I like to think that the likes of St Aelred, St Brigit, and St Teresa of Avila nourished my roots even before I was aware of them.' John Boswell's monumental works, *Christianity, Social Tolerance and Homosexuality* and *The Marriage of Likeness: Same-sex Unions in Pre-modern Europe*, argue that for the first millennium of its life the Christian Church neither condemned nor punished homosexual behaviour – and that same-sex relationships were celebrated with Christian liturgies until as late as the nineteenth century.

While the reconstruction of homophobic religions is definitely still a work in progress, what is noticeable is the enthusiasm that queers are bringing to the task. Catherine Hopper found this when she was the religious reporter for *The Pink Paper*:[28] 'it's clear that lesbians and gay men are not just surviving within religions, they're flourishing; they're taking all kinds of initiatives, and many would argue that their end of religion is where it's most lively. Certainly some of the most dynamic and new stuff is coming out of radical lesbian and gay Christianity.' There has been an extraordinary proliferation of books for and about lesbian and gay Christians; the Metropolitan Community Churches and LGCM have both grown rapidly. This unleashing of creativity parallels, for Rabbi Elizabeth Sarah, the way women have challenged religious patriarchy. 'The men took it for granted for so long. Women are excited: they're realizing "it's mine!" Suddenly, the doors are open.'

REDRAWING THE BATTLE LINES

Too often the battle lines are drawn with lesbian, gay and bisexual people on one side, and religion on the other. Queers are oppressed: religion is oppressive. It's not a very constructive way of looking at things, and it's too simplistic. Some religions are on 'our' side, and there's some of us in most religions. If Catholicism wheels out its guns to attack homosexuality, who is to say that Buddhism doesn't have a bigger artillery to defend us? If Christianity is intrinsically homophobic, where does that leave Quakers and Unitarians? Religious homophobia must be seen not just in relation to secular morality, but also contrasted with the thinking of some of the great spiritual traditions (including, often, alternative traditions within any one religion). Some things are seen as a good idea by pretty much all the world's religions: compassion, for instance. Homophobia has no such universal seal of approval.

Not all religions are the same; not all people who identify themselves with any particular religion are the same; and so not all religions, or all followers of any particular religion, will be homophobic. And if the ranks of religious believers include not only homophobes but also queers, we steal their trump card. Instead of saying we don't want to play your stupid game, we're saying, we're already playing, and what makes you think you can set the rules here? Just as the Church is the people, so religion is queer people (and straight people as well, of course). 'We' are Christians, Jews, Buddhists, Hindus, Neo-Pagans, Sufis and others – as well as atheists, humanists and people who don't care or haven't really thought about it.

This more complicated model of religion and homosexuality actually gives us a stronger position from which to argue against religious bigotry. Quaker Robert Crossman explained that 'when I encounter people in other religious organizations I've felt very strong, as a gay person and a believer – because the Society of Friends is a very queer-friendly organization'. Pagan Gordon Hunt takes this argument to a blunt extreme: 'If Christians tell you you're no good, you counter by saying well, you're only a Christian'.

Dirk de Klerk also draws strength and confidence from his spiritual practice: 'Buddhism gives one a system of morality. It's very important to me to maintain high moral standards. I think it is essential that gays feel morally justified in terms of their own conscience. Buddhist morality is very clear. One way of summing it up is: treat others in the same way you would like other people to treat you. If you behave in that way you are behaving in a moral way. When people say to you homosexuals are wrong, you take the moral high ground. Do not give anybody else the status to judge. This is not saying: "the judge may be right but I don't give a fuck" – which is a tacit acceptance of the judgement. It's saying: the judges have no right to see themselves as judges, they do not have moral grounds that are worthy of my respect.'

Maitreyabandhu is convinced that Buddhism has more moral authority than any of the arguments that can be used against his sexual orientation. 'As Buddhists do not believe in God, there is no concept of "sin". Buddhist ethics are quite different to society's conventional morality, which may have little to do with real morality. Cross-dressing, for instance, has nothing intrinsically unethical about it – it simply flies in the face of convention, so society disapproves. Examples of real immorality would be hatred or dishonesty. Without this distinction, you just act out of prejudice or assumption.'

Maitreyabandhu makes a distinction that queer people have long known the truth of: the conventional will not necessarily have any firm foundation, or relation to the life we live. In addition, the previous three chapters have argued that conventional religion will not necessarily be spiritual. Our most effective strategy, therefore, is not casting ourselves as the 'opposite' of religion, playing the godless sinners they want us to be – but to question on what authority they make their claims, and counter them with spiritual authority of our own. We do not need to play the victim when it comes to our own spirituality: the truth of our experience cannot be challenged. Michael Seán Paterson has seen people living with AIDS come to this realization: he calls it 'the journey from victim to victor, oppressed to free, survivor to thriver'. It is a journey we all need to make.[29]

Notes

1. Lionel Blue, *A Backdoor to Heaven* (London: Fount Paperbacks, 1994), p. 143.
2. Arthur Evans, *Witchcraft and the Gay Counterculture: A Radical View of Western Civilization and Some of the People It Has Tried to Destroy* (Boston: FAG RAG Books, 1978), p. 55.
3. From an interview in *Gay Times*, July 1995, p. 49.
4. The Radical Faerie movement is found mainly in the USA. Groups of gay men gather, chiefly in isolated rural environments, to support, love, nurture and care for each other. Their gatherings usually have spiritual elements drawn from a wide range of traditions; through tribal rituals (such as chanting, drumming and dancing) they seek to rediscover the ancient spiritual powers and visionary role of queer people.
5. From Bernard's essay on 'Religious and Spirituality Conflicts' in Dominic Davies and Charles Neal, *Pink Therapy: A Guide for Counsellors and Therapists Working with Lesbian, Gay and Bisexual Clients* (Buckingham: Open University Press, 1996), p. 206.
6. When I started this research I assumed that drug-related experiences would figure prominently in gay men's spirituality. This was not the case, at least among the people who have contributed to this research. There may be a number of spiritual clubbers whom, despite my best efforts, I simply failed to reach: they were perhaps unlikely to respond (too busy clubbing?) to the published requests that yielded the majority of contributors; there is no equivalent organization to, say, the Christian or Jewish lesbian and gay groups that I approached; and I'm not a serious enough clubber (or drug taker) to make the contacts personally. A more likely reason for the absence of a rave-based spirituality, in my opinion, is that it is so difficult to articulate

anything coherent or useful about the experience, and there is no concerted attempt to do so amongst gay people. There are plenty of people around who might say that going to a hardcore venue like Trade in London is a 'religious experience', but cannot say much about how this influences the rest of their life and under-standing. Nicholas Saunders's comprehensive research into ecstasy use has uncovered people who use it as part of their spiritual practice, as well as reporting how gay people use it when clubbing: significantly, there was no overlap between these groups. Lynette A. Lewis and Michael W. Ross attempt, in *A Select Body* (their study of 'the gay dance party subculture and the HIV/AIDS pandemic'), to look at 'ritualized behaviour', including ideas of sacred space and time, and rituals for initiation, transformation and healing. However, the weight of their theory – drawing on sociologists of religion like Elidae and Frazer – is not supported by the evidence given by the clubbers they quote from. What the authors refer to as transcendence sounds more like escapism, or simply having a laugh – both of which are essential when living in the midst of a pandemic (or when living anywhere, for that matter), but neither of which would generally be understood as 'spiritual'. Though a rave experience is shared, the interpretation of it – and consequences for life outside the club space – cannot be. If anybody thinks differently, please let me know! Cf. Lewis and Ross *A Select Body* (London: Cassell, 1995) and Saunders, *Ecstasy and the Dance Culture* (London: Nicholas Saunders, 1994).

7. Buddhists, of course, do not believe in God.
8. Evans, *Witchcraft and the Gay Counterculture*.
9. As quoted in *SheBang*, April 1994, p. 30.
10. *OUT* magazine.
11. Paul Gordon Schalow, 'Kukai and the Tradition of Male Love in Japanese Buddhism', in José Ignacio Cabezón *Buddhism, Sexuality and Gender* (Albany: SUNY Press, 1992).
12. For the sake of brevity, throughout this book I refer to 'Nichiren Buddhists', 'Nichiren Daishonin Buddhists' and 'Nichirens'; in all cases I am referring to members of SGI, rather than any other Buddhist sects.
13. In Japan, however, Sokka Gakkai has close links with a right-wing political party it created, and which stands firmly for 'family values'.
14. Bert Herrman, in his book *Being, Being Happy, Being Gay* (San Francisco: Alamo Square Press, 1990), notes that Aquarius was another name for Ganymede, the beautiful boy with whom Zeus, father of the Greek gods, had a fling.
15. As Sister Mary-Anna Lingus of the Order of Perpetual Indulgence points out, Louise Hay curiously stops short of saying that we can grow missing limbs back if we love ourselves enough.
16. The Joseph Rowntree Charitable Trust consists of Quakers, and is guided by Quaker principles. They generously funded the research for this book; a very practical – and welcome – example of how Quakers are committed to lesbian, gay and bisexual people.
17. Elaine Willis and Ian Dunn (eds), The *Dunblane Papers: Report of the Second Pastoral Approaches to Lesbian and Gay People* (London: Institute for the Study of Christianity and Sexuality, 1990), pp. 35, 37.
18. Dr Elizabeth Stuart, *Daring to Speak Love's Name: A Gay and Lesbian Prayer Book* (London: Hamish Hamilton, 1992), p. xvi.

19. From Bernard's essay 'A Land Beyond Tears' in Ide O'Carroll and Eoin Collins (eds), *Lesbian and Gay Visions of Ireland* (London: Cassell, 1995), p. 218.

20. Lynch, 'A Land Beyond Tears'. Bernard stresses that he 'cannot judge those who choose otherwise'.

21. Alison R. Webster, *Found Wanting: Women, Christianity and Sexuality* (London: Cassell, 1995), part III.

22. Some of Sue's contribution here also appeared in Webster, *Found Wanting*.

23. Robert Goss, *Jesus Acted Up: A Gay and Lesbian Manifesto* (San Francisco: HarperSanFrancisco, 1994), p. xx.

24. An evocative phrase used by 'Jennifer' in Webster, *Found Wanting*.

25. I'm very grateful to Simon's sister, Rosemary, for providing me with a paper that Simon wrote on the subject of gay spirituality and giving me permission to quote from it. A collection of Simon's stories and writings about AIDS, death and spirituality has been published under the title *The Well Within* (London: Darton Longman and Todd, 1996). Rosemary's book about her brother's work, and the responses of the parish he worked in to his illness – provisionally entitled *Scarlet Ribbons: A Priest with AIDS* – is to be published by Serpent's Tail in late 1997.

26. LGCM, *Order of Service* for Southwark Cathedral, 16 November 1996, p. 6.

27. Stuart, *Daring to Speak Love's Name*, p. xv.

28. Catherine was still using the surname Treasure at the time.

29. Michael Seán Paterson, *Singing For Our Lives: Positively Gay and Christian* (Sheffield: Cairns Publications, 1997).

4

'This is My Body'

*The body does not lie. Flesh-body can indeed
be the place of truth, and can be
the best means of grace.*

(Jim Cotter)[1]

So perhaps it is not impossible for queer people to follow spiritual paths;
perhaps they might have reason to do so. But doesn't it require leaving
behind too much that we hold dear? The body is the one thing queers feel
comfortable about worshipping; whereas religions appear to hate the body,
or at best, are embarrassed by it.

We come out partly in deference to the longings, needs and stirrings of
our bodies. Once out, we can enjoy, and act upon, our attraction to the
bodies of others. Queer people are expected to be – and thus, *allowed* to
be – physical: to have sex, obviously, but also to present their bodies in a
conspicuous style (whether drag diva or diesel dyke, clones or cravat-
queens). Lesbians, in the best traditions of feminism, have fought
patriarchy's attempts to objectify and control women's bodies. Many gay
men (ignoring those feminist insights) have invested heavily in grooming
and building their bodies. Our position in relation to the mainstream
culture – and, particularly for gay men, the forms our own culture has
taken – give us a particularly acute consciousness of the body.

These insights – that our bodies are important, cannot be ignored if we
are to live whole and healthy lives, and can be a source of joy – are shared
by practically all queer people, whereas some heterosexuals can live their
whole lives without realizing them. And, despite what you may have heard,
most faiths argue that valuing the body is crucial to our spiritual growth.
It is through our bodies that we relate to creation; our 'sense of being' is
experienced through and within our bodies. Many traditions suggest that
by working with the body we can become more enlightened, or nearer to
God – whether through yoga, Tai Chi, fasting, or ritual exercises. Once
again, something that queer people take for granted turns out to be a sign
of spiritual maturity; again, we have a spiritual headstart.

The idea that the body is just a disposable shell for the soul is not found in many faiths. The early Christian church, however, embraced this dualism – with profound consequences for Western culture. It is a particularly bitter irony because, of all religions, Christianity is the one which might most be expected to value embodiment; as Michael Seán Paterson explains, 'at the heart of Christianity is the astonishing claim that God became *fully human* in Jesus and took on human flesh. With a body, circumcision, erections, ejaculations, sexual attractions. With eyes that noticed beauty, skin sensitive to the massage of oil and the touch of a woman's hair. Spittle that he rubbed on the eyes of a man born blind. A taste for a good wine and feet that could dance the night away at Cana. Is this *bodiliness* or *holiness*? Is there a difference? Is this not what Jesus took on in the Incarnation?'[2] 'In the early Church when the prestbyter administered the holy communion to the faithful, saying *Corpus Christi* – "the body of Christ" – the response was not "amen" as we now have it, but "I am",' points out Father Bernard Lynch. 'Can you see how radical that is? You – I – we are the body of God, in our humanity. No other religion I know states so unequivocally that God is found in and only in the human.' Over the centuries the Church has played down this message, Bernard believes, 'in case people like you and I would believe it – and live it'.

Lesbian and gay Christians argue that our bodies are a gift from God – and essential to spirituality. 'Our bodies are for the embodying of our loving, one to another,' says Father Bill. 'It is impossible to love totally if we deny the value of our body and its sensualness'. To repress 'sensual wonder in our lives, including our erotic and ecstatic experiences, is to destroy our innate capacity for recognizing and welcoming the divine'. Simon Bailey wrote that 'our bodies pray too, not just our "souls" so-called – God made it all, after all.' Mike Fox, a gay Catholic, is clear that the physical and sensual are vital for his prayer life. 'For me, being gay, admitting and accepting my sexuality, means accepting my full humanness. I cannot live by existing merely in my intellect. I am a person, I am incarnate, I am in the world of sense, and that is where I find God. If I find God in my sight, smell, taste, touch and hearing, why should I not find God in worship in this way? It may sound clichéd, but I am a "tat queen". I firmly believe that all worship should be an assault on the senses.'

Whereas queer Christians are still fighting for the body's value to be recognized, other faiths have fewer hang-ups. In Judaism, according to Rabbi Sheila Shulman, 'there's a realization that it's good to be bodies. When we celebrate, we eat, we dance. The whole material world is validated and appreciated.' 'Paganism across the board is a celebration of the earthy things – the tangible – including the body,' according to Roberta

Wedge. 'I see spirituality as integrated with the physical, and I think that is in general a pagan perspective.' For Roberta this understanding that 'pleasure is its own reward' is one of the connections between her pagan and bisexual identities: an overlapping of two body-positive philosophies.

Gary has studied a number of esoteric traditions. He explains that in these the body is seen as having a unique value. Before birth 'we're all floating around in the astral world, slightly separated from God. (I have memories of the astral world from before I was born.) Your soul wants to learn; but the classroom of the astral world isn't intense enough. So you manifest physically as an animal.' Although the physical is limiting in some ways (not least because it is finite), 'it's a much more focused way to learn'. To pay attention to the body is 'like giving thanks to God. This is the level where we have chosen to be – so let's use it.' 'The spirit would be nothing without its connection to the earth,' says Amneon, a Tantric masseur who has also studied a wide range of the world's spiritual traditions; 'the body is the spirit's temple, and its vehicle'. 'A lesson learned in the body is worth two out of the body,' says Steve Graham, a spiritual healer. 'I need to be in the body to get more and more clarity about karmic lessons.'

MASSAGE

Gary, Amneon and Steve all work as masseurs; massage is very popular amongst queer people, a sign of how highly we value the body. 'My body leads me, and I can get wisdom from it', says Gary. 'When I do a massage, it's like my hands listen to the body. My hands will go to the place that needs work, and I'll realize afterwards what's happened – it's that way round. Sometimes it's like you enter a magical space. When there's a flow between you and the other person, it's beautiful, it's a cosmic dance. You're completely in synergy.' Ben Stevens, a gay Christian in his sixties, has also discovered the joy of massage. 'As I weave my hands over a stressful body, slowly watching him relax, I can see a transformation which I can truly call healing. A lot depends on how one behaves, as to whether the massage is just horny or spiritual or both. It is easy to manipulate someone into a sexual drive. I have friends who on a one-to-one basis ask for a massage with this in mind. This is a totally different form of release and when done in private, comfort and warmth is very loving and helpful.' The sexiness of massage is, of course, one reason for its popularity; but Ben emphasizes there can be more to it. 'The relaxation the person experiences – the healing – is also felt by myself as I work on the massage. I have a feeling of quietness and nearness to God. When done properly I feel that, even with a total stranger, there is a tremendous flow of love and to me that is about God, and not about getting one's rocks off.'

'Sex needs to be integrated with the rest of our existence,' argues Gary, who specializes in erotic massage. Like Ben, he sees massage as healing – and 'healing is bringing things together. Generally we experience our sexual lives as quite "other". We need to embrace our sexual energy, to be whole.' Steve Graham takes a similar approach to his work. As a child Steve wanted to be first a priest, then a physiotherapist. 'In a way, I'm now both. I help people's bodies, which is what physiotherapists do; and I try to bring people to spirituality, but I don't do it under Christianity. My job is to integrate. The important thing is to bring the spiritual down – not just to the heart or the gut, but really down to the pubic bone, the base chakra, the perineum – for a lot of people that's beyond the pale, it's to do with piss, shit and sex, three of the taboos. Spirituality to me is integrating the lot. If you do it properly, you bring together the God source with the earth. Part of my job is to bring people into their bodies and help them to be happy there.'

DANCE

Another way in which people bring themselves into their bodies – and are happy there – is by dancing. Dance has long been part of religion; from the sacred dances of Hinduism to the dizzying folk-dancing of Judaism. Jesus, I was made to sing in school assemblies, is 'lord of the dance'. Aziz, a mathematics teacher, leads the sacred dances at the London Sufi Centre (Sufism is essentially a mystical form of Islam; the order Aziz belongs to draws upon other religious traditions as well). 'Meditation doesn't have to be sitting: you can also enter the state by chanting and moving. One aspect of the dance is companionship, friendship, sharing in the joy. Another aspect is losing your self-importance and self-identity, and releasing it into the group. It's very healing, especially in our individualistic society. It can be very powerful.' Aziz does not believe that all dancing is automatically worshipful; Sufi dances came to their composers in visions, and the holy words that accompany them are sung by the participants. The benefits he describes, however, are not unimaginable to lesbian and gay people who have danced in more secular environments, like clubs.

'Sometimes I get spiritual experiences when dancing,' says Trevor, a gay Londoner. 'When my mind's switched off, the music is rhythmic and tribal, I've got a bottle of poppers, hands in the air – I can feel energies flowing around me. I feel the music dancing me rather than me dancing to the music.' Another gay man recalled an experience where 'I got carried away to the point where I felt there was no distinction between me and the music – after a while there wasn't even any music, there was just this sense of oneness and this flow of energy in this huge dark space, this experience of somehow being connected to everyone else, in a way that I couldn't be just walking down the street.' Not many clubbers would claim to be seeking spirituality when larging it of a weekend. But for some, dancing may none the less generate unsought feelings of transcendence and unity. There are also a few people who use dance consciously as a spiritual practice.

'The ritual of dance, the repetitive nature of the movement, the rhythm that drives your mind into submission, eventually allows the kundalini energy to rise through you, and also through the community dancing around you,' says Amneon who dances to trance and ambient house. 'You just keep going. You feel the rhythm and you ride it. You relax into it. It sensitizes you. You feel it with your whole body until you forget the body – it goes – and you are only in that feeling of the rhythm and the dance and all the sounds that move you through it, until eventually you go even beyond that and you become so light that you feel waves of ecstasy moving through you. And you can have visions: and all of the sudden you realize the truth. You feel the truth. The truth is beyond your body, beyond the music, beyond the light. It's there all the time.'

In Jewish thinking an awareness of God should imbue everything that we do: Rabbi Mark Solomon finds his occasional nights out on the scene conducive to prayer. 'Although I don't set out to the disco to have a religious experience, the euphoric effect of the music and the movement – for me that expresses itself in some kind of prayer. You can transcend yourself a little bit because of the atmosphere. It just seems a good opportunity to get out of my usual self-absorbed preoccupations and direct my thoughts to God. A lot of the time I close my eyes; when I don't, I'm looking at these nice bodies, and there's a huge sense of gratitude, saying I'm really enjoying this, thank you for the opportunity to be alive and to be dancing.'

The energy that Roberta Wedge can feel when dancing is very similar to the life-force she connects with in her worship of the earth. 'I remember dancing in one ritual outdoors with dozens of other people around, who I didn't know very well, and going outside myself; feeling an energy and a power that I don't normally, and going wild with it, and leading these strangers on a spiral dance. It wasn't specifically sexual, but most people there were in varying states of undress, and the energy there was the same energy that I feel during the highs of arousal – except it wasn't turned towards a partner, it was used together with everybody there.'

SEX AS SPIRITUAL

Both massage and dance have qualities that people have argued are 'spiritual': they are intense experiences that take us out of the everyday (by bringing us much deeper into the body than we're used to), increase awareness of a sense of being and lead us to feel connected to something greater than ourselves. There is something we can do with our bodies that is even more likely to lead to such experience: have sex.

'Making love with somebody is a religious experience,' says Steve Hope. 'That's the sort of language the Church is beginning to use but doesn't really believe. It's a feeling of barriers being knocked down, the expansion of consciousness, participating in something absolutely essential.' Michael Seán Paterson agrees, 'I'm utterly convinced that for most people spiritual experience happens between the sheets, because that's the closest encounter we have with the Other, the Transcendent, the More Than Self. Love making is *the* sacrament for gay men. I could argue from Christian terms that that is what "this is my body for you" is about. The Churches have copyrighted that to mean bread and a cup – it doesn't mean that at all: it means this is all of me. That total whole person experience where you give everything to one that you love, it's not just that you're physically screwing: there is nothing to hide behind, no fig leaves, no barrier, no fear of consequences. That is the sacrament of spirituality for many of us, certainly for me. It's certainly far more nourishing than going to be told who my God should be and how He should look. The numinous – that "something-out-there" thing – is out there permanently; in those highly privileged moments of love making, I know it to be present in an immediate way. Love making gives it form, gives it a moment of articulation.'

Occasionally the transcendent potential of sex finds truly mystical fulfilment. Peter Cooper, now in his seventies, recalls one such occasion from many years ago. 'I was a Wing Commander in the Royal Air Force. Carl was a Commander in the United States Navy. We had been lovers for two years.' One summer, on leave in the mountains and forests of Turkey, 'We swam naked in a river. Afterwards, as we lay in the sunlight, we made love. We had done so many times before, but there was something specially intense about this occasion. Our bodies smelled and tasted of the cool fresh river. We could see a magnificent oak tree, whose leaves danced and rustled. Carl reached his climax inside me. He brought me off with his hand at the same time. We had simultaneous orgasms of explosive force. At this instant our gaze was drawn to the tree, which had undergone a change. It was ablaze with mysterious life, as if our release of energy had somehow triggered off a reaction in the tree so that sap raced upwards through it, filling it with power. The best analogy was that a mighty wind was blowing vertically through it and rushing into the blue sky. I thought of the wind of the Holy Spirit which filled the house of the apostles in Jerusalem on the day of Pentecost. Our sex act had been the expression of our intense love. Love was the force that flowed through the tree and through us. Our bodies were melded. Carl was still inside me. There was a change in consciousness, so that we were at one with each other and with the tree, which seemed to ramify gigantically into outer space. It was a tree of life. The whole landscape – river, forest, mountains, sky – was lit from within. Colours glowed with extraordinary vividness. All was vibrant. Paradise was here and now. Never had we been so full of life, seemed so beautiful to each other, loved each other so tenderly, been so fused together in body and spirit that each experienced the existence of the other as his own. We saw how everything and everyone was connected in a unity.

'Then the vision vanished as suddenly as it had begun. We felt that the mysterious activity was still going on, but that we had lost our awareness of it. It was only now that we realized that during our change in consciousness we had seen no physical motion, heard no sound. For a moment we were dazed at returning to the familiar universe. We discussed what had happened. We had each, independently of the other and yet together, just had an experience that had been virtually identical. Carl said: "The force, whatever it was, obviously didn't mind our being homo-sexual." We had felt our love (love, not just sex) to be in perfect harmony with the manifestation, indeed to be a part of it. I am a Christian, but I cannot explain it in Christian terms, although I feel it to be in no way incompatible with Christianity. It changed our lives. We could "make connections" as never before. We had more empathy with people. It was one of the reasons why I later retired from the Royal Air Force and became a probation officer.' Carl died in the following year – 'I feel that he was part of the *mysterium fascinans* which we once glimpsed together, and that we shall one day be reunited in it.

'I don't mean to imply,' adds Peter, 'that this happens to me every time that I have sex!' He does, however, believe sex to be 'a sort of ritual, not totally dissimilar from a religious ritual, and also to have a sacramental quality – "an outward sign of an inward grace". I cannot see that God can be kept apart from the sexual act of love, as if it would somehow dishonour him to have any connection with it. It seems to me appropriate to ask for a blessing beforehand, and to offer a heartfelt thanksgiving for love (or even just good sex) afterwards.'

Not all sex is transcendent or sacramental, as some of us well know. But if few of us experience the spectacular heights described by Peter, much of what he describes has probably felt within our reach, albeit at a lower intensity. For many of us sex is where we feel most alive; where we experience awe, joy, gratitude, awareness; and where we encounter a mystery far greater than ourselves. Orgasm in particular, involves these feelings. 'The peak moment of sexual orgasm is similar to that of spiritual experience: both for a fleeting moment take you completely out of yourself,' says Father Bill. American Joseph Kramer, who founded the Body Electric school, has said that 'it takes something extraordinary to bring the different facets of ourselves together . . . I feel orgasm – not ejaculation, but orgasm – is a major aligning process . . . so powerful that we get pulled in and we're fully present.'[3] Lesbian theologian Carter Heyward is of a similar opinion: 'Sexual orgasm can be literally a high point, a climax in our capacity to know, ecstatically for a moment, the coming together of self and other; sexuality and other dimensions of our lives; a desire for control and equally strong desire to let go; a sense of self and other as both revealed and concealed; the simultaneity of clarity and confusion about who we are; and tension between the immediacy of vitality and pleasure and a pervasive awareness, even in moments of erotic ecstasy, that the basis of our connection is the ongoing movement – that is, the friendship – that brings us into this excitement and releases us into the rest of our lives, including the rest of this particular relationship.'[4]

The Reverend David Allen is another person who learned, through sex, things they didn't teach him at Sunday school. 'In a physical relationship I discovered "this is what love can mean", and that was a profound spiritual experience for me. I felt like the person in the healing miracle reported in Mark 8:24. Suddenly people were alive – and I could look into their eyes and see them as living beings. I distinctly remember the feeling of elation, liberation – scales were gone from my eyes.' Contrary to the assumption that sexuality and spirituality are somehow opposite, it would appear that our sexuality – and sexual experiences – can be a way into the spiritual and religious. As Rabbi Lionel Blue says, 'it is right to unite your sexuality and spirituality. The price of castrating body or soul is too high. Fanatical religion and compulsive porn recommend this divorce. I have met people who tried it but were wrecked.'

Mike Fox has struggled to unite his sexuality and spirituality: from the conflict he has experienced a better understanding of his religion, and felt a closer relationship with God. It was particularly difficult for Mike to come to this acceptance because, although a devout Catholic who trained for the priesthood, his sexuality is sadomasochistic. He was 'turned on' by the Crucifixion. He told his spiritual director (another priest), who was understanding. 'He said you can either be sensible about this, find someone who cares for you and is prepared to explore this with you; or you can try and bottle it up inside you, get angry and get guilty, try to repress it – then it will ruin your relationship with God. He told me – thank God that you are a randy bugger, and thank God that you're a pervert. I left him thinking, woh! This is not Christianity! That was my gut reaction – this is completely opposed to everything I have ever been taught.'

Mike slowly became more grateful, as his director had suggested; but he reached a crisis point one day when he came to prayer full of anger. '*I have had enough* – that was my attitude towards God. Second mystery, the flogging – "they took him, stripped him, tied him to a pillar, and whipped him". I can see myself standing there dressed head to toe in rubber with a huge great big whip in my hand flogging Jesus saying "you deserve this you bastard, you really deserve this you bastard". I had to stop. I remember breaking down in tears and throwing myself on the floor and saying, I really do not want to see myself in this situation, I can't cope with this any more, I don't know what you are doing, I don't like this, show me the way out. Then I couldn't feel the floor any more. All I could feel was this tremendous sense of peace, of joy, of tranquillity. God was saying that is how you are, that is how you are made, that is how you respond to the world sexually. God has given me my sexuality and it's as much part of me as my belief in God. There is absolutely nothing which God cannot accept of me.

'I can try to cut those feelings off from God; but then I'm not being honest, I'm not allowing the relationship to grow and become real. So I have decided that God is going to cope with my desires. There are still parts of my life that I try to keep God out of. To have them illuminated by divine light is not a pleasant process, but it's got to be done. I had to go through that stage of being revolted by my own sexual fantasies to realize that I am redeemed as a whole person – that means that my desires, my emotions, my lifestyle are also redeemed. God knows all of me, including my desires, and loves them as part of me. So, no matter how sadistic or masochistic they are, they can still be beautiful, wholesome, pure, positive, life-affirming and valuable, because as part of the whole of what I am they are being worked upon by God.' Mike, for whom S/M is not about hurting and punishment but about the pleasurable inflicting and experiencing of pain, does not feel that his desires are inferior or somehow more 'sinful', because of the form they take – 'all desires – even perfectly "vanilla", so-called "normal" sexual desires – are transfigured and transformed and glorified by the operation of grace on the soul'.

Orthodox religions are still getting their heads around homosexuality: so S/M will presumably trouble them (and not just them) until the day of judgement. Mike's story illustrates, however, that the presence of the sacred in sex cannot be limited to the missionary position in the marital bed, as those religions would like. John Pierce argues for the spirituality of another sexual practice that religion prefers not to think about. 'Masturbation . . . can on occasion lead on to something more inspirational and touch in to our deeper, more spiritual nature, bringing a sense of harmony with ourselves and the world around us and for the religious person a sense of thankfulness to God who so delightfully created us . . . It is to be approached with reverence. It is a clue to our physical selves which are not to be regarded as less than the best, degrading or filthy. Our physical selves involving our sexuality and our masturbation even, are the gateway to our spiritual selves: flesh and spirit are inextricably woven together.' The fact that self-stimulation is a solo activity does not make this any less true. John compares it to prayer, in so far as both are acts of 'personal exploration.'[5]

SEX-POSITIVE SPIRITUAL TRADITIONS

Some religions recognize that the sexual and spiritual cannot – and should not – be kept apart. Adam Sutcliffe points out that 'It is a *mitzvah* [commandment] in Jewish law to make love on the Sabbath – sex is part of God's gift, particularly to be enjoyed in the time set apart for worship and rejoicing rather than work. I love going to synagogue on Friday evening, to mark the beginning of Shabbat, a day devoted to celebration and enjoyment of Creation. Afterwards, I sometimes slip out to a bar or club on the gay scene, for a late night cruise.' A Jewish lesbian who also tries to observe this divine commandment notes it makes further demands: 'Foreplay is required. I don't necessarily follow the rule that you have to be naked and that the lights have to be off.' In the mystical Jewish texts of the Middle Ages a great deal of thought is given to the spiritual and mystical meaning of sex; according to Rabbi Mark Solomon, the Kabbalah sees sex 'as the human representation of the divine paradigm – human sex helps things happen in the divine realm. Everything to do with sex is regarded in the Kabbalah with the utmost mystical awe and terror – so when it's done right, it's very good and helps to give life to the universe; and when it's done wrong, it has the opposite effect.'[6]

Representations of the creator's cock are commonly found in Hindu temples. Siddharth Deva, a gay Hindu, tells the story of the lingam, the smooth black phallic shape that bursts proudly out of the ground in temples throughout India. 'Shiv was caught one day making love to either his wife or mistress. A group of gods saw him and they were disgusted. He was killed and became ashes. He comes back to life, and says to them: this is important, you can't have me without this, it's the human element of the god. And the lingam has been worshipped ever since.' Sexuality in Hinduism is more pervasive than eternal erections. 'In the temples you have many depictions of scenes of sex, which are very erotic. As a teenager I used to think about them while masturbating. I never, as a child, came across anything in Hinduism that said that homosexuality was wrong. Whenever you did read things like that, it was from Christians. I think Hinduism helped me to have sex with men without feeling guilty about it.'

Some spiritual traditions – especially those with Oriental origins – go further than sanctioning or representing sex; they see it as a sacred art. Most famous amongst these are certain versions of Tantra, in which a variety of sexual (and non-sexual) rituals and techniques are used to awaken ecstasy and awareness: the word, and some of the practices and philosophy, can be found in both Hinduism and Buddhism (although 'orthodox' forms of both disown the sex-centred Tantric teachings that have become popular in the West).[7] Not dissimilar is the Taoist approach developed in ancient China, in which deepening the pleasure of love-making brings unity with the infinite force of nature (the 'Tao', which means the way). Taoism is contemplative – emphasizing the holistic experience of sexuality – while Tantra is more ritualistic, using sexuality to attain heightened states. Both traditions are esoteric: how fully they can be incorporated into a modern Western lifestyle, removed from the (very different) cultures that created them, is questionable. There are, however, queer people who draw upon their insights.

'Tantra is an expansion of oneself, and a union of oneself with a partner,' says Vieta, who combines it with Nichiren Daishonin's Buddhism in her own life, as well as teaching it to others. 'It wakes up the sexual and spiritual energy that everyone has.' According to another practitioner, Amneon, it 'uses sexual energy to expand consciousness. Raising the sexual energy, which is at the base of the spine, through a system called the kundalini and the chakras (which are different energy points going up the spine) to your spirit.' Tantra is more than just 'having sex': it includes exercises, visualization, chanting and breath work. Vieta has a mantra that she chants and a mandala that she worships; she sometimes calls out the Nichiren mantra, *nam myoho renge kyo*, during sex ('it helps to have a partner who chants too – because he doesn't think it's odd'). But sexual pleasure is central. 'Everything that comes out of the body is embraced,' explains Vieta. 'Tantra had a bad name in the past because it would include scat games, urine games, playing with one's menstrual fluids. Everything's done for the pure pleasure of doing and being done. The basic rule of Tantra is nothing is ever done for orgasm. If you're doing it for orgasm you've missed the point. If there's a purpose for sex, it's very sad – it's like saying sex is for procreation only.'

'Taoism is a sex-positive spiritual tradition,' according to Gary. 'It takes sex further than our culture. It uses erotic energy in a different way. Men don't come: you remain charged. You're completely stretching your whole experience – not just having sex, or just having mystical experience – but bringing the two together. We're unfamiliar with the idea in our culture, because sex is seen as something separate – it's under-utilized.' The idea that sex can be 'refined' seems strange to Westerners, who place high value on a (somewhat spurious) notion of spontaneous passion. But to Gary it is the difference between merely moving to get around, and dancing. 'Like with dance, you apply awareness, control, pattern, shape, form – it makes it beautiful, so it's a holy act because you're bringing together earth and sky, animal and spirit.'

Gary has attended workshops given by the Body Electric school in America, which incorporates Native American as well as Tantric and Taoist traditions to teach gay men to access their full erotic and ecstatic potential. He remembers it as a 'liberating' experience, coupling intense breath work with massage, including close attention to the cock (or 'magic wand' as they call it) 'in very formal, ritualistic ways'. This is done in groups – and not just with people you fancy. 'Every other man is your sacred brother. You diminish all those socialized judgements and you increase your love for other men. You look into their eyes and you see their soul. We are all part of each other.' These practices can eventually lead to the experience of non-ejaculatory or 'dry' orgasm. Another Body Electric student, Lev, describes what this was like for him: 'It's an orgasm, but a hundred years away from the orgasm you experience when you come. The sexual energy flows everywhere. I left my body. I don't know where I was. I had the most intense transcendent experience. I went way up into the heavens.'

For Lev this was a breakthrough in his spiritual growth. 'I came away from that experience feeling all this Jewish stuff I'd been involved in for all these years was only scratching the surface! What that work showed me was the value of the body in spirituality. The body is another important vehicle for reaching one's core, for knowing oneself. I actually felt that erotic massage was a more powerful experience of God – in the true sense of God – than any other I'd ever had.' Gary also found this bodily experience took him further than the philosophies he had studied. 'You come out a bit more. Before I did Body Electric, I thought I'd come out as much as I could – but I hadn't. It's something about a profound sense of acceptance. You get outside your everyday consciousness, and you start to feel things differently. Awareness increases.' Amneon teaches that through Tantra 'you unify yourself. You'll become androgynous for a time, and you'll enter deep spiritual states – you'll go into trances, have visions, go astral travelling, have very profound experiences.' Tantric practice can apparently stimulate the sort of experience that Peter Cooper described as occurring spontaneously with his lover in the forest.

These experiences are, of course, equally available to women. 'Tantra is for women, men, any sexuality,' says Vieta, who is herself bisexual. 'Tantra is only taboo for narrow-minded people. For women Tantric practice can bring empowerment. It can open women up to their needs. Women sometimes see sex as a means to something else, instead of just pleasure: women have been very good at using sex to manipulate, because they've been so put down by men. Women I have lived with still had this need to manipulate me. Tantric practice aims to break through all that: to bring women in touch with themselves.'

The intensity described by practitioners of Tantric and Taoist sexual techniques can be harnessed and used for our own ends, according to some Pagans and occultists. 'Magic works best in a high emotional state,' explains Gordon Hunt. 'Emotion changes things and the sequence of things.' Orgasm is a high emotional state and, according to Gordon, 'you can actually focus this power, in what is known in Wicca as shape-shifting, where you change the nature of events. You can alter circumstances, there's no doubt about it.' Jason explains how sex magic can be set in motion. 'You create a symbol beforehand. There is a rune that looks like a diamond which represents the god Frea, who gay men have an empathy with. Before you start having sex, you imagine this rune hanging in the room in red fire. Both partners say – all the energy, and all the love, and all the intense feelings that we experience while having sex, are going to be contained in that rune, and at the moment of orgasm that rune is going to explode and all the energy is going to pour out into the desired end. You set it up then go and have sex – you don't have to think about it again.' Although he cannot reveal the details of any of the occasions where he has used this technique, Jason is convinced sex magic is effective. As Martyn Taylor, another gay Pagan, cautions though, 'People do have to be focused, otherwise it won't work!' Which explains why Hampstead Heath is not the site of nightly miracles – people don't usually set up runes in the sky before getting their hands down each others' trousers. Despite this general ignorance amongst queers of the possible potency of our sex lives, Gordon Hunt thinks that Church homophobia is partially based on the fear that 'we will unleash all sorts of magic. The anal chakra is the one associated with magic. Are you aware of the Sufi's kiss? Also known as rimming. Stimulation of the anal chakra has some very strange shape-shifting effects . . .'

MORE THAN SEX: SEXUALITY AND SPIRITUALITY

Sexual acts can be a source of spiritual insights, even revelation. Furthermore, sexuality can be of spiritual significance even when you're not having sex.

When the American theologian Carter Heyward came out, concerned friends warned her that, by going public, her sexuality would be seen as the defining aspect of her personality. She worried about this herself – other aspects of her life, such as her politics, were also important. Why give sexuality such prominence? What eventually impelled her to come out was her belief that 'the celebration of the erotic and of our desire to express it sexually *ought* to be a major issue in our life together, because it is the primary wellspring of our capacity to be creative together – to love one another, write poetry, struggle for justice and friendship.'[8]

Anyone who identifies as lesbian, gay, bisexual or queer is likewise saying that their sexuality is important. At the very least we mean by this that sex is important to us: that we desire sexual pleasure. We know that sex is more than nature's way of keeping the species going; we may decide, like Father Bill, that 'sex is about filling the world with love, not about filling the world with children'. But coming out also, usually, involves some sort of articulation of the idea that our sexuality is more than genital activity, or the desire for it. 'Sexuality includes sex and the biological organs,' Father Bill says, 'but it also goes beyond those to involve the total personality. At the heart of sexuality is not the biological dimension but rather the personal and spiritual, functioning through the physical dimension in a creative way. While it does not determine our feelings, thoughts and actions, it permeates and affects them all.' Peter Wyles, a bisexual Quaker, shares this broad understanding: 'Sexuality is an element in what we do, who we look at walking down the street, our friendships and other relationships, our understandings of ourselves, how we love and get hurt and grow. I even realize that my sexuality colours how I watch a film, look at an Old Master, how I read a text. I am more than my sexuality, but it is more than what I do in bed.' This leads him to ask 'how can my sexuality and spirituality be separate?'

If spirituality is our sense of being, and sexuality so pervades our being, then the two must be intertwined. A Christian lesbian told me she felt they were 'interwoven somehow: when I'm aware of my spirituality I'm also aware of my sexuality – because it's about being aware of all of who I am.' 'Sexuality is who I am,' another lesbian told me – 'whereas sex is what I do with that, the action that results. Likewise spirituality is who I am, while religion may be what I choose to do with that.' Which means that, while sex and religion may be very different, sexuality and spirituality are likely to be very similar – both are about who you are. As Bernard Lynch says, 'all free and responsible sexual behaviour is about the discovery of self'.

When Carter Heyward talks about celebrating 'the erotic', she is using the word as Audre Lorde defined it in her classic essay on 'The Erotic as Power'- a combination of 'sexual' in its broadest senses with qualities that might equally be referred to as spiritual. Lorde, an African-American lesbian feminist, describes as erotic 'those physical, emotional, and psychic expressions of what is deepest and strongest and richest within each of us, being shared: the passions of love, in its deepest meanings'.[9] It is in this broader sense of sexuality that the deepest connections with spirituality lie. 'If it's just about who we fuck, then sexuality and spirituality have no automatic links,' contends the Reverend Niall Johnston. 'If on the other hand sexuality is something much deeper than its physical expression, something than informs our whole being, the person we are, and how we relate with other people – then it must have an intimate relationship with spirituality.'

'In both sexuality and spirituality I live out my own personal truth, my own personal myth,' says Peter Cooper. 'I allow myself to accept who I am and to be who I am. I have life more abundantly. In both I become more fully human. To become fully human is to share in the divine life. God is present at all peak moments in my life, both sexual and spiritual.' John Pierce, a gay therapist and lay preacher, similarly emphasizes how both are about being fully human. 'We share these in common with one another: they are essential elements in our humanity and yet in each of us they represent our uniqueness. Sex and spirit are the personal features which enable us to relate to one another. As the forces around us tend to isolate, depersonalise and dehumanise us, the development of our sexuality and spirituality becomes an increasingly important task.'[10]

Sexuality and spirituality are both experienced as 'deep within one's being', in the words of Vieta. 'These very "spiritual" people who haven't a clue about their sexuality haven't a clue about their spirituality – they only know about an Outside God. What's an Outside God got to do with an Inside Life? It's not out there. If it is out there, you'll never find it until you find it within.' The spiritual journey involves going within; sexuality is experienced as a force somewhere deep within us – from a source deeper than the thinking mind, even beyond the more predictable mechanics of the body.

And yet these deep inner feelings both reach towards something outside the self. A drive towards relationship is at the heart of them both; sexuality is the seat of our relationality,' according to Father Bernard Lynch. The late Robert Crossman, a Quaker, equated 'sexual attraction' with 'being drawn to people'; for him, this was 'another way of the light showing itself'. Another Quaker, Damian Entwhistle, expands upon this line of thinking: 'I think that this gift [of sexuality] is the dynamo for human relationships; it is what makes one individual go out from self towards the other. It is the power that enables us to relate to one another. It may also be viewed as the impetus that leads us to God. Some would regard that as the ultimate in going out of self towards the other. I feel that the mere fact of our existence places us in relationship with God; sexuality is the dynamo that moves us to respond. Sexuality is the power to go out from self in love.' To go outside the self is to transcend – the experience of transcendence, of encountering a reality beyond the self, is spiritual. Ecstasy – an experience associated with both spirituality and sexuality – literally means 'standing outside oneself'.

There is a further paradox: through ecstasy, through transcendence, through going beyond, through relationship, we find out more about the self. We see that the spirit outside us is also the spirit within us (that Brahman and Atman are one, in Hindu terms). Sexuality and spirituality both lead beyond the self and back to a deeper experience of the self. Thus, for Lorde, the erotic was both connection and self-connection: and 'self-connection shared is a measure of the joy which I know myself to be capable of feeling, a reminder of my capacity for feeling'.[11]

'The sexual has so often been described in religious literature as a helpful way of making comparisons with the divine, the divine which is thought to be something wholly different from and other than the sexual,' Jim Cotter notes. He doesn't hold with the idea that sexuality and spirituality are entirely separate and just happen to resemble each other. 'I am suggesting that the sexual is a *parable* of the divine, a sample of the divine, a "knowing" of God: it is not the fullness of eternity, but it is at least a foretaste of it.'[12] Many would go further even than this. Vieta says 'sexuality and spirituality are the same energy for me. You can't separate them.' Father Bernard Lynch decries a world that is not only homophobic but 'erotophobic', in which 'sexuality and spirituality are seen not only as split but in continuous and constant conflict. I believe, through my work with people with the virus, that sexuality and spirituality are the one energy, the same pure water of the uncreated life of God. They are the alpha point from which we live and move and have our being. The sacredness of sexuality, the holiness of sexuality, the mystery of sexuality speak to the fact that we are one body. We are already one in our spirituality and sexuality (relationality). Our separateness is an illusion.' Bernard feels that organized religion is primarily to blame for fostering this illusion. 'Hence the experience of most queer people that they cannot be queer and religious, or even spiritual.'

The connections between spirituality and sexuality are virtually innumerable. Beauty, for instance, can be both a sexual and a spiritual term. Both sexuality and spirituality can be ritualized. Both provoke moral and ethical questions. Both can be felt privately or expressed publicly. Both require and increase vulnerability and intimacy. Both can be fearful and abused. Both connect with our mortality. It is beyond the scope of this book to explore these in full, although many are touched on in later chapters. What I want to stress here is that queer people may be in a better position than most to make these connections, because we have identified – publicly, loudly and proudly – as sexual. We have already gone beyond the straight orthodoxy that sexuality is simply what you do with your genitals. Only having discovered that sexuality has other qualities can we realize that those qualities are also intrinsically spiritual. This is why Bernard Lynch thanks God for being gay. 'I am able to experience sexuality in a way that wouldn't be possible if I wasn't. And I see that as a way in to God, not a way out.'

SPIRITUALITY CAN BE SEXUAL

If sex and sexuality are so closely connected to spirituality, it should not be a surprise that spiritual practices and spirituality can feel 'sexual'. 'The phenomenon of having a sexual experience as part of your religious ecstatic experience is recorded in the rulings that are given to nuns and monks in medieval times,' Methodist minister Neil Whitehouse points out. 'Personally I have experienced a warmth of sexual arousal concurrent with spiritual arousal. I don't know why – except that everything that one experiences in the religious mode points towards wholeness and interconnectedness. It can be distracting, and bring your religious thoughts to an abrupt end, especially if you feel guilty about it – "oh my God, I'm getting an erection, how base" – if your doctrine is that sexual feelings are wrong. Sexual feelings for me are part of loving feelings, often, and they're God-given energies. As a gay man, there's no doubt that feeling drawn to the character of Jesus includes my body as well as everything else.'

Mike Fox argues that this is valuable. 'If we're going to relate to Jesus, we have to remember that he is perfectly human as well as perfectly divine. Therefore he had a perfect sexuality and a perfect sexual desire – if you ignore that, you are making Jesus to be less human than he is. So there is absolutely nothing wrong in relating to Jesus in sexual terms, or with images where one cuddles, kisses, fondles. Some of the saints have used incredibly erotic images – Teresa of Avila, or John of the Cross. If you try to cut that off, then you are saying that sexuality is fallen, sexuality is irredeemable – whereas, of course, it isn't. It's very easy to forget that beauty is a theological category. God is the supremely beautiful thing, otherwise how could you fall in love with him? How could the saints' sexual desire have been aroused unless there was something attractive, aesthetically pleasing, beautiful about God? When I was training for the priesthood, the way I used to rationalize mass was as the only way I could shag God.'

Moira is a lesbian who welcomes the sexual element of her relationship with her higher power: 'I do, at times, feel embraced, caressed, held and loved by my higher power, as if I were with a lover. In fact, one of my most sensual, spiritual and energizing sexual experiences came from embracing a tree in a fierce rainstorm. I felt connected to my higher power in a very loving and erotic way.'

What better way could there be to relate to God?

OTHER WAYS OF SEEING SEX

Away from the exalted heights of sexual–spiritual theorizing, it must be admitted that queers for whom sex is a deliberate spiritual practice are still a small minority. As Basho observes, 'there are a lot of guys around who don't want sacred, conscious, gracious, beautiful sex'. This can (but doesn't necessarily) reflect an underlying discomfort with their bodies, or with their sexual orientation. Steve Graham feels that 'a lot of the time people think they're in their bodies but they aren't, they are in a place they have constructed for themselves that feels safe.' Growing up hating ourselves and our homosexual feelings – as well as being part of a society that has problems with physicality – we are sometimes guilty of using the body only for 'genital acts'. It's interesting that 'masseur' is practically a synonym for prostitute in gay papers: it's as if the only time gay men have permission to touch and be kind to each other's bodies is when it will lead to ejaculation.

Self-hatred aside, not all spiritually identified queers see sex as sacramental. Buddhists such as Varabhadri from the Western Buddhist Order claim that such talk is 'a spiritualization of a very basic activity. You can bring more love and awareness into sexual relationships, but sex isn't innately spiritual.' Catherine Hopper, a Friend of the same order, doesn't deny that 'sex can be associated with all kinds of wonderful feelings of great closeness, and in so far as it helps you be more honest about who you are as a gay person, it could help you in your spiritual development. But in itself, it's just an instinct, which can equally be used for quite basic gratification, like scratching an itch.' Maitreyabandhu takes the same line – 'Sex can be fun – but no more than that. The whole thing that it's a gift from God is silly.'

Roberta Wedge makes a distinction between the joy of sex and other spiritual experience: 'for me sex is a connection with one other person, and recognizing the specialness of that other unique human being, which can be very tender. The charge that I feel from nature is about me as part of something much bigger than myself. Any spiritual connection that I make during sex is of a humbler, human kind. It's not the connection with everything that I feel at other times.'

Without doubt most sexual experiences are 'humbler' than many of those referred to in this chapter. This does not mean that such experiences are without worth. All sex – the good, the bad, the ugly, the casual, the anonymous, the drunken, the surprising, the regretted – can tell us something about what it means to be human. There is the physical pleasure, of course, which, even if it doesn't involve interplanetary orgasms, cannot be a bad thing. And this pleasure can be experienced with a stranger just as it can with someone who is intensely beloved. Anglican Eric Bond feels 'I have learned a lot from casual sex and there have been times of real, albeit brief, encounter'. Fernando Guasch has discovered the same: 'I think when you're cruising – not when you're feeling bad about yourself or want comfort – but on a day when you can make space to play – you can get encounters with other human beings that are raw and fresh. It's a dangerous situation morally: there are no rules at all, you could treat each other like shit, you could reject and abuse one another. If, in the midst of that vacuum, you can afford some humour or tenderness, it's charged in a way that's made me feel close to gay men. You can catch people so stripped of all their personas, the rules and games, the communication can be tremendous. It can equally be tremendously damaging; but for me, at times, it has been a very humanizing experience.'

To rely upon the sexual kindness of strangers goes against everything that men are taught about appropriate intimacy. All but the most selfish of casual sex involves some element of giving – a mutual concern for the other person's pleasure, if only for that moment, which, some of the time at least, deserves to be called 'compassion'. Casual sex can also be deeply honest – an acknowledgement of need and desire, without pretensions. By any standards, truthfulness and realism are more spiritual than deceit and escapism.

THE EXPERIENCE OF SEXUALITY

Whether sex is God-given or sex is mundane, queer followers of all faiths are convinced that sex is no sin, nor is it bad. Whether sex is a quick shag or eight hours of Tantric ritual, it is not separate from spirituality, any more than the body is separate from the soul. Unhealthy religion may encourage the mortification of the flesh; but a healthy spirituality requires us to listen to our body. 'Really love your sexuality,' advises Vieta. 'Really celebrate it. What you have to do in order to become spiritually or sexually aware is follow your bliss, as Joseph Campbell said – without any shame, without any fear. Live off your pleasure, and give off your pleasure.'

In a chapter about the body – and about sexuality, and about spirituality – it is often hard to find the right words. Saints and romantics throughout the ages have been pushed to the limits of language by their experiences. 'To a certain extent language breaks down,' admits Mike Fox. 'We do not have language for dealing with transtemporal realities, for sensations which involve the entire person – not just the meat of the body but also the feelings, desires, everything else. We don't have a language that deals with that in religious terms, we don't have a language that deals with that in sexual terms.' Ultimately, to *talk* about the body, and the forces within that reach beyond the body, is to miss the point, because it involves retreating back into the head. As Mike says, 'The only way to understand the experience is to have the experience.'

Notes

1. Jim Cotter, *Pleasure, Pain and Passion: Some Perspectives on Sexuality and Spirituality* (Sheffield: Cairns Publications, 1993), p. 39.
2. Michael Seán Paterson, *Singing For Our Lives, Positively Gay and Christian* (Sheffield: Cairns Publications, 1997).
3. Mark Thompson, *Gay Soul: Finding the Heart of Gay Spirit and Nature* (San Francisco: HarperSanFrancisco, 1995), p. 178.
4. Carter Heyward, *Touching Our Strength: The Erotic as Power and the Love of God* (San Francisco: HarperSanFrancisco, 1989), p. 33.
5. John Pierce, *Sex and Spirit* (Drewsteignton: Charisma, 1992), p. 40.
6. Unfortunately for gay men, a number of sexual practices, including mutual masturbation, are taboo in kabbalic thought because of what semen represents – when it doesn't go into the proper receptacle and is 'wasted', it gives birth to all sorts of demons.

7. In particular, Tantra as a cross-religious set of beliefs and practices – as popularized in the West since the 1960s – should not be confused with the 'Tantric Buddhism' of the Vajrayana tradition. Although there are Buddhist texts which include highly sexual images, 'orthodox' Buddhists (if that's not oxymoronic) argue that these should be understood allegorically or archetyally – rather than as a sex guide.
8. Heyward, *Touching Our Strength*, p. 27.
9. Audre Lorde, 'Uses of the Erotic: The Erotic as Power', in James B. Nelson and Sandra P. Longfellow (eds), *Sexuality and the Sacred: Sources for Theological Reflection* (London: Mowbray, 1994), pp. 75–9.
10. Pierce, *Sex and Spirit*, p. 6.
11. Lorde, 'Uses of the Erotic'.
12. Cotter, *Pleasure, Pain and Passion*, p. 43.

5

Relationships

'Forms, of course, are a lot easier to administer than content, so all institutions, whether religious or secular, concentrate on them.' According to Rabbi Lionel Blue, this is why orthodox religions so often focus on (heterosexual) marriage, to the exclusion of all other relationships. Gay people, he argues, pose a valuable question to religion: 'whether one can define relationships by their content rather than by their form'.[1] Once again, being lesbian gay or bisexual can help us focus on the internal rather than the external. Our queerness means that we will not conform to the dominant models. We cannot take for granted that our primary relationships will be with a spouse, or with blood families. Instead, Elizabeth Stuart suggests, we judge our relationships – and our Relationships – 'on the basis of quality of the friendship . . . not on conformity to traditional institutions'.[2] Just as our exclusion from the traditional forms of religion can liberate us to search for real spirituality, so our lack of social conformity can liberate us to see the true value of our relationships. By doing so, it may be easier for us to perceive their spiritual, as well as social, value.

MARRIAGE

For most faiths marriage is still the ideal – according to the Church of England House of Bishops' report, it is the ideal that queers inevitably (and pitifully) fall short of. Interestingly, the recent debates over lesbian and gay marriages have largely concerned legal rights and political status rather than its spiritual significance. A lot has been said about why we should be allowed to marry, rather less about why we might want to and very little indeed about whether religion has anything to do with it (beyond opposing us, as it does at present). Because of this, the 'right to marry' campaign can cheerfully co-exist with the widespread queer hostility towards religion; this no doubt reflects the perception in society as a whole that marriage is only tenuously connected with religion, the main role for churches and synagogues being to provide a pretty backdrop, a bit of gravity and an official stamp of approval.

According to Elizabeth Stuart, the defining feature of marriage for queer people is that we can't do it. The obvious reason for this is that we're not allowed to by any religious organization. Elizabeth Stuart argues that there is a theological reason as well: 'marriage' is *ipso facto* a heterosexual institution. 'Whereas it is perfectly possible for lesbian and gay relationships to fulfil the other purposes of marriage given in the [Church of England's *Alternative Service Book*] – mutual comfort, bodily union and the building up of community', queer people cannot meet other crucial criteria – 'marriage is a relationship between a man and a woman' and 'generative in character'.[3]

Some queers argue that this exclusion is to our advantage. The Reverend Malcolm Johnson argues that only a few lesbian and gay couples would want to 'copy slavishly the model of heterosexual marriage'; most want 'the freedom to develop their own unions around their own talents, gifts and shortcomings'.[4] Elizabeth Stuart likes to quip that to campaign for the right to marry shows a singular lack of ambition. 'Some would want to disassociate themselves from an institution which has historically been based upon structural and legalized inequality, specific gender roles, and which seems to impose at least a degree of conformity and uniformity and unrealistic expectations on those who enter it. And, of course, as a modern institution marriage seems to be in a state of grave crisis.' For once, 'bishops and gay men and lesbians agree . . . lesbian and gay relationships are not marriages'.[5] Queer relationships are very different.

All the same, some queer people do hold holy unions, affirmations, partnership blessings and commitment ceremonies. And sometimes, while recognizing all the objections, we call these occasions weddings, and the relationships that they celebrate marriages: maybe to be camp, to be provocative or because certain elements are so obviously the same (two people in love, exchanging rings and commitments). The Lesbian and Gay Christian Movement, which puts Christians wishing to have such ceremonies in touch with ministers who are willing to lead them, has made over five thousand such referrals in the last twenty years. The Metropolitan Community Church performs hundreds of such services each year, including a 'mass blessing' at the Pride festival where couples line up for synchronized ring swapping. Some Unitarian ministers and Quaker meetings officially support same-sex celebrations. Queer Pagans have held 'handfasting' rituals of union.

Why are all these queers tying the knot? Many of the reasons are the same whether the couples concerned are religious or secular.[6] It is an impressive and memorable way to say 'I love you' to each other, and to make a commitment. People want their relationship to be publicly recognized: by friends, and by family where possible. It's a good excuse for a party. Partners know that their love is at least as real and deep as in heterosexual marriages, and they do something similar to acknowledge this. Some people want to make a political statement: we can do it too. Some couples do it to try to paper over the cracks in their relationship. And amongst gay men there is the reason that Sister Latex (of the Order of Perpetual Indulgence) gave for his marriage to Sister Sadomystica: 'we'd been to too many funerals; one marriage celebration helped. I love weddings. They make me go goo-goo.'

But are there any specifically spiritual reasons why queers would want to commit to each other? Sue Vickermann is a Methodist who wants to 'marry' her partner. 'It's not the attraction of the wedding day itself: far from it. The ceremony as imitated or modified by same-sex couples has always looked like a slightly ridiculous parody in my opinion. But wedding traumas apart, we would like to have a politically respected commitment on not only a legal but also a deeply personal level. I see the Christian ideal of marriage – a life commitment on an emotional, practical and spiritual level – as a challenge that I would like to rise to. When the marriage terms as spoken in a Christian ceremony are taken literally and unambiguously, it looks like a more difficult vocation in many ways than being a monastic – a strenuous and endless discipline. It's not for everyone, gay or straight.' The late Robert Williams, who led many lesbian and gay marriage ceremonies, wrote that 'When a marriage is good and healthy, it becomes a source from which the partners draw, as they go out into the world to do the work of justice and love to which we are called by God.'[7] The Rev Malcolm Johnson – a member of the Anglican General Synod – has been officiating at same-sex unions since 1973. The Christian couples who come to him 'believe, as I do, that their love is divine in origin and needs to be acknowledged as such in God's house. They want, quite rightly, to thank God for giving them their love and for giving them to each other.'[8]

In addition to giving thanks, a religious ceremony may also ask God's blessing, a concept which Elizabeth Stuart explains: 'In the Hebrew tradition all creation is the expression of the extravagant, unconditional, gracious, loving nature of the creator. When human beings co-operate with God in the continuing act of creation by treating each other with the respect and love due to beings created in the image of a loving, just God, then we say their relationships and actions are blessed. When we recognize a relationship as blessed, we are affirming that we recognize the presence of God in that relationship, bringing order out of chaos, life out of death, wholeness out of brokenness. We recognize the mysterious power of divine love operating between the people involved and flowing out to enrich the world around them. We recognize that relationship as a contribution to the furtherance of God's reign on earth. We also affirm our responsibility, as the community in which the relationship has been born, to nurture and support the relationship. To bless a relationship is also to pray for God's continuous presence and protection from forces which threaten it. It is a statement of hope as well as affirmation.'[9]

Rosie remembers the day of her blessing ceremony – which celebrated her relationship with Chris – as 'so *reverent*, so deep and emotional (most of the people cried at the beauty of it and the words spoken) – so religious! The religious, to borrow Julia Kristeva's words, "relates to an exaltation beyond eroticism". Everyone felt a "special" atmosphere, a warmth, an electricity, a joy beyond the earthly, real interpretation of the term joy. If God is with/in us all then the coming together in Celebration of Love can only produce a heightening of the "normal" state of belief or joy. The many separate parts, separate loves we each have, come together in an intense "oneness" celebratory of Love, God, God's Love. We needed to know that our gathering was about love and not about gender politics, not about a focus on "difference" or our sexual labels. God loves people and therefore people should be free to meet and love in the true spirit of that.'

Strictly speaking, in Judaism and in Western forms of Christianity, the rabbi or priest does not marry the couple – they marry each other, and the priest or rabbi simply blesses the union (the Society of Friends do away with even this minimal role for religious authority). Queer people have taken this power into their own hands: we can celebrate our relationships regardless of whether certain institutions want to give their approval. Religion cannot get in the way of our relationship with God (where God figures in people's spirituality), and cannot diminish the meaning of our relationships with each other. We 'marry' each other. Because we are denied the off-the-peg service – and form of relationship – supplied by the religious authorities, we have to think more carefully about what it is that we want and how that should be celebrated. Elizabeth Stuart collected various texts for relationship ceremonies for *Daring to Speak Love's Name*; she observes 'the beauty of planning a service of this kind is that there is no set formula, so the service can truly reflect the uniqueness of the relationship'.[10] A lot of lesbian and gay couples design their own rituals: they choose music that is significant instead of hymns that are expected, read from favourite texts as well as the Bible, and invite the participation of friends and family instead of making everyone listen to the local vicar who's only met them on a handful of previous occasions.

People also write their own vows, which can vary widely according to what people are willing to promise. For instance, not everyone wants to make a lifelong commitment. 'In some forms of Wicca you only marry for a year, which is much more realistic for modern society', according to the Reverend Dr Gordon Hunt, who has conducted handfasting ceremonies for gay Pagans. 'The Romans had seven different forms of marriage, only one of which was for life. I will not lay down the rules. People must formulate the vows that they wish to make. I am not into spiritual unions for life and eternity: I think to stand up and have pride and mutual confidence before a group of your friends is the essence of the marriage ceremony. All present are recognizing that two people are making a commitment.' Malcolm Johnson suggests that couples 'follow the example of monks and nuns and make a one-, three-, or five-year commitment', although all the lesbian and gay relationships he has blessed have disregarded this (unromantic?) advice, and opted for a life-long commitment.[11] Unitarian Dudley Cave shares the same concern: 'I try to avoid till death do us part, I think that's a dreadful mistake; if it's the only thing keeping them together, it's a bad thing,' as we have learned from observing heterosexual marriages. Everything is negotiable, even the number of people in the relationship. A Metropolitan Community Church preacher once blessed a partnership of three people 'because it seemed the right thing to do. The important thing is that our relationships have integrity.'[12]

According to MCC's Reverend Elder Jean White, the integrity of lesbian and gay relationships – and the ceremonies that celebrate them – is so palpable that straight people feel they can learn from them. 'We've found a lot of people who are heterosexual saying "we wish our marriages had been like this". Parents of some of the couples have come back and said, "would you be willing to let us make new vows?"' It is often argued that lesbian and gay partnerships are potentially more equal and fluid than their heterosexual equivalents, because we are not forced into fixed roles according to gender: everything's negotiable. As such, queers are perhaps in a better position to meet the Christian requirement for marriage to be mutual.

The most important element of marriage, for spiritually identified queers, is not the ceremony or even the legal status, but the acknowledgement of the significance of *relationship*. Rabbi Mark Solomon notes that 'the first thing that is identified in the Bible as "not good" is being alone. So the idea that humans are made for relationship is enshrined in the account of Creation, however one understands that – (I don't take it literally). I think that most people – not everybody – can achieve their human potential most fully in a personal relationship with, generally, one other person. I think there's a whole dimension of human life which is about giving, about sharing, about being in relationship – and, the longer a relationship lasts, the more different aspects are going to be uncovered and experienced. In a short relationship you may not have to encounter the full reality of another person – it's in facing and transcending conflict after conflict, and experiencing the times of peace and happiness which come between and after the conflicts, that you gradually deepen. The temptation so often is to say "that's it, I can't stand another night of this". The sense of completeness, of real *sh'lemut* (which means wholeness) that you can find in a human relationship at its best can contribute greatly to a sense of *sh'lemut* with God.'

The Buddism of Nichiren Daishonin also teaches the spiritual value of relationship, even in times of conflict. 'Partners in marriage bring out the three poisons in each other (greed, anger and stupidity),' says Bryan, a gay man, who has learned the hard way – from six years with his boyfriend. 'It's through confronting these that we can do our human revolution and fulfil our potential as human beings.' [13] Marriage is frequently defended by modern religion as an important commitment, to attempt to confront any difficulties rather than give up altogether. You don't need a ceremony to make a commitment, but some queers like to have a formal recognition that it has been made – and to name it.

AGAINST MARRIAGE

The Reverend Jacqueline looks to her lover for spiritual sustenance. 'Supremely, my relationship with my partner points me to God – not that she is God! But so much of my growing and learning have come through our relating. Her loving helps me to love and accept myself. I would hope and pray that my relationship would manifest the fruits of the spirit mentioned in Galatians chapter 5: love, joy, peace, patience, kindness, goodness, faithfulness, gentleness and self-control. I would like to think that both of us are working towards a greater demonstration of those qualities in ourselves, and in our relationship.'

So far, this may sound like a defence of marriage. But Jacqueline concludes, 'you don't need a service to do that'. Like many lesbian and gay people, while fully conscious of the spiritual importance of her relationship, Jacqueline does not feel she needs a ritual to celebrate it. The fact that some queers want to walk down the aisle and others run in the opposite direction should not come as a surprise: a commitment to the inner quality of a relationship can be expressed in a variety of external forms (whereas insisting on just one external form could limit the inner content). If we all agreed that relationship ceremonies were necessary (whatever form they took, whatever the relationship was called), it would suggest the conformism that we're supposed to have been liberated from.

As Elizabeth Stuart pointed out, some queers are uncomfortable with the idea that we might be aping a deeply flawed heterosexual institution – even if we are attempting to remake it in our own image. A major drawback of the marriage ceremony for heterosexuals is that it can distract them from the content of the relationship. 'I perform a lot of weddings and I get more and more cynical about marriage,' admits Dennis Fraser, a Church of

Scotland Minister. 'Couples spend three years planning the marriage, one day doing it and fifty years talking about it afterwards.' One of the great gifts of being queer is that we are liberated from social preconceptions, and burdens. To set up new models – however worthy – may be regressive: moving away from internal qualities, and back to external forms. Not being able to marry at least prevents us from becoming idolatrous – and sentimental – about it, as heterosexuals have done. No less a figure that Jesus implied that marriage wasn't so important – he said there will be no marriages in heaven (Luke 20:34), hardly the future you would expect for something which his Church is so keen on.

Rabbi Lionel Blue is wary of the gay marriage bandwagon for a different reason. 'Gays like a party, dressing up and ritual – but that's only the froth of religion. You don't really need much religion for a marriage. You can do it yourself; your own desires, longings and love will carry you through it. But to be able to see it over the hurdles or part decently, that's where religion is really required.' If we have gay blessings, we must be prepared for gay *get* (divorce). 'You can't just invoke religion when you happen to want it and then say it doesn't concern us later. The break-up of a relationship affects and unsettles many people besides the parties concerned. It is not just their business. If you want gay marriage, that has consequences. You have to have conditions for it: you promise that you will go to some kind of counselling before you split up, and you think of the consequences for yourself and others.' The current debates about marriage rights have scarcely mentioned divorce. Some sort of legal provision would obviously be necessary; but also, if relationships have spiritual significance, this must also be true of their termination. Christianity has yet to address this issue properly for people of any sexual orientation. Elizabeth Stuart and a few others have written liturgy for the occasion, involving the smashing of plates and burial of seeds – 'opportunities for those going through a parting to make sense of the experience' – but the concept of separation needing religious acknow-ledgement is still so alien that the practice of it is rare. Painful and acrimonious partings, unfortunately, are far from rare among queer people (in this respect, we're no different from straights); ritual destruction of crockery may not be the answer to this, but the problem needs addressing.

ROMANCE

Most Buddhist lineages have no marriage ceremony. 'Buddhism does not see sexual relationships as a spiritual matter,' says Maitreyabandhu, 'and for this reason does not engage in pseudo-spiritual fantasies about the loving couple.' He rejects what he describes as 'the "cotton wool world" of sentimental affection, neurotic dependence, and rationalized craving'. If this doesn't sound very romantic, well, it's not supposed to. Buddhism – along with various other spiritual traditions, as well as many psychologists – rejects 'romance' as deceptive and destructive. This is not to say that they reject love – which is (theoretically) at the heart of most spiritual traditions – but they are suspicious of 'falling in love'. Varabhadri, a Buddhist and lesbian, describes the process: 'When we see another person, almost without knowing it we make judgements. If we like the way they look, we're attracted to them. If it's sexual, before we know anything about them, we want them, we want them to want us. If we get to know them, we decide she likes me, she doesn't like me, based on how we hear what they say. The world had been dark before we saw that person, now it's hard to live one day without a phone call. We seem to be living for one particular person, a few days without seeing her is an impossible eternity. That's projection. We all suffer from it.' 'You have no idea who this person is,' argues Nagaraja on the same theme, 'but there's just this desire to hand control over like you would to father or mother, to say, just look after me. This is a ridiculous way to treat another human being. It's unkind and inappropriate. I would never treat friends the way I've treated people in relationships.'

Another Buddhist practitioner, Fernando Guasch, admits that this may seem 'depressing', even 'chilling', 'because it runs so counter to the notion in the West that the Other Half is our true fulfilment, the fundamental fiction that this person is so special, and without them I couldn't live with myself'. Sex and sexual attraction 'can lead you to believe things that are phoney; such as that you're not alone, that another person is so unique and so important and so perfect for you that you could not be yourself without them. It's wanting to be looked after like a little baby.' Although we might protest that falling in love is natural, and glorious, Maitreyabandhu counters that it 'can so often come off badly – it can actually be the cause of immense suffering. You're not really seeing them for who they are at all: you're relating to someone who isn't there. So when that projection breaks down, and you start to realize who they are, you start to hate them. That's the acid test of falling in love – what happens when you fall out of it, what happens to that "love" when you break up?'

We're persuaded – by advertisers, by films, by our conversations with each other, by songs – that all we need to make us happy is a partner. There are many joys and strengths in relationship, as has been made clear already, and most same-sex relationship ceremonies are probably celebrating more than romantic love. However, joyous and strong relationship is not the exclusive preserve of two people, let alone two people 'in love'. The limited self-transcendence of being in a couple is not the same as the deeper transcendence of self spirituality calls for; nor does having a significant other express all the significance of Other. It is tempting think that it does, because, where once people would have turned to religion, they now turn to romance, or sex, to meet the same needs. The lover can be seen as our world, our meaning, our everything – our salvation.

The problem is that lovers, however great, cannot meet the spiritual needs that religions, however flawed, attempt to address. And, as Maitreyabandhu warns, 'people are not just trying to meet their spiritual needs, they are very often trying to meet *all* their needs through their "significant other" – psychological needs, financial needs. Which on a purely commonsense basis is a silly thing to do – it's putting an incredible weight on the sexual relationship, all your eggs in one basket. No one other person can fulfil all those needs.' Quaker Steve Hope is adamant that 'human beings deserve to be treated as human beings in relationships – not as gods. It is actually very oppressive to them – and when they behave as fallible, they get far more severe punishment for it than they deserve, because they're expected to be gods.' Much of the time we find it difficult enough to manage to behave humanely towards one another, so expecting people to be godlike is bound to end in tears. This is not to say that everyone should be single; but it is questioning the notion – supremely epitomized by contemporary theology about marriage – that there is something intrinsically holy about shacking up with someone. As Nagaraja puts it: 'A boyfriend is fine as long as you treat him as a boyfriend; but don't think he's your existential plug. He's not going to satisfy your neurotic inner craving for intimacy, for positive affirmation, for meaning.'

Queer people might be expected to be more alert than most to the romantic myth. We do not automatically accept the dominant values of heterosexual culture. We have developed alternative forms for relationships: the 'open relationship' and the proud promiscuity of some gay men, as well as women's communes, oppose co-dependent partnerships. But we need only look at the sheer number of lonely hearts advertisements, the speed at which some dykes move in with each other, the fondness of gay men for torch songs and show tunes, to see that we have not escaped contamination from our culture's idolatry of romance. How could we have done, when it is so pervasive, and when there are factors which make us particularly vulnerable? 'The myth becomes extra potent to us because we've been made to feel so lonely, so abandoned,' suggests Fernando Guasch. 'For people who've felt excluded and emotionally desolate as adolescents, the temptation to see the solution to all that in one solid thing – one person – is overwhelming. And there's an equally overwhelming temptation, once you've found a person, to imprison them.' And as Steve Hope observes, 'we can have so few sources of support we tend to put far too much on one central relationship – it's a pressure which most straight relationships haven't got.' We have escaped the limitations of marriage; but the 'loving couple' is a traditional form that is harder to shake off.

Rupi is a bisexual who admits that, in the past, 'I was desperate for a relationship. I thought it might make me a better person. And I wanted to give love, and share.' Jason, a gay man who lives in London, tells a similar story: 'From my late teens until . . . my mid-twenties, I had a series of relationships in quick succession, all motivated by my quest for self-respect. I was seeking happiness through the approval of partners whom I perceived as somehow better than me.' Jason discovered Nichiren Daishonin's Buddhism. 'When I started to practise I began a relationship which typified that tendency [to seek happiness through his partners]. This relationship lasted for the first nine months of my practice, by which time it had become very clear to me what the problem was. So for the next three and a half years I didn't have any relationships at all. During that time I went through a process of developing self-respect and discovering my own direction in life. I was learning to base my life on the Gohonzon [a Buddhist scroll used as a spiritual mirror – and one's deepest self], and learning that this was a process I had to go through on my own.'[14] Rupi's desperation was put in perspective when he discovered the work of Louise Hay; he can now say 'a relationship's not the most important thing in my life'.

Rupi's process of learning to love himself included very practical steps like buying flowers for himself and going to see movies on his own. Religions suggest various techniques to bring people to the same realization. Tibetan Buddhists practise a long visualization meditation in which everyone is imagined to have been your lover, and enemy, and mother, and father, in previous lives. For Fernando, this leads to the realization that 'there is no one person that ought to be treated with any greater or lesser degree of respect or compassion'. The Western Buddhist Order uses a similar technique called 'Metta Bhauana', which Maitreyabandhu claims cultivates 'the emotional positivity you can get from falling in love, that sense of aliveness', but for more than just one other person – 'you imagine having that for everyone you come into contact with'. Buddhist practice helps one become more aware of the 'projection' that fuels romantic love. 'Nobody in the FWBO says that there is anything wrong with relationships,' explains Catherine Hopper, 'but you may outgrow them, and there is no virtue in keeping them on just because you said you would. You wouldn't be encouraged to promise someone you would love them for ever, because romantic love is fleeting. Friendship actually endures much longer than love does. Sexual attraction certainly is even more capricious. My relationship is very important to me, at this stage; and to my partner as well. But we try to keep hold of the idea that this relationship will not always be valuable in the same ways, and one day the sex will fizzle out completely, and we'll be left with deep spiritual friendship, to the grave and beyond, which we have already begun. We don't have any plans to live together – we have these moments when we think we'd like to settle in a little cottage with the roses round the door, but I think we both know that would be limiting.'

Buddhism is perhaps the faith with the most vehement suspicion of romance, but its criticisms are not unique. Rabbi Sheila Shulman calls the story of Adam and Eve a work of 'romantic fiction' – which is no praise, for 'romance inevitably involves a kind of sinking of the self in the other that for us [women] would mean a betrayal of the self we struggle so hard to find, to make, to cherish'.[15] Rabbi Lionel Blue asserts that 'Judaism is not a romantic religion. It is less concerned with people being in love than with "the love" which, a text from the Jewish Reform Prayer Book says, "you earn, as you earn your living, with the sweat of your brow". This love is the end, not the beginning, of a relationship. It is the fruit of loyalty, and of being able to appreciate the otherness of the other. It is an antidote to the kitsch and the inflation of love which occur in cheap religion, cheap romance, and cheap porn.'[16]

ROMANCING GOD

Lionel Blue recalls in his autobiography, *A Backdoor to Heaven*, an occasion when even love that had been earned with the sweat of his brow was not enough; the day when he realized that, having lived with a man for many years, that partnership was at an end. 'I wandered into a church to absorb the shock in quietness, and that's when my voice started up again.' (Lionel communicates with God through something like the Quakers' 'still, small voice' within.) 'It said, "All the loves you will ever have in this life are only reflections of the love between us. One day when this world dies on you, you will have me, love itself, not just reflections. So don't take this world too heavy."' Earlier it was argued that other people are not, in themselves, enough to meet our spiritual needs; but realizing this may point to some sort of force that is. 'One thing that relationships have taught me', says Rabbi Mark Solomon, 'is that no human relationship can be a substitute for a relationship with God, you can't put your ultimate reliance on your human relationship however good it is – you have to have some other resources to fall back on.'

Eric Bond, an Anglican, shares this view. 'I believe that people are a sacrament, a form of the presence of God. However, God is ultimately more important than my partner; I believe all our desires are part of our natural thirst for God, that S/He satisfies through people, treasured objects and through the planet on which we live.' Nagaraja similarly claims that his

Buddhism is more important than any boyfriend would be – which perhaps sounds callous or repressed, unless it is understood as part of a deeply compassionate philosophy. It must be reiterated that none of the lesbians or gay men whose opinions make up this section, nor the faiths they represent, are arguing that we should all be single, let alone celibate. They are however, stating that, by definition, spirituality – which concerns itself with the whole of being, all our relations – will, if taken seriously, inevitably be more important than the fragile intimacy which exists between two people – although that intimacy is part of the whole, and can be a valuable contribution to our understanding of the whole.

'Longing, ultimately, is not for somebody else, it's for the one that is behind everybody else,' thinks Aziz. 'Sufis believe that there is only one being – God. I'm so attracted to you that my heart leaps out to you; then three months later I think, oh, he wasn't as great as I thought he was, let's find another one who doesn't have these faults and who gives me this buzz. Of course we can never find this perfection in another human being, because by definition we are limited. What the Sufi believes we are really looking for is the perfection of the beloved, which is God; when I love you, what I really love is the manifestation of God through you, which is unique – so I do love you, but in a deeper sense I love that which is behind you. This is quite a leap to take, from the personal. You still love the personal; but you appreciate beauty as an expression of the splendour that comes behind it, as an expression of the divine that has translated through us in a unique way.'

The Reverend Michael Vasey, an evangelical Christian who controversially broke rank by writing an affirmative book about homosexuality (*Strangers and Friends*), suggests that we can consciously utilize this connection between desire for another person and our ultimate desire; we can see romantic love 'as an intuition of beauty, a moment of revelation both about God and about creation. As an emotion it should be seen as an awakening – a summons to other emotions and other commitments. As a revelation of God it should lead to worship. As a revelation about creation it should lead to an appropriate engagement with the created order – possibly art, poetry or political endeavour; possibly, but not necessarily, to relationship with the person whose beauty has been seen.'[17]

FRIENDS

Jim Cotter – a gay priest, therapist and liturgist – admits that not 'every human relationship *automatically* reveals God', but is sure that 'there is no better place to look if you are searching'.[18] Romance, clearly, does not guarantee the presence of a deeper love. But if romance is not to organize and motivate our relationships; if we do not want to marry, and even have reason to be suspicious of 'exclusive' coupledom; and yet we recognize that relationship is central to spirituality – then what should we aspire to? Queer Buddhists, Jews and Christians disagree, to some extent, on the aim of a spiritual life; and the way I have quoted them in this chapter has perhaps suggested more of a consensus among them than can truly be found. But, in answering this question, they are unanimous. 'The Buddha said that the whole of spiritual life is friendship,' says Nagaraja. 'God is friendship,' according to St Aelred of Rievaulx, who encouraged same-sex friendships among the monks he led in the twelfth century – and who is an inspiration for a number of lesbian and gay Christians.

Friendship is a concept that we can readily understand. 'Gay people have learned that your friends are your family; gays create their own family,' notes Rabbi Lionel Blue, even though (or maybe because?) 'it is not an official relationship'. Elizabeth Stuart agrees: 'for lesbian and gay people friends often offer the kind of physical and emotional support that society expects of families'. Friendship 'emerges as a relationship which, as it grows between people, results in mutual and equal acceptance, respect and delight . . . Friendship has a social and political dimension, and is always subversive in a social and political climate which devalues friendship and promotes other relationships.'[19] Stuart, along with other feminists and lesbians including Mary Hunt and Carter Heyward, has been developing a theology of friendship, based on 'friendship as the fundamental and ideal relationship between God and humanity, among human persons, and between human beings and the rest of creation'.[20] Friendship, not marriage, should be the 'normative' Christian relationship: since an unmarried life, as we know, can be fulfilling, but who could survive without friends? Friendship 'acknowledges no barriers and locates the dignity of each person in their being, not in their status, in *who* they are, not *what* they are.'[21] 'The one advantage to living in a context where friendship is not held up as the ideal is that more effort is put into "policing" other relationships, with the result that friendship can become a sacred space in which people encounter one another, freed from the conscious and unconscious assumptions, prejudices and expectations that we are taught and bring into other relationships.'[22]

'I believe if people need anything – even more than meditation and awareness – they need friendship,' argues Maitreyabandhu from the Buddhist perspective. (His name means 'twice friendly' – '*Maitreya*, the name of the future Buddha, means "the kindly, friendly one", and *bandhu* means "friend" or "friend like a brother".') 'Today's fractured society has left many people sorely isolated. It is through human contact that we become fully human. I don't think you can effectively change without genuine friendship. The word in Buddhism is *kalyana mitrata* – which means auspicious friendship, friendship with the beautiful. It is quite an ideal: a mutual recognition of the good in each other, a response of virtue for virtue. But you can start with having a cup of tea.' 'If you can be a friend to the world,' says Nagaraja, 'you'll be someone who is compassionate. The Buddha is a friend – not a king, not a hero, not a conqueror. A friend wouldn't lord it over you.' (Along similar lines, Elizabeth Stuart ends her book on a lesbian and gay theology of friendship, *Just Good Friends*, with a chapter on 'Friend God' – arguing that this might be a more appropriate metaphor for the divine than Father or Lord.) The Friends of the Western Buddhist Order, to which both Maitreyabandhu and Nagaraja belong, has no marriage ceremony – but does have 'friendship ceremonies' (in which two experienced Buddhists and one less experienced Buddhist undertake to support and encourage each other until death – and beyond). 'My partner has had two friendship ceremonies,' says Catherine Hopper – neither of them with her. 'The movement is a network of friendships, and we're trying to develop deeper friendships with a wider number of people, to get away from this awful nuclear couple idea which is so unhealthy – it's very exclusive.' Friendship, by contrast, is inclusive.

One of the ways in which friends are commonly differentiated from spouses/partners/lovers/significant others – and one of the ways in which friendship is deemed inferior – is by assuming that friendship is not sexual. Sexuality is 'permissible' only in one relationship. Queers are less likely to fall for this idea (although we too may sometimes be guilty of diminishing the significance of people we don't have sex with, or, at least, giving our sexual relationships an undue significance). Since our sexual partners aren't our spouses, we're more inclined to the obvious truth that our sexual partners should be friends. Queers may choose to have sex with a number of friends – in addition to, or instead of, a central 'partnership'; and may develop friendships out of sexual encounters. We can also acknowledge, however, that many friendships have a sexual dimension, even if it this is not physically expressed. 'I think friendship nearly always has an erotic tinge,' says Maitreyabandhu.

LOVE

Queer people bring to any relationship – whether marriage or friendship – a commitment to looking at its inner content not its external form. And the inner content that we aspire to – the depth we desire – is a word that is used (perhaps too freely) in both personal and spiritual contexts: love. Thomas Merton is one of the most influential spiritual teachers of the twentieth century: a Christian monk with Zen leanings, who has already been cited by a couple of this book's contributors. He wrote that 'love is our true destiny. We do not find the meaning of life by ourselves alone – we find it in another. We do not discover the secret of our lives merely by study and calculation in our own isolated meditations. The meaning of our life is a secret that has to be revealed to us in love, *by the one we love* . . . We will never be fully real until we let ourselves fall in love – either with another human being or with God.'[23] (Merton is not advocating romance here, nor is the love he writes of necessarily sexually expressed.) According to Richard Woods, love is 'our most radical capacity for transcendence'.[24] Lest any of this should sound mushy or trite, it is worth remembering the insistence of gay priest Robert Williams that 'love is not just a warm fuzzy feeling; love is taking action, making decisions, negotiation, sometimes altering your needs and desires in order to accommodate those of another'. He wrote that 'the more we experience the love of another human being, as unconditional as it is possible for human love to be, the more we can understand and experience God's love for us.'[25]

Queer people ought to know about love. Ours is the love that dared not speak its name, but is now shouting it across the world. It is something we have proclaimed so necessary to our lives that we have taken considerable risks in order to make it possible, leaving behind the continuous denial of the closet, where love is suppressed and murdered. Love is also is a spiritual necessity. Perhaps this is another of our head starts on the journey. Sometimes it may seem – especially to queers who experience religious persecution – that we know more about love than religions do. 'Love knows no bounds,' says Father Bernard Lynch. 'Within the institutionalized religions, of course, it knows lots of bounds. I think its up to us on this side of the rainbow to move the boundaries.'

Notes

1. Rabbi Lionel Blue, *Godly and Gay* (London: Gay Christian Movement, 1981), pp. 8, 14.
2. Dr Elizabeth Stuart, *Daring to Speak Love's Name: A Gay and Lesbian Prayer Book* (London: Hamish Hamilton, 1992), p. 19.
3. Stuart, *Daring to Speak Love's Name*, pp. 18–19.
4. Stuart, *Daring to Speak Love's Name*, p.66.
5. Stuart, *Daring to Speak Love's Name*, p. 19.
6. Organizations such at the Gay and Lesbian Humanist Association have also registered a massive increase in demand for 'affirmation' ceremonies.
7. The Rev. Robert Williams, *Just as I Am: A Practical Guide to Being Out, Proud, and Christian* (New York: Crown Publishers, 1992), p. 214.
8. Stuart, *Daring to Speak Love's Name*, p. 65.
9. Stuart, *Daring to Speak Love's Name*, pp. 22–3.

10. Stuart, *Daring to Speak Love's Name*, p. 25.

11. Stuart, *Daring to Speak Love's Name*, p. 66.

12. Reported in the *Edinburgh Evening News*, August 1995.

13. *UK Express*, October 1993, p. 16.

14. *UK Express*, October 1993, pp. 15–16.

15. Sheila Shulman, 'What is Our Love?' in Jonathan Magonet (ed.), *Jewish Explorations of Sexuality* (Oxford: Berghahn Books, 1995), p. 110.

16. Blue, *Godly and Gay*, p. 9.

17. Michael Vasey, *Strangers and Friends: A New Exploration of Homosexuality and the Bible* (London: Hodder & Stoughton, 1995), p. 236.

18. Jim Cotter, *Pleasure, Pain and Passion: Some Persepectives on Sexuality and Spirituality* (Sheffield: Cairns Publications, 1993), p. 17.

19. Elizabeth Stuart, *Just Good Friends: Towards a Lesbian and Gay Theology of Relationships* (London: Mowbray, 1995), p. 48.

20. Stuart, *Daring to Speak Love's Name*, p. 6. Other works on the theology of friendship include Stuart, *Just Good Friends*; and Mary Hunt's *Fierce Tenderness: A Feminist Theology of Friendship* (New York: Crossroad, 1991).

21. Stuart, *Daring to Speak Love's Name* p. 6.

22. Stuart, *Just Good Friends*, p. 49.

23. Thomas Merton, *Love and Living*, as quoted in Lucinda Vardey (ed.), *God In All Words: An Anthology of Creative Spiritual Writing* (London: Chatto & Windus, 1995), pp. 137–8.

24. Richard Woods, *Another Kind of Love: Homosexuality and Spirituality* (Fort Wayne: Knoll Publishing Co., 1988), p.138.

25. Williams, *Just as I Am*, p. 214.

PART II

. . . to Eternity

So far this book has suggested ways in which being queer, far from making religion out of bounds, is actually useful to a spiritual life. Being queer can set us going on the journey within; and give us experiences that are useful to work with. Queer people have – to borrow the words of Richard Woods – 'uncovered the mechanics of social determinism in their own lives and had to face the limits of their previous social conditioning. To that extent they are free of them.' But what replaces that social conditioning? What do we do with the freedom? What are our values, and how do we determine them? Where do we look for support? Can lesbian, gay or bisexual 'identity' of 'community' or 'lifestyle' fulfil these needs? Woods reckons not: he fears that queer people 'may not have access to an alternative integrating framework – except that of the gay world itself, which is fraught with its own social determinants'.[1]

Quite how fraught is made clear by Mark Simpson, in an essay subtitled Inside the Gay Underwear Cult. He suggests that 'gay' – or, more accurately perhaps, gay lifestyle – can seem like a religion, with many of that word's negative connotations (especially the unquestioning acceptance of orthodoxies, and pressure to conform). He turns his withering attention to the idea that coming out is the end of all our problems, that any unhappiness after leaving the closet is clearly the result of straight oppression, or self-oppression:

> And best of all, the newly emerged out person also discovers that a sense of difference and apartness, feelings of aloneness and hollowness common to most at some time or other and exploited by all nasty religions – especially the anti-gay ones – are in fact a product of being homosexual but unable to become gay. It is surely a great consolation to know that the real reason for your sense of smallness and strangeness in the universe as a child was not because you were human and frail, or separated from God, but because you were meant to dance till dawn in a Spandex all-in-one, surrounded by young men with mobile hips and chemical smiles, and yet were stuck in a Gap-less town in Cleveland where the only place open after 11pm was the deathburger van outside the Young Farmers Club.
>
> And it has to be the case, doesn't it? If coming out isn't a coming home, then it would mean that homos were still lost souls who have to face the universe alone. And that would be a bit of a downer, really.[2]

Actually, in spite of Simpson's sarcasm, I think coming out is at least a step towards coming home; and that he understates the extent to which feelings of 'aloneness' can be massively, even fatally, intensified by being in the closet, especially in circumstances where homophobia is more of a daily reality than in the columns of lifestyle magazines. For many gay men (especially those over the age of forty, and those living outside big cities) not to mention lesbians and bisexuals, dancing till dawn in a Spandex-all-in-one is not what they came out for. I also don't think it as ridiculous as Simpson obviously does (elsewhere in his essay) to describe 'the transition from homosexual to gay' as a choice of 'light over dark, truth over falsehood, reason over superstition, rationality over convention, expression over repression': it certainly brings *more* of these qualities into the life of whoever comes out.

Where I entirely agree is in questioning *how much* more. I think we need to admit, more than we do, that 'aloneness and hollowness' are indeed feelings common to most of us, and this 'human frailty' doesn't disappear when we come out. While I'm convinced that my sexuality is a good thing, I agree with Simpson that it is not sufficient 'consolation' in the face of problems that are existential, universal, probably timeless – and, perhaps, spiritual. For Richard Woods the development of 'an explicit and authentic spirituality' is 'perhaps the only genuine alternative' to becoming 'a creature of the ghetto', and subscribing to the gay 'religion' Simpson derides.[3]

Coming out is not the end of the spiritual journey and our sexual orientation does not make the journey for us. Being queer does not guarantee the presence of spirituality. Being queer does grant us insight into certain problems and injustices: being excluded from the mainstream – including mainstream religion – enables us to see its faults, and that's good. But being queer isn't, in itself, automatically an alternative to those faults. It *may* make us less likely to make the same mistakes. It will not necessarily prevent us from making many other mistakes. Running through so much queer discourse – including some lesbian and gay theology – is an underlying assumption that being right about some things (the validity and pleasure of our sexuality, the evil of homophobia) makes us right about everything else. Sometimes lesbian and gay Christians seem to imply that they'd have the spiritual journey sorted out, if the Church would only get out of the way. Similarly there are New-Agers and Neo-Pagans who portray queers as perfect saviours of an imperfect world. Either way the argument is *they* need to change, *we* don't (at all). Of course, it is not only 'spiritual' queers who display this triumphalism; to read the gay press sometimes, you would think that paradise on earth had been built (albeit with occasional interference from the straight barbarians at the gates). But there are problems other than religious corruption; there are problems other than homophobia; and some of these problems are of our own making.

So, while the first part of the book was about how the strengths and pleasures of being queer can help us on the spiritual journey, the second part concentrates on how spirituality connects with the difficulties we face. These may be challenges that all people must confront, that we cannot avoid no matter how proud and justice-seeking we are – such as mortality and suffering – or they may be problems specific to our lives. Since there is nothing inherent in homosexuality that will solve these problems, some people turn to spiritual traditions in an attempt to address them. The fact that life is difficult is another answer to this book's initial question: why do queers want spirituality in their life?

Part one focused chiefly on the individual: the inner life, and the body. Part two concentrates more on the ways we relate to one another, the groups we form, our collective identities. 'Religion is not just about me being Christian or a Buddhist or whatever; it's about relatedness,' says Catherine Hopper. Spirituality is about the connections that we make. The previous chapter concluded with Thomas Merton warning that the meaning of life cannot be found alone. A gay man who was involved in setting up the London Lighthouse, Andrew Henderson, has written that 'AIDS reminds Christians to be suspicious of any tendency to over-individualise or to privatise conversation, belief or spiritual practice . . . we are most fully ourselves, the people God made us to be, when we are members one of another.' He criticizes ' the secular heresies of individualism and the glorification of independence', and yet both are concepts that would seem dear to the hearts of modern queers.[4] Here spiritual and sexual identity would appear to make conflicting demands. The chapters that follow investigate how people attempt to resolve this clash.

Acknowledging that there are problems, even suggesting that they may have spiritual solutions (or may not be soluble without spirituality), does not mean that we are somehow betraying our queerness. The strengths that were outlined in the first part of this book do not get thrown away. People do not stop listening to the authority of their individual experience. Rather, it is listening to this experience that obligates us to acknowledge the problems. Audre Lorde predicted that this was the consequence of being alive to the sexual–spiritual power she named 'erotic'. 'Our erotic knowledge empowers us, becomes a lens through which we scrutinize all aspects of our existence . . . And this is a grave responsibility, projected from within each of us, not to settle for the convenient, the shoddy, the conventionally expected, nor the merely safe.'[5] Unfortunately, shoddiness and convenience – and, above all, convention – are not the exclusive preserve of heterosexuality.

Notes

1. Richard Woods, *Another Kind of Love: Homosexuality and Spirituality* (Fort Wayne: Knoll Publishing Co., 1988), p. 125.

2. Mark Simpson, *Anti-gay* (London: Freedom Editions, 1996), p. 6.

3. Woods, *Another Kind of Love*, p. 125.

4. Andrew Henderson, 'Members One of Another', in James Woodward (ed.), *Embracing the Chaos: Theological Responses to AIDS* (London: SPCK, 1991), pp. 36–7.

5. Audre Lorde, 'Uses of the Erotic: The Erotic as Power' in James B. Nelson and Sandra P. Longfellow (eds), *Sexuality and the Sacred: Sources for Theological Reflection* (London: Mowbray, 1994), pp. 77–8.

6

Belonging

'Evangelical Christianity offered me something I'd never experienced before: acceptance.' This is what Drew Payne recalls as being so attractive about fundamentalism when he was an insecure teenager. There was, however, a price on this acceptance: 'more and more I was told by others that Christianity and the Church had to be the most important things in my life – actually my whole life had to revolve around them.' He could belong only if he conformed to the group he wanted to join, which meant denying his sexuality. Nick Williams had a similar experience of the Welsh Baptist church he belonged to when he was younger. What he liked was the 'companionship'; but 'I felt I could stay only as long as no one found out what I was thinking a lot of the time': as long as he did not disagree, and as long, of course, as he wasn't homosexual. Although Drew and Nick wanted to belong, they knew that in truth they did not.

For the Reverend Diana Reynolds, coming out is 'moving from not belonging to belonging, from a bad to a good experience of community. I think at the deepest level of humanity we all have a need to belong somewhere. A strong community is really valuable.' In her work she has witnessed strong religious communities; she feels that their strength, and the strength of the lesbian and gay community, comes from 'a real sense of commitment to the same thing, sharing something so powerful in one's life with other people'.

Glenn Palmer, who has been active for many years in gay politics (particularly in his native Australia) greatly values 'a sense of community and identity, a place where I belong'. To find this he now looks, not just to his lesbian and gay comrades, but to the Church. 'I don't think gay identity is very fulfilling, and it's certainly not complete. I'm searching for a more fulfilling community. Our relationships with other human beings are an integral part of the human experience that we cannot live without. To what extent does the gay community facilitate those relationships?'

All these people agree that humans have a deep need to relate to others, and share some sense of belonging with them. They have had varying experiences of where that need can be met. We experience and confirm our membership of a group by holding certain things in common: sharing spaces, attitudes, beliefs, behaviour, rituals, language, even appearances. This is as true of lesbians and gay men as it is of Christians or Jews. As the stories above illustrate, there can be a clash between the expectations of the group and the truth of our individual identity. Spirituality has been defined in terms of being the whole of who we are, and of becoming more fully human. The value of queerness, it has been argued, it that it encourages us to do this by valuing our individual truth more than conformist orthodoxies; which is why Drew and Nick have discarded the fundamentalist Christianity of their past. But where else can our need to belong be met? Can we look to a community of lesbian, gay and bisexual people?

Our sexuality alters any relationship we have with religious institutions, but it is also the case that our spirituality can alter our perception of gay and lesbian life.

WATCH THAT SCENE

There is much more to gay male life than 'the scene'. There are switch-boards, befriending groups, health projects and numerous social, religious and political organizations. For any gay man there is more to life than being out on the scene. And yet, the scene – the bars and clubs, the media that promotes them and their influence on how gay men perceive themselves and look and behave – continues to represent a central part of our identity. The scene is where we are visibly a collective (the only other place being Pride, which these days is the scene writ large, and moved outdoors). It is one of the few things that almost all gay men share, in as much as it is something that we all relate to – even if we distance ourselves from it, there is still an awareness of what is being rejected. And it exerts an enormous pressure to conform.

'My whole life people have tried to make me fit into boxes.' This was true of the religious traditions Seamus explored when he was younger; but also of the London scene when he arrived there in the early 1980s. He went – with long hair – to the most fashionable pub of the time, The Bell. No one talked to him for months. 'I bought some 501s, a white T-shirt, and shaved my head. I went into the pub and it was like flies to shit; the same barman who had served me for months suddenly asked me for a kiss. It was a confirmation that people don't want to accept me for who I am; and this was the community that I really wanted to be accepted by. I got what I wanted – I got sex – but I'd traded down from my standards. People are so focused on "getting it right" they're not interested in who we are.' Maitreyabandhu agrees: 'I think the group eventually is a power structure: if you don't fit into it, you'll get pushed out, or you start to feel you're not wanted.' He felt this both about the Church he sang in as a teenage choirboy; and about the scene he came out on to, when still called Ian. 'I went to The Bell where everyone acted as though they had just popped in to buy a packet of cigarettes and were far too good looking to actually talk to anyone. I felt a mere mortal in a world of unattainable gods. At the LA[1] I wandered around trying to look tough – among a lot of other men trying to look tough. I went home wishing I bore even a passing resemblance to a Tom of Finland drawing. I went to my local gay pub, got anaesthetized by inane music, bored by bitchy conversation and bemused by cheap innuendoes. I had seen the gay scene as the light at the end of the tunnel, now I saw it as another tunnel (albeit better lit). The scene is quite a totalitarian situation. You know when you go in there's certain criteria that you've got to meet, and you probably don't.'[2]

Richard Kirker has spent much of his life fighting Church homophobia as General Secretary of the Lesbian and Gay Christian Movement. Surprisingly, he feels 'very much more a stranger in some gay contexts than I do even in the most hostile of Christian environments, and I feel that there are elements in the lesbian and gay community which run perilously close to being judgemental and exclusive, just as the Church is rightly criticized for being judgemental and exclusive. I think lesbian and gay people could perhaps take a leaf out of some of the examples which the better church communities offer of being a place where all are welcome. Get things in proportion: how we dress really should not become the goal of our whole lives. Just as tat and a particular type of praying should not become an obsession of our lives as Christians.' What Richard criticizes in both the gay and the Christian worlds is ritual behaviour that has no inner meaning – but serves as a means of drawing the lines around who belongs, and keeping undesirables out of the exclusive club. Yet the people who are responsible for ostracizing are people who have experienced the pain of being ostracised.

'As a gay man I feel an outsider from the rest of society,' says David, a Buddhist. 'Within gay society, I feel further marginalized because I don't want to buy into the scene. I've found myself socializing a lot more with Buddhists than with other gay men – but that isn't ideal, there's a gay side of my life that I want to be integrated with the rest of it – if you find yourself spending most of your time with straight people there is this tedious element of being the odd gay man. Yet when I go back into the gay scene, it can be difficult to form close contact with people if their whole attitude is so completely different from your own. I don't like aspects of gay culture which seem to diminish the human spirit. I like to have the opportunity to talk to people. I want to know more of what the person's like than a snap impression against a huge amount of noise and buying them a drink then dragging them back for sex. I've done the rounds of social groups; they can be absolutely horrendous, then you start beating yourself up because you're making judgements about other people being socially inept. So for me, the problems with being a gay Buddhist have come from other gay people rather than Buddhism.'

Normality is a myth that everyone fails to achieve; we know that is true of heterosexuality, but as gay men we sometimes set up an alternative, self-imposed standard, even though the majority of us will always fall short of it. One reason why so many gay men feel disappointed by the scene is that the gay world isn't supposed to be like this; from its rhetoric, you would think it a place of joy and togetherness. 'The scene imposes its own conformity while proclaiming a message of liberation,' complains Peter Wyles. 'Despite all the claims that the "community" wants sexual freedom, the "community" is a home for everyone oppressed by straight society, people must be free to be themselves and so on – bisexuality can be unwelcome. Fat bearded people are supposed to stay out of the way, or at least dance only with other fat bearded people. For men anyway, the scene seems driven by appearances.'

MATERIALISM

'To be one of us, you must look like this' is the creed of body fascism, as summarized by Dennis Fraser. It is something a lot of men feel the burden of. 'The dogmatism around having to have pecs – it's another tyranny,' complains Michael Seán Paterson, a therapist and pastoral worker. 'I do acknowledge it's my agenda – I haven't got The Body. But what happens to those who don't fit? We're allowing ourselves to be abused by ourselves, we are giving people our money and our energy and saying beat me up any way you like. I'm just amazed at how much like sheep we are. Why are we giving away our freedom so quickly? If I saw every guy in Old Compton Street looking happy I'd say fine, but I see a hell of a lot of sadness, the deep sadness of having to keep up, and I get a lot of them coming to me in my professional work.' London's Old Compton Street, sometimes claimed as a triumph of queer visibility, is really the scene in a shopping precinct, and what it's selling above all is how gay men should look. 'I grew up with gay baiting, but worse is walking down Compton Street,' maintains Nagaraja. 'I feel like shit: oh God, I'm not as stunning as they are. It's like being six or seven again.' Louise Hay, the New Age guru with a big gay following, writes perceptively about the causes and effects of this behaviour. 'If you are not young and beautiful, it's almost as though you don't count. The person does not count, only the body counts. This way of thinking . . . is another way of saying "gay is not good enough". Because of the ways gay people often treat other gays, for many gay men the experience of getting old is something to dread . . . It is almost better to destroy themselves first; and many have created a destructive lifestyle . . . While it is often deplorable the way straights treat gays, it is *tragic* the way many gays treat other gays.'³

Needless to say – or rather, it should be needless to say but is all too rarely said among gay men – body fascism is the antithesis of any worthwhile value system. 'People are of inherent worth in themselves, not because of the size of their pecs,' states the Reverend Niall Johnston. To believe otherwise is materialistic – as if the physical is all that matters – and superficial, a concentration on the surfaces of things instead of their potential depths. Spirituality opposes both superficiality and materialism: it prizes the inner, and often intangible, 'spirit' of things.

'We live in a society which divides the mind from the body,' laments Mike Fox, 'where we are encouraged to view our bodies in a purely instrumental sense. One extreme of this leads to neuroses, diseases like bulimia, anorexia. It also leads to body fascism: the body is what the mind wants it to be.' To Mike this philosophy is not compatible with Catholicism, for it has 'no real understanding of what it is to be human. Christianity teaches that the body is the temple of the holy spirit and the soul is the form of the body. I am the body. The matter, the stuff, the sinews, the muscles, the hairs, the forty feet of gut – even that is redeemed, that is preserved into eternity. You have to view the body as the self. You can't treat the body any way that you like – it has to be treated with a certain amount of respect, and if you love yourself it has to be treated with love and care. Sometimes I am horrified at the things that people will do to their bodies believing that the body is merely an instrument for the mind.'

'The body fascism that rules gay identity I can't even aspire to,' says Glenn Palmer. 'I don't even have a choice – the average person who is maybe a bit overweight and doesn't dress very well can beat themselves over the head. I can't.' Aged thirty-two, Glenn has a muscular wasting disease which is progressively weakening his body. 'I haven't chosen not to have a physique of Atlas – it's denied me. That makes me angry. How do you carve a gay identity in that? So much of the lifestyle revolves around physical activity – being able to fuck, looking good enough to fuck, being able to dance, being able to drink, being able to cruise the streets. If you can't do that any more, what are you living for? And maybe, in my search for the spiritual, I'm looking for a reason to live. What brings the spiritual struggle for me into sharp relief is that for the gay community quality of life is a very physical concept; but a human existence that is focused around physicality and what the body can do is, for me, very tenuous. So I'm faced with the question well, what am I?'

There are other gay men who, by default, do not belong because they are physically incapable of matching the ideal. Kauldip Singh, a Sikh in his thirties, is one of them. 'If you don't fall into that whole gay stereotype, which obviously many of us don't because we're not blond haired and blue eyed, you're on the periphery. It's very difficult for me, as an Asian gay man, to relate to that – it's very rare that you see positive images of Asian or Afro-Caribbean men. A lot of Asian gay men when they come out think this is what I'm supposed to like, and I'm going to meet, a blond hunk on the scene. They're soon brought down to earth. "He's standing there; he's not even looking at me; what's the problem here?" I know a couple of Sikh men with turbans on the gay scene, and the nightmare stories they come up with make me very angry. They're so visible – they get racism from the bouncers and the punters. But they're very clear about their religion; and they are not going to give up their turban because they are gay. In the gay community there's so much pressure to look and act in a certain manner. Whereas when I go out with my family, I can drink and stand and sit in the way I want.'

The Sikh faith sees modesty as a virtue – an interesting alternative to the prevailing ethos of the scene. 'It all comes back to self-respect; that's one of the things with spirituality; you've got to learn to love yourself, irrespective of how you look. If you feel the way to love yourself is to go out wearing tight jeans and not breathing for four hours while you stand against a pillar in a club, and going overboard to get people to like you and admire you, where are you going to stop? You should be able to be who you are, the care should come from within. If you're good looking and handsome, use that as an inner charm; don't flaunt it. There's nothing *wrong* with wearing tight jeans – as long as you know who you are'.

Another group who are not accepted, in many gay environments, are older men; there comes a point when no amount of weight-lifting and shopping for beauty products can defeat the inevitable ageing process. Again, this rejection is in complete contrast to traditional religious thinking, which revered older people as (potentially) wiser. The spiritual journey is about growth, which takes time, since we can learn only from experience – and there's no experience without growing older. Gay men's obsession with youth is idolatry; it is the worship of something which has no intrinsic value. 'Why should being a gay man reach its apogee at being a disco bunny?' asks Sister Latex (who is in his forties). 'I teach young people; they're extremely undeveloped, they've just come out of being teenagers, which is borderline psychotic. Why have we got a culture in which borderline psychotics are the finest? Gay middle age can crash in very suddenly. Straight men can distract themselves from it because they have the status of fathers. Whereas some gay men think "this is the end of my life". They can only see themselves as a desirable young thing. Tough on them. They better wake up to life and discover new ways of validating themselves.' The habits of the Sisters of Perpetual Indulgence 'are anti-gay fashion. We cover up our gay signifiers: our hair, and our toilet areas. That is very equalizing. So Mother Molesta, the oldest nun, is equal with disco-bunny nuns.'

'The materialism of the gay and lesbian scene is partly cultic in origin – the need to produce a clearly defined identity,' suggests Niall Johnston. 'Partly, it's a recognition that we live in a capitalist society where money is often seen as the ultimate source of status; for those who sit on the margins, to claim status is crucial, and how better to show that than with the power of the Pink Pound?' The gay scene's materialism is manifest in commercialism and rampant consumerism as well as body fascism. Spiritual traditions generally have little truck with the accumulation of wealth (although their leaders often make a fine job of doing so). Glenn Palmer provides a reading of one of the most famous comments on the subject, Christ saying it was easier for a camel to get through the eye of a needle than for a rich man to get into the kingdom of God. 'I think it isn't so much about someone who has a lot of money being less worthy than someone who doesn't; it's about how people whose whole life is focused on the physical rather than the spiritual aren't going to get into heaven – not because God is going to turn round and say, no you can't come in, but simply because they're not going to look for it. It's not just about God judging you good or bad, it's about how you identify yourself and understand life, and how that informs your life. Gay people spend an enormous amount of energy and effort in the satisfaction of the physical senses.' 'Materialism is a blindness to a fuller reality,' argues the Reverend Neil Whitehouse along similar lines. Christopher, a Tibetan Buddhist, calls this materialism an 'alternative religion', one that he feels is especially appealing to gay people. 'I say this primarily from personal experience: once I had realized my sexuality, I wanted all that it could bring me; I bought magazines, watched videos and objectified people for the kicks that I could get.'

The comparison with religion is instructive, because inherent in materialism is a powerful alternative view of how life should be lived. Spirituality is about making connections beyond the self; materialism is centred on accumulating things for the satisfaction of self. Most faiths would argue that materialism is misleading, because it distracts you from the real questions (the questions that being queer can alert us to); it says that material things, and the satisfaction of your desires, are enough to make you happy. The experience of contributors to this book – and of human beings for millennia – is that this approach will simply not work. Stewart Harrison was struck by this realization in the basement of the London Apprentice, at 2 a.m. one morning. 'I said to myself, there's more to life than this, and more to life than just going to work to earn money. There's another dimension. It's all about what you really value in life. My religious journey started then.' Stewart is now a clergyperson for the Metropolitan Community Church.

Materialism is the prevalent ethos of the scene, however, because the scene is an intrinsically materialist phenomenon: it is driven by commercialism. You cannot make much money out of genuine spirituality (and presumably wouldn't want to). The scene encourages the objectification of human beings – through its advertising, through the environment it offers. People in chapter four argued that sexuality is a God-given gift that draws people into relationship with each other: capitalism redirects sexual attraction away from human beings, and into commodities that can be consumed. The reality that spiritual traditions urge us to address – the genuine diversity of human beings, the fact that we age, our need to care for each other – slows down the rate at which money can be made: so any such reality is numbed by loud music, dim lights and drugs. It's much more efficient only to deal in a Standard Model Gay Man. 'It's not as if human beings were not given enough temptations to make fundamental mistakes about their happiness,' argues Fernando Guasch. 'It's a particularly sore point that it happens to people who ought to have that extra sense of suspicion about myths. A community of people that have been given nothing very much by the capitalist value system is being conned into making the same mistakes – to see themselves as what they own, how they look, or what clothes they wear. From a Buddhist perspective, all these things – the 0898 numbers, the clubs, whatever lands us in the "hungry ghost realm"[4] – are problematic, because fundamentally they are telling you need something you don't have. You're incomplete, you're not right as you are: come and get a better body, come to the Fridge.[5] Gay people are psychologically vulnerable in any case. We're being peddled *as a solution* something that tells us we're not good enough as we are. It's a fundamental affront to human dignity. It's our neurosis and hurt that drives us to those bars. People go there because they are desperate, because they've got no place to go.' This may sound a bit extreme – some people just go out for a beer with their mates – but what is undeniably true is that the scene uses our very deepest desires – our sexual–spirit need to experience something beyond ourselves – in order to make money. 'Some well-known writers in the gay press defend club culture with "let the poor kids have fun",' Fernando continues. 'Don't they understand what it does to somebody, to be filled with these needs and to find this false, phoney substitute for the inescapable hard slog of having to trust another human being when you're feeling vulnerable? You can't just pop a drug and bypass that experience. Trusting means fear, it means exposure. That's what the moral experience is.'

Peter Wyles sums up the scene with the phrase 'drugs, dick and dancing. Now enjoying yourself is not wrong, and fun is part of the more abundant life we are required to lead. There is, however, more to life than worshipping the three Ds.' This is, potentially, the worst blasphemy of the scene – it's narrowness of vision. There is, in Peter's words, 'more to life' than sex, certainly more to life than the cruisy/sleazy sex that the scene sells. 'The prime directive is getting sex: everything else falls by the wayside,' observes David. 'You want a raunchy atmosphere – so let's lose the tedious bit of having a conversation. What do you get in the end? Monoculture without diversity.' Maitreyabandhu fears the effects of this monoculture: 'Sometimes we can feel sex is compulsory – that if you haven't got a boyfriend or aren't on the scene there's something wrong with you. Instead of saying you can't have it, we're told we have to have it. There's still no freedom in that.'

SUPERFICIALITY AND FANTASY

Much of the scene is inimical to true communication. In many of the spaces gay men have created, it is difficult to hear what anybody is saying. Even when verbal communication is possible, concern about keeping the image up, and fear, can conspire to keep us silent and strangers from one another. 'Going out to a gay pub can be a bit like going to church,' says the Reverend Bruce Kinsey, 'because we go there to meet people and end up not talking to each other.' 'Gay men can communicate very easily on a sexual level,' says Adam James. 'But where is the expression from the heart? It's unbelievable really that gays who say they are persecuted by the mainstream choose to go to places where they cannot speak.' We campaigned for the right to be ourselves and then created spaces where we can't be. Why, in the public space of our 'community', is it so easy to participate in intimate sexual acts, but so difficult to say 'I'm scared, I'm lonely, how do I get through another day'?

The scene doesn't pretend to be about the whole of life: at most it can serve only a few specific desires, at best it would be somewhere we go, sometimes, to have fun. The problem comes if what it offers is taken to be the summit of our aspirations, or the only worthwhile recreational activity for the happening homo. The scene is still where gay men are most likely to seek to meet partners and friends; it may still, especially outside big cities, be the only place people can be gay at all. So we end up associating being gay – with all the spiritual (not to mention sexual) potential that has – with the strictly limited pleasures of the scene. Gay men seem to be faced with the choice, in Maitreyabandhu's words, between 'painful superficiality or isolation.'

The scene sells fantasy; spirituality, the queers in this book maintain, is about engaging with reality. 'I find aspects of the gay scene antithetical to integrating my life, not because it's immoral, but because it's so false,' says Buddhist David. 'It gags in your throat to be involved in that much triviality, that basic lie; so much of it is to do with distraction – particularly from emotions. If you do get a chance to talk to people, their lives revolve around the scene, so they haven't got very much else to say. There's this emphasis on being completely OK – it's nauseatingly false.' 'I never had a night out without waking up the next morning smelling, with wrinkles on my face,' admits Nagaraja. 'Real life isn't like the magazines. Well, my life isn't. Maybe for some people it is. So what do you do – sit around the sidelines weeping? Or find something that *is* meaningful to you?' Fernando is angered by the escapism of gay popular culture: 'You could for ever live your life in London as a gay man and be on this conveyor belt of ready-made identity. The community that gay people are inventing for themselves is one that is absolutely the antithesis of any spiritual values.'

This is a long way from the vision that Edward Carpenter had for us. In *The Intermediate Sex*, written in 1908, he predicted that queers (or Uranians, as he called us) would form 'the advance guard of that great movement which will one day transform the common life by substituting the bond of personal affection and compassion for the monetary, legal and other external ties which now control and confine society'.[6] Instead of displaying the 'extraordinary humanity and sympathy' that Carpenter thought was an evolutionary trait of ours, we have substituted ties of our own for those with which heterosexuals confined and controlled us. For me the scene is one of the strongest arguments against the essentialist notion that queers are some sort of spiritually evolved sub-species of humanity. As Adam James puts it, 'if gays think they are on a higher level, why don't we show it, why don't we make something beautiful?' There are some queers who are creating beauty, of course; and the political progress that has been made and genuine community organizations that exist were created by some remarkable people – but they are a minority. What we see in the scene is our lowest common denominator.

For all its mundanity and lack of aspiration, the scene is not without value. In spite of the problems he sees with it, Maitreyabandhu is still grateful. 'I know that coming out for me would have been so much more difficult without the gay scene. The emergence of the gay scene and the gay community with all its groups and sub-groups, has vastly improved the lives of millions of gay men . . . and given gay men a chance to live a whole life – so unlike the damaging secrecy and pretence that goes with being in the closet. We need to rejoice in all this and feel gratitude to all those unknown people who made it possible.' Steve Hope warns that it is impossible to generalize, even about individuals. 'Leaning on the same bar are people who strike you as dreadful superficial twits, and people who have a profound appreciation of life – sometimes they're the same people at different times, sometimes you find yourself in either group.'

Neil Whitehouse, a Methodist, emphasizes that 'the underlying realities of life, however rich you are, are painful for lesbian and gay people, and if someone's made a success of their life materially it can often hide a great deal of pain and struggle.' Pagan Jason Oliver feels that 'gay people have to hide so often when they're in straight society, it continues into the gay scene; and because gay people are insecure, they have to put on an image, how they want to be perceived instead of how they really are. People are just scared really, they don't want to get hurt – they've probably had a load of shit anyway in their lives, and they don't want to get isolated on the gay scene as well.' Some people find true friendship – and the love of their life – on the scene. Gay men's experience of it varies widely, according to temperament, age, location and appearance.

ALTERNATIVES

The spiritual traditions followed by some gay men offer alternatives to the values of the scene. Awareness of the potential of others – perhaps as divine, certainly as a genuine equal – is helpful. 'It's very easy to lose any sense of holiness – of transcendental joy, and of transcendental ethics – on the scene, where we tend to resign ourselves to treating each other pretty badly,' says Adam Sutcliffe. 'Try to bring heaven into things,' is Rabbi Lionel Blue's advice. 'Bring God into a crowded gay bar, sit Him there, see what effect He or She has on you. Do you see people differently? A lot of religion is fantasy, but it becomes reality when you see God in other people and in yourself.'

Robert Bristow is a Nichiren Buddhist who has chanted (albeit under his breath) in his local lesbian and gay centre. He says it 'brings you back to where your determination, your energy, your life force, are coming from. What I'm doing there is going to be the best I can do, I decide that I'm going to influence that atmosphere and make it positive'; practically, this may simply be a matter of smiling and chatting to people. Before he discovered the Nichiren practice Rob felt he was 'allowing the environment to carry me off. I'd just get pissed basically.' He used to find the scene shallow and cliquy; but chanting has helped him 'see beyond the superficiality, and treasure the great things about people – it's helped me integrate into the gay world a bit more'.

Rupi feels that Louise Hay has helped him 'seize back the power'. 'If you start saying the affirmations, and you believe that you are loved, loving, and loveable, then you don't have to take on board the baggage that the gay scene is placing upon you: about youth, about race, about wearing the right thing, being in the right places, doing the right job. It puts things into perspective. It's made me more aware of how the gay scene manipulates you. I've changed my whole attitude to how I behave when I'm out. I refuse to buy into it now.'

These people do not look to the scene to be accepted, or for their sense of belonging, although they still visit it as part of their social lives. They identify with something else; their spiritual lives give them a sense of acceptance that the scene cannot. People may find a sense of belonging with a group that isn't gay at all. 'Over the last few years I have been gathered in to a family, a family that I've chosen and who behave like friends – all the time,' said Robert Crossman (shortly before his death) of the Quaker meeting he attended. 'It feels like I'm being taken care of. I know there are other Quakers I can ring up and talk to when the going gets tough – they won't judge me, and they will listen to me. My faith base helps me when I encounter disappointment on the gay scene.'

The criticism here is not that the scene is 'bad', but that it is limited, and limiting: and we are people who ought not to accept limitations, having fought them so hard when they are imposed by homophobes. It is less than thirty years since it has been legal for us to come together publicly; the scene is in its infancy, and there are many reasons that can be given for why it's in the state it is. But we should not apologize for wanting more. A Buddhist monk, the Venerable K-N, concludes: 'Don't be afraid to be yourself. If the scene's not what you want, you can guarantee it's not what most other people want either. It's only a prototype, not the finished job – so get on and finish it.'

LESBIAN LIFE

It is not a gay man's place to write about the specifics of lesbian life. In the light of what some women have told me, however, I want briefly to indicate that not all the pressures and issues described above are exclusive to gay men. Women socialize in different ways to gay men, and lesbians come together in different contexts. The difficulties gay men have simply communicating do not seem to be shared by women. But having said as much, acceptance can still be conditional – on appearance, politics or sexual practice.

The 'lipstick' debates of the mid-1990s are only the latest in a venerable tradition of arguments about what a dyke 'should' look like. Whereas gay men's image is probably created by a mixture of lust and greed, lesbian discourse is more likely to draw on political analysis and feminist idealism. But the bottom line is the same: some people are excluded simply on the basis of the way they look. Women have also felt excluded – or been forced to take sides – because of their attitude to pornography, sadomasochism, bisexuality or other concerns of lesbian/feminist politics. 'My experience of being a dyke in the late eighties was that it was all to do with politics and not to do with people really,' says Catherine Hopper. 'Alongside the desire to change the world and make life fairer for lesbians was this horrible policing of ourselves. The lesbian feminist movement could be so cruel, it was so unkind. In retrospect, it wasn't allowing me to be myself. It was asking me to be A Lesbian Feminist.' Catherine experienced a lot of hostility for not being working-class (something she didn't have much choice about). 'You still had to conform.'

Although feminist 'censorship' largely vanished along with the 1980s, Carol, a lesbian Nichiren Buddhist, suggests that this element of righteous judgementalism can still persist. Coming out over the past couple of years she has experienced 'amazing prejudice' from other lesbians, and concludes 'there is a lot of narrow-mindedness within the lesbian and gay community, which I think is sad'. Pam Mears has also been told she doesn't belong: 'Lots of my lesbian friends won't have anything to do with me now, they consider me a traitor because I also sleep with men.' This influenced her quest for spirituality: 'Because I don't fit in to the "norm", the little boxes we like to put everybody in – I found somewhere I could fit in.' Pam has turned to various New Age philosophies – she follows a shamanic path, and is a professional aromatherapist. 'Once I found my spiritual path, I gained an awful lot of confidence in myself. I realized I don't have to "make up my mind", there's nothing to make up my mind about – why can't I love *people*? Right and wrong within my spiritual path has nothing to do with your sexual orientation – it has to do with how you relate to other people on the planet. You have to be yourself first.'

COMMUNITY

Whether the lesbian, gay and bisexual community is anything other than notional has been the subject of debate for several years. It is a concept thrown into sharp relief by people who have experienced what the word can mean in contexts related to their religious beliefs. 'There isn't a comparison between the community I grew up in and the lesbian and gay community,' says Kauldip Singh, a Sikh. 'A lot of Asian guys feel there isn't the support within the wider lesbian and gay community that one has seen within one's own family. I couldn't see myself, as a Sikh, not being attached to a family.' The usual model for lesbian and gay people is that your blood family might reject you but the lesbian and gay community will accept you instead. This is not Kauldip's experience. 'I know my family will always be there for me irrespective of what happens, but I can't rely on the lesbian and gay community. A lot of the guys I speak to say the same thing. If they need assistance or advice, their family and friends will be there to give it to them, the family will never shut the door in their face. Whereas in my experience of the lesbian and gay community, if you have a problem or want to talk about something, people don't want to know if you're not in the right clique or not wearing the right clothes. If I meet anyone at the temple, they will say "hello, how are you, how's your family?" – real, genuine concern. I feel so immersed in that community, because I know that community accepts me and welcomes me. If you walk down Old Compton Street there isn't that warmth; if you're not sitting in the right place at the right time, you're not part of it.' It is impossible to separate how much this community is connected to religious values from how much it has to do with culture and race. 'When you come to a society like Britain where you can't ignore the racism. Your family is a protection against that.'[7]

Although he feels more accepted by his religious community than any grouping around sexual orientation, conflict remains, because 'you cannot really live your sexual life within that family system'. Even in a community as valued and loving as the one Kauldip describes, there are always rules to be followed. While the Sikh faith has little to say about homosexuality, it puts a lot of pressure on its followers to marry. According to Kauldip, it is remaining unmarried rather than sexual orientation that will cause rifts with Sikh parents ('we don't care if you're gay as long as you're married'). Partly because the Sikh community can be so much more real than anything lesbian and gay people can offer, however, some Sikhs prefer the compromise of marrying and having same-sex affairs on the side to the prospect of ostracizing themselves from their religious culture. 'If you choose to be gay there's no guarantee that when you get out there you won't face other discrimination – you're becoming a minority within a minority, because you're an Asian or "politically black" gay man in a predominantly white lesbian and gay community. If you choose to live with your family and live a life where you get married, you're still not living your life as you wish – but you've got some security.'

Kauldip's sense of belonging to his religious community partly derives from having grown up in it. Some people choose to join communities as adults. 'I think the men's community that I'm living in – where some of the men are gay, some are straight, some are bisexual – is a community in a real sense,' says Maitreyabandhu, who lives in a converted fire station in East London with other Buddhists. 'Men trying to relate to each other, living communally, sharing a life with a common ideal. It's not that we all happen to share a house: I'm not living *near* people, I'm living *with* people, more and more deeply. I had hoped I'd come out into the bosom of this gay 'community' that it would welcome me. But it wasn't like that at all. Gay men have their sexuality in common with other gay men, but I don't see how that adds up to a community in any genuinely meaningful way. I think even the word "community" is a fiction. It's just an idea in people's heads.' Catherine Hopper, although not as yet living communally, none the less argues that the Friends of the Western Buddhist Order is more of a community than whatever the word means in lesbian and gay contexts. 'I so revel in this spirit of being able to trust people, and I never found that in the gay community: it wasn't all right to say some things, or people weren't interested. The FWBO is the best expression I've yet found of really healthy living – a group of people who are committed to each other and to a set of ideals. I don't mean they're flawless – obviously not everybody in the movement loves gay people, black people find there is some racism – but it's the best thing I've found so far. We're living in an environment of psychological nakedness, where we should feel absolutely free to own up to how we feel without feeling stupid, and where other people should listen to us without judging us. That involves ideally a spirit of absolute trust. We really can be who we are.'

Although the Sikh and Buddhist experiences just described represent different concepts of 'community', in both cases the word indicates something tangible and supportive. These queers identify more readily with their religious communities than with a lesbian, gay and bisexual 'community' because they find more commitment, trust and acceptance from people who share their beliefs (and, crucially in Kauldip's case, culture and race) than from people who share their sexual orientation. The precedence of spiritual community over sexual one makes sense if the two identities are compared. While sexual orientation is only part of our life – albeit a very important one, for some of us – religious systems refer to the whole of life. They have ideals, and ethics, neither of which are inherent in being queer.

BEING BOTH

A group of people who share your spiritual beliefs can give you the sense of belonging that gay or lesbian life fails to provide. But they may not put an end to a troubling sense of being out of place. If you felt marginalized by the queer world before, you risk even greater isolation once you take up a faith: ironically, the rejection that causes people to seek somewhere else to belong intensifies when they find somewhere. 'There are people at the Coleherne and the Anvil who won't talk to me because I'm a practising Catholic,' testifies Mike Fox. 'I've come in for a lot of stick from both gays and straights.'

Drew Payne finally broke away from the evangelical Christianity of his adolescence when his Church tried to exorcize the 'demon' of his homosexuality. While his concept of God and the role of religion in his life changed dramatically, he did not lose his faith; but 'the process of coming out led to me entering another closet – this time it was my beliefs I closeted away. The people I worked with, my family, my flatmates, all knew I was gay but very, very few of them also knew I was a Christian. I was afraid of having to constantly justify my beliefs, and I was still more afraid of rejection. Rejection does not become easier to bear the more you experience it.' Kate also feels pressure to give up her faith. 'Like many lesbians I find that my friends from the feminist and lesbian communities struggle with my desire to maintain my belief in the Christian God. How can I, when it has been so oppressive to me in the past?' But Kate is determined to keep her faith because she has first-hand knowledge of the cost of self-repression. 'All those years I spent trying to deny my sexuality I lived in a two-dimensional world. Now that I am celebrating the fact that I am a lesbian and love women, I do not want to live in another two-dimensional world. My desire is for my life to be three-dimensional; a seamless garment incorporating my love of God, my love of women, my love of myself.'

The obvious question prompted by such experiences is: why should it have to be a choice? If religious institutions push queers out, that's prejudice; is it any more justifiable for queer people to reject other queer people because of their beliefs? Religion is a good test of any claims made by the lesbian and gay community (whatever/wherever it might be) to be tolerant and inclusive, and the radical claims of activists and theorists that queers are anarchic and subversive. Is 'Queer' open enough – is lesbian, gay or bisexual identity pluralistic enough – to include Jews and Buddhists as well as sadomasochists and gender-transgressors?

Spiritually inclined queers respond to the prejudice they sometimes face, and the pressure to keep their beliefs quiet, in the same way that they responded to homophobic pressures: with pride, and by telling the truth about who they are. A man training for the Jesuit priesthood recalls being in a gay pub with a fellow novice – who was busy chatting someone up. 'He said to me – "for goodness' sake, shut up about me being a trainee priest". I felt really angry – I said "look, I haven't come out of the closet as gay to go into the closet as religious – I am me." Once you start deceiving others and deceiving yourself, "you give free rein to the enemy of our human nature", in Ignatius of Loyola's words.' Glenn Palmer refuses to keep quiet about something as important as his spirituality. 'I'm not a proselytizing homosexual and I don't think I'm going to be a proselytizing Christian. But I'm not going to hide my Christianity, because I can't; if I am a Christian it will inform the way I behave, just as I don't have to have a badge saying I'm a gay man for people to know I'm a gay man.' Lesbian witches talk about the need to come out of the broom closet. And for Varabadhri, 'when I first spoke the words "I am a Buddhist", it felt like coming out. It's the difference between knowing something about yourself (even for a long time) and making it more public.' It is a statement of greater truth about who you are. 'It's not so subliminally compartmentalized – and it means you believe it.'

'I'm not sure I would like to be Ms Average. There's no way that I would ever feel comfortable being in the centre of something,' says Rabbi Elizabeth Sarah, to some extent making a virtue out of necessity from her 'double minority' status of being Jewish and lesbian. 'I don't think it's a distortion to say that proportionately lesbian and gay people, and Jewish people, have been more creative; and that creativity has come out of that experience of otherness, difference, marginality, constantly having to cross borders and deal with conflict and change.'

Feeling doubly marginalized can bring twice the creativity; it can also been doubly isolating. The need to belong remains; we still need to find People Like Us, but cannot look to the compromise of ready-made 'communities' to do so. Just as we couldn't disregard our sexual experience in order to fit into religion, so we cannot ignore our spiritual experience in an attempt to fit into lesbian or gay social groupings. We need to find places where we can be more of who we are. Crucially, we need to share honestly our experience: 'before we begin to talk about God we should learn to speak to each other,' as Dennis Fraser puts it. Communication is vital for both healthy sexuality and for spirituality. 'Talking to one another more,' says the Reverend Jean White, 'we'd get to know more about each other, which would help us be more whole, healthy, spiritual people – because we'd have an understanding that we're not alone in the things we think and do, and a collective strength in being able to share'. Her colleague Stewart Harrison sees the Metropolitan Community Church as 'a place where we can care and support each other, where through Jesus we can heal and tend the spiritual wounds and brokenness many of us have suffered'. As Jean says, 'being there for people, that's what it's all about isn't it? That's what has happened with HIV and AIDS groups.'

Michael Seán Paterson, as pastoral worker at the London Lighthouse, has observed the formation of informal supportive networks comprised of HIV-diagnosed people, friends, partners, family, complementary therapists and volunteers: 'What happens in these new *communities* is that a safe place is created where nothing that is human is found to be strange, where the depths of fear and self-annihilation can be excavated in good company.'[8] 'I turn to friends more than anything,' says Seamus, who attends a 'spiritual drop-in' for HIV-positive people in south London. 'We all come with our own understanding. Our understanding isn't necessarily fixed – it's something which is constantly evolving and changing, we share our experience, and hopefully grow through that as a group, as individuals. We support each other. I find the Narcotics Anonymous and Alcoholics Anonymous programmes useful, and very spiritual – being honest with yourself and other people. Communication is the key – other people can relate because they've been there. People who are not saying they've got the right way, but who are coming together and sharing experience. I might have something in my experience that can give you an insight into something you're struggling with. And you very probably can reflect something back to me.'

Neil Whitehouse, the Methodist minister who is setting up Kairos, a social and spiritual project in London's Soho which will serve the lesbian and gay communities, hopes it will offer 'chances for people to be honest about where they're coming from, and to explore more deeply what it means to be who they are. Community arises out of an understanding of yourself as well as an understanding of other people, and demands responsibilities to one another to be meaningful. You accept that you are your sister or brother's keeper – it's moving away from individualism.' The motivation behind the project comes from Neil's own experience and needs; he sees it as 'a bridge between two families, my Church family and my gay family. I know I belong to both, yet there's no tangible expression of that truth.'

Groups which do allow people to express both 'truths' about themselves are highly valued by their members. 'It was amazing to be in a place where so much of me was represented in other people,' recalls Lev of his first meeting with other queer Jews: at an assembly of the world's gay and lesbian Jewish organizations. Because Lev's Judaism takes a less than traditional form, he felt an even stronger sense of connection when he led a Shabbat service at a Radical Faerie gathering in the United States: 'It was more like coming home than anything I could imagine. It felt like I was really getting to the core of who I am. It was probably one of the most healing experiences of my life: being in this radical spiritual environment, as a Jew, with Jews, with gay men.' For Steve Hope, coming together with the Quaker Lesbian and Gay Fellowship (QLGF) was 'one of the most profound religious experiences I've ever had. It was very moving and very illuminating; and gave me a sense of there being ways to be gay socially which also encompassed something to do with religious sensibility, something that's usually conspicuously lacking in pubs, clubs, discos, even gay political groups. I realized how important it was to share not only one's sexuality, but also one's values. When one finds oneself in a group of lesbian and gay people who value themselves and are also obviously profoundly schooled in the ways of the spirit, it gives one a little vision of what the world might have been like if none of this homophobic shit had happened. That extraordinary discovery that the wellsprings of the spirit of the universe belong to you as well – it's what you keep saying to yourself but never quite believe – and yet in QLGF, it happens. And needless to say, men who are sexy are even sexier when they're spiritual as well!'

Catherine Hopper recalls that on a Buddhist retreat for lesbians 'when we had our meditation periods we had rarely experienced such deep concentration. It was a more devotional and deep experience than I think many of us had had on any retreat before. We had brought absolutely our whole selves to this retreat; there was nothing left behind.' Maitreyabandhu explains that 'because you know that everyone on the retreat is gay, you can just get on with living – for a moment you're the majority, in a positive context, where people are doing something more than being gay.'

To come together in an genuinely accepting environment does not necessarily require a specific religious intent. There are groups such as the Edward Carpenter Community (named after the great man rather than founded by him). ECC brings people together in pursuit of personal growth, and encourages greater trust and intimacy amongst gay men. It chiefly does this on week-long retreats in areas of rural beauty, where gay men eat and play together, dress up, run around naked, have workshops and discussion groups and cabarets and balls, and form bonds with other men that can last for a lifetime. 'ECC represents huge new possibilities for me,' says Nick Williams. 'Being more open, being with gay men in other than sexual ways, positive role models, feeling accepted and "normal". I imagine that a lot of these things are mirrored in the lives of people who embrace more conventional religions. It's all part of the need to connect, not to be alone in our experiences, to feel loved and to align ourselves with the part of us which grows towards the light and seeks fullness.' Drew Payne – who, along with Nick, shared his adolescent experiences of Christianity's conditional acceptance at the start of this chapter – has also attended a gay men's week and found 'a realization of belonging, and slowly opening myself up to others as they did towards me, slowly lowering the barriers and protection. I felt safe and relaxed. The judgemental pressures of the gay scene were gone. It was not Christian, but very spiritual.'

What is most important – more so than the beliefs and practices of the specific faith – is the sense of belonging without preconditions. We need this, and we need to provide this. As John McNeill says, 'Acceptance, originally denied us in the family setting, is not something that we can give ourselves; rather, it is something we give each other.'⁹

Notes

1. The London Apprentice – a butch gay pub in London.
2. Some of Maitreyabandhu's words here were published in *Rouge* magazine.
3. Louise L. Hay, *You Can Heal Your Life* (London: Eden Grove Editions, 1988), pp. 138–9.
4. Hungry ghosts are pictured on the Tibetan 'wheel of life'. Their stomachs are far larger than their mouths, so they can never be satisfied.
5. A gay club in London.
6. Edward Carpenter, *Selected Writings, Volume 1: Sex* (London: Gay Men's Press, 1984), p. 238.
7. It is interesting that Kauldip associates the lesbian and gay community with scene values – in spite of the fact that he works for an AIDS organization, which might be thought of as more community-spirited. For me this confirms just how central the scene is to gay men's self-image.
8. Michael Seán Paterson, *Singing for Our Lives: Positively Gay and Christian* (Sheffield: Cairns Publications, 1997).
9. John J. McNeill, *Taking a Chance on God: Liberating Theology for Gays, Lesbians, and their Lovers, Families and Friends* (Boston: Beacon Press, 1988), p. 68.

7

'Love your Neighbour as Yourself':
Sexual Ethics

*A religious education is obtained not just in seminaries
and synagogues, but wherever people have to choose
between what is selfish and what is selfless, what is
generous and what is mean. I had such an education gratis
in the bars, cafés and saunas of the continent. For some
sex was a way of mutual giving and fun, a way of
warming others, a way people comforted each other
against the cold and the dark, a way people touched each
other's souls through each other's bodies. For others sex
was an addiction, a forlorn escape. It meant manipulating
others and letting them down in the rush for self-
gratification. The choices talked about in the textbooks of
spiritual literature became obvious and apparent in the
steamies. Through the mist, I was fascinated as I saw
heaven and hell at work before me and in me.'*

(Rabbi Lionel Blue)[1]

THE NEED FOR ETHICS

Sex can be great, as various lesbian, gay and bisexual people in this book
have already said. Giving and receiving bodily pleasure can be a source
of profound spiritual insight. Lionel Blue's experiences in Amsterdam
(where, as a young rabbi he went to escape his closeted English existence)

suggested to him that not all sex is great, however, and that the difference in quality is a spiritual concern. There are choices to be made: ethical choices.

Religious institutions have traditionally attempted to help people make those choices – or, more often, have told people what they can't do. One of the simplest sexual ethics is, of course, 'no sex outside marriage'. This is obviously not much use to queers, although some fundamentalists – including, unhappily, certain fundamentalists who know themselves to be attracted to the same sex – deduce that, since homosexuals cannot marry, homosexuals cannot have sex. Such an ethic exemplifies the worshipping of tradition for tradition's sake, rather than listening to experience, which is more characteristic of queer people. 'Liberal' religious figures like the (straight) American Episcopalian Bishop Jack Spong have suggested an ethic based on queers being able to get married – or on relationships which correspond to marriage. This would also not be very satisfactory for most of us. (Indeed, the low rate of marriage, and high rate of infidelity and divorce, suggests that it is not very satisfactory for heterosexuals either.)

If the guidance offered by religion is so out of touch with how we are living, can we therefore conclude that we have no need for ethics at all? No, argues Peter Wyles (a Quaker): 'Just because conventional sexual morality is wrong in parts (sexism and homophobia being the most obvious), that does not mean that there is no case for morality.' 'Morality' is a concept that has long been used to condemn queers, and consequently we may be suspicious of its use. Surely we have fought, and continue to fight, for sexual liberty, for the right to be who we are and do what we want? No one contributing to this chapter would disagree with that. But just because all our activities are deemed by society as a whole (let alone religion) to be beyond the pale, does that mean we shouldn't bother to distinguish between them ourselves? To say that morality is the exclusive preserve of straights is, of course, to be trapped by the hetero–homo binary again. The most compelling argument for sexual ethics is that we should care about ourselves, and each other. A desire for ethics can be prompted by an awareness that we are all capable of sex which falls short of the ideal – not just 'spiritual' ideals, but also the more modest ambition of pleasure. Sex can be unsatisfactory, even harmful or destructive (to ourselves or others). Ethics may be the answer to the question: how can we avoid soulless or soul-destroying sex?

'I don't know whether good sex is spiritual,' one gay Christian told me, 'but I do know that bad sex is spiritually crippling.' 'Wherever you have the potential for positive you have the potential for negative,' is the reasoning of Vieta, a Nichiren Buddhist and Tantric practitioner; because she uses the power of sexuality as part of her daily spiritual practice, she is in a position to know that 'sex can also be extremely negative'. Sue Vickermann has come to the same conclusion: 'Even the most sizzling of orgasms has never left me with new insight into the meaning of life, the universe and everything. I've never had a dazzling moment of spiritual realization. But I *have* experienced, through a chain of sexual relationships and encounters (mainly with men), a sensation of the ebbing away of my spirit until I can practically chart my life and graphically illustrate the point of lowest ebb. My present-day sexual morality is informed by my personal experience of losing any sense of the spiritual dimension of life, and of ultimately regaining a perception of some ultimate meaning and goodness to aspire to, which you can call God if you like.'

'Sex is never value-free, it is never without its human and emotional consequences,' asserts Father Bill, one of the founders of the Streetwise Youth project which supports male sex workers in London. 'It is unpredictable, and vulnerable to misuse and abuse.' 'It's not just a question of getting your rocks off, you see,' says Transcendental Meditator Henry Giles. 'Sexual energy is part of your whole being: if you're using it in inappropriate circumstances, that will have spiritual consequences.' The late Simon Bailey argued (using more conventional theological language) that queer sex 'like all the rest of sex is not an unadulterated gift of God. There is something wounded about *all* sexuality, not evil of course and yet not perfect either. Sex is always exploration towards God, not the experience of God: so we go on wounding each other in it, wounding ourselves, longing to heal. And so we also sometimes glimpse the glory.'

We know that sex can be wounding and wounded only because it also has the potential to be so good. If queers seek an ethic it is in pursuit of more joy, not an attempt to restrict pleasure. It is the search for real pleasure that may be the best guide to ethical behaviour – rather than any amount of rule induced guilt. Father Bernard Lynch recalls how C. S. Lewis's fictional devil figure, 'Screwtape', wants to stop humans feeling pleasure, 'for pleasure gives us a touchstone of reality'. Bernard believes that 'fundamentally all consensual behaviour is good'. But 'while all consenting adult behaviour may be permitted, not all is necessarily helpful'.

A WAY OF GOING

To develop (or acknowledge the existence of) sexual ethics is not to return to a situation where desire is legislated against and circumscribed or where one group of people tells others what to think and do (which often is how religious sexual ethics have worked). Lesbians, gays and bisexuals know all too well the destructive effects of prohibiting sexual acts, and deciding that some things should be taboo, while others are 'normal'. What some gay people are seeking, however, is not a new set of rules but perhaps some sort of collective wisdom. Rabbi Lionel Blue has spoken to fellow gay and lesbian Jews about the need to establish a sexual *halakhah*. '*Halakhah* means "way of going" in Judaism; *din* is law. I think the whole of Jewish society is moving away from law now; what is becoming more established is this "way of going".' In contrast to law, a 'way of going' is a body of knowledge formed by, and responsive to, personal experience. As Bernard Lynch puts it, 'here on the mountain there are no laws, no trodden paths. We find the path by walking.' This chapter is not a treatise on what queer sexual ethics 'should' be: apart from anything else, the contributors to it employ a variety of different religious frameworks, and these cannot be easily amalgamated. But I do hope to give some idea of the 'ways of going' spiritually identified queers have come to in their lives.

It is, of course, perfectly possible to arrive at a secular ethic. There may, however, be less incentive to do so if you are not consciously striving – as religious queers are – to live a deeper and better life. For Adam Sutcliffe, although 'any explicit notion of spirituality is far from my mind when I'm in bed with someone, trying to be genuine, respectful and aware when the exposure of sex can make it much easier to hide behind masks and emotional armoury isn't easy. Without an ethical framework in which to think about sex, I think that much more often I'd forget to even try.' One lesbian contributor who rediscovered her childhood religion welcomes the new ethical dimension it opened for her: 'becoming more religious was a part of becoming more ethical, and vice-versa. The mantra "as long as you don't hurt anybody" no longer seemed enough.' (It's not that avoiding harm is not a basic aim of any decent ethic; rather, that there are additional factors that need consideration, if you aspire to more than damage-limitation.) A faith that sees life, and the body, as sacred is likely to offer an ethical framework which respects those beliefs; whereas there is no reason to expect that a lesbian and gay 'community' will automatically do so, or that lesbian and gay people will automatically be ethical – something made clear by the negative experiences recounted in the previous chapter.

In approaching sexual ethics, as with anything else, queers have to start with their own experience. It is our experience that tells us religions are wrong if they attempt to limit sex to procreation or marriage. I am equally suspicious when I see claims – regardless of the sexual orientation or ideology of the person who makes them – that sex is truly worthwhile only between long-term, loving, exclusive partners. My suspicion is based on the evidence of our experience: so much sex happens outside such relationships. Certain religious ethics set up ideals of behaviour that bear no relation to the way people actually behave: there's an air of wilful delusion about them, as if they believed that sex takes place only when their permission is granted. Queer sexual ethics can start with the reality of sex as practised, with an acknowledgement that *sex happens* – and happens in a variety of circumstances. Admitting this truth is a very firm foundation; and this much, we are good at – because we have had to 'admit' at least something about our sex lives by coming out in the first place. As such we have a head start on many ethics, which are paralysed by hypocrisy.

If personal experience is so central, we have to acknowledge that there will not be a full consensus between lesbian and gay ethics. Female and male experience differs. The Reverend Jean White sums up the stereotypical perception of this difference: 'Men have one-night stands and women have one-week relationships which didn't work out. Women nest, men hunt.' Crude though this division might seem, and however numerous the exceptions to the rule among both sexes, there still seems to be some basic difference between the way men and women think about sex – and behave sexually – in our society. Among contributors to this project, men were far more likely to talk about casual sex, women to talk in terms of relationships.[2] Some women might question how far you can isolate 'sexual ethics' from broader relational ethics, as I am doing here. Our queer understanding as outlined in the previous three chapters – of the body, relationships and belonging – is crucial to any ethical approach to sexual behaviour.

INTENTIONS NOT ACTIONS

The Judeo-Christian religions have traditionally claimed that sexual acts have an objective value. Sex was a sin outside marriage, it was a gift from God within marriage. Anal sex is a sin. Sex between people who don't have a penis isn't sex. Such sexual ethics are based on the idea that there are divine do's and don'ts, and, if you follow these, you'll be all right. This is, in fact, the fundamentalist approach to religion as a whole: follow the letter, not the spirit, of the law, and don't question who wrote it.

A different approach is taken towards sexual ethics by lesbian gay and bisexual people; there is considerable consensus on this approach amongst people coming from a variety of different faiths. Sexual acts are neutral; what makes them otherwise depends on what we as individuals bring to them. In Nagaraja's words: 'Sex is not a virtue or a vice – it's just an activity. What you use it for – that's where the problem starts.' Human relationship is the central ethical concern for most queer people. This is in keeping with the earlier contention that sexuality is broad, complex and a force for relationship – even if religions sometimes attempt to reduce it to genital acts.

This book has avoided Biblical exegesis so far, but for once it is worth making an exception. There is a text which neatly illustrates the difference between an act-based ethics and a relationship-centred ethics, a sacred text for Jews and Christians which is frequently used to condemn homosexuality: Leviticus. Much has been written about the weakness of using Leviticus to justify homophobia;[3] but Rabbi Elizabeth Sarah offers a new approach which moves the debate away from quibbling over what acts are forbidden, and on to how we should be behave towards each other. 'If you look at the Bible, Leviticus 18 and 20, which deal with sexual prohibitions, have another chapter in between them. Leviticus 19 is full of ethical principles about how you should treat people. In the centre of that chapter is the major statement, echoed by Christianity as the most important statement ever made – "you shall love your neighbour as yourself". We never think of that in a sexual context, but its place *between* chapters 18 and 20 suggests that it should also be applied sexually. How do you love your neighbour? By behaving in a way that respects their integrity, which is caring and compassionate. You treat the person you are with as an individual human being *like you.*' This rules out relationships which are abusive or exploitative. The prohibitions of chapters 18 and 20, as many scholars have argued, attempt 'the preservation of the separateness of the people of Israel' and reflect 'the need to ensure the people do not follow the ways of Canaan or Egypt' (*not*, it must be said, a pressing issue for twentieth-century lesbian and gay people). But in chapter 19, 'the need for right conduct in social relationships is stressed again and again'. Loving someone as yourself is a commandment to equality, an ethic everyone can aspire to, whereas the prohibitions in Leviticus are (bar one quibble about bestiality) all addressed to men (with women as prohibited objects). 'For the spirit of Leviticus 19:18 to infuse the sex laws would mean . . . perceiving sex, not as a series of acts perpetrated by one party on the body of another, but as a means of expressing a relationship. It would mean seeing the expression of love and desire as one of the primary purposes of sexual activity.' All relationships should be evaluated 'according to the identical criteria of love, equality and reciprocity.'[4]

Buddhism has always concentrated on intentions rather than any actions which result from those intentions. The third of the 'five precepts' for ethical living is 'abstain from sexual misconduct'. That misconduct is not necessarily defined in terms of specific acts or even prohibited relationships (unlike the Biblical commandment against adultery). As Fernando Guasch argues, 'only you know what the psychological consequences are, only you yourself know when sex becomes a means of doing the dirty on oneself and on another person'. A Buddhist approach to sexual ethics requires 'being very alert to what you're doing, and your motivation.' For instance, 'no two acts of cruising are the same. The Western model would be that what is wrong in cruising is the very act itself. We know that's not true: it can be a very beautiful, compassionate, kind encounter with another human being. To me that proves quite directly it has to do with the quality of mind that you take to the encounter, and the spaciousness you can afford to deploy in the situation. I don't say something's wrong because Big Daddy Buddha is watching. But something in me is watching. If I bring to the situation a mind that is angry or hurt – it could be that I've had a bad day – I can end up using the other person, and deploying power over them in order to make them feel small or controlled. I've learned over the years that such sex is not particularly pleasurable. You come away feeling strong, validated – he was gorgeous and I had him – but what is wrong about it, in the Buddhist analysis, is what you've done to your mind. You've blinded yourself to all sorts of things, and the mind you take away from the encounter is actually quite limited, arrogant and scared – because, the more you build up an ego, the more vulnerable you feel in case somebody smashes it. You haven't really been awake to the other person: you haven't done justice to what it is to encounter another human being.'

The same approach underlies the classical Christian understanding of 'sin'. 'I don't view sin as a list of things,' says Catholic Mike Fox. 'The act of sinning arises from a sinful intention, which arises from a disordered desire. If you start off with a good desire, which leads to a good intention, which leads to an action which has good consequences, then the act itself must be good.' John Pierce, a therapist and Christian priest, recalls that, when he was younger, he would buy for a penny a list of all possible sins: to help him make sure that he didn't forget to mention any in confession. 'I do not now believe that the nature or the extent of sin can be contained in such a list. And so by implication I do not now believe morality consists in keeping to a code of pre-determined rules . . . In that change I have found a liberation every bit as great as the sense of liberation of the first absolution I received . . . The only law that can be universally applied is that of love: it is the key to an appropriate responsibility in our relatedness to one another and to the happy integration of our own sexuality and spirituality.'[5]

The gay theologian Norman Pittenger, now in his nineties, describes sin as a 'refusal to move on in becoming truly human, as God proposes us to be' (according to the process theology that Pittenger subscribes to, 'human existence is intended to be a movement or process towards the . . . making real of God's image in man'). 'A penetrating and disturbing question, which might well be asked after every sexual contact of the physical sort, is this: "Now that I am leaving this person, am I leaving a body with whom I have had gratification *or* am I leaving a person with whom I have shared something of the joy of mutual existence, expressed in physical fashion?" If you answer person rather than body, you 'can be sure that the act has been right and good – and I dare say in accordance with the purpose of God for his children. The Latin liturgy for Holy Thursday includes the splendid words, *ubi caritas et amor, ibi Deus*: "where loving care and self-giving are found, there is God present".'[6]

Queer people might be expected to adopt an intention-centred ethic almost automatically, since by coming out we have already rejected orthodox sexual conventions. In practice we have sometimes taken the easier option, which is simply to redefine what is acceptable. To over-simplify, lesbians have argued fiercely over whether certain 'acts' (such as S/M) are allowable; while many gay men seem to assume that any act is acceptable in any circumstances. Perhaps unconsciously, we are still thinking within the terms of our oppressors. As Fernando Guasch says, to do otherwise is to 'ask people to think very radically afresh about ethics and morality'.

VALUING THE HUMAN

Yet although it may be a radical approach to morality, the aims are very simple: to be more human, and to acknowledge the full humanity of the other person. 'I am beginning to feel that maybe this whole sexual liberation trip is simply trying to recover some pretty fundamental, pretty obvious ways of having sex,' says Fernando. 'I for one spent years not knowing anything about having sex with somebody as an act of kindness or communication or sex involving feelings of tenderness, friendship or goodwill.' He says we should avoid the temptation – which is given the hard sell to gay men – to objectify. 'The reason there's so much promiscuity,' reckons Nagaraja, 'is that we can treat people as objects. The last thing you want when you're out cruising is for someone to turn round and talk to you – then he's a librarian, he's a real person.' The aim, then, is 'to humanize yourself. Maybe moving from having to use lots of pornography and poppers to actually having sex with human beings – and then maybe having sex with human beings without the drugs; maybe being content to then move on to more physical intimacy, and not being orgasm-orientated. I'm just talking about me here, rather than having to generalize about the gay community! Becoming more human means being more open, honest and truthful. But it's not to do with the Christian mind-set, "good" and "bad" – it's about developing awareness, and responding in a positive and creative way. Buddhism would advise you to become aware of your patterns and the games you play.'

For gay men, 'humanizing' sex could start with something as basic as talking to sexual partners. Mother Molesta of the Sisters of Perpetual Indulgence has made this his mission. 'When gay men have charver[7] with each other in a cottage or cruising, they don't talk. Sometimes because they've got their mouth full of course – or you might want to fantasize – but underneath the excuses, I wonder why we don't talk to one another, even while pleasing each other's bodies? As Sisters we work at that shame. We insist on talking to people when we're shagging.'

Any spiritual system suggests that there is far more to ordinary human life than we generally acknowledge; so to objectify another person cannot possibly do justice to the full potential of the situation. Rabbi Lionel Blue learned this through experience: 'I remember asking God in a sauna "is this all there is to it? All this desire and all over in a minute? Is this what it's all about? I'd prefer a meal." I got the message that you don't get much if you don't give much. I had to learn to give. I remember praying – and my prayer always takes a conversational form, which makes it a bit schmaltzy, but that's the way it works – what order do I make out of this? The inner answer was well, Lionel, the best thing to do is keep your promises. If you make an appointment to see somebody, you keep it even if you've met someone nicer in between. If you say no, say no nicely. In practice, sex does not always require love. It is wonderful, but arbitrary; it sometimes comes at the end of the relationship, not at the beginning. Respect is more basic, and so is compassion, which is as necessary for sex as it is for prayer.' Buddhist Dirk de Klerk agrees on this point: 'A central standard of morality is compassion. Respecting the other person with whom you're having a sexual encounter. Actually loving a person while one is making love to them. How selfish are you feeling while you are actually having sex, how obsessive are you? Can you say, "I wish everyone the happiness that I wish upon myself"?' As Dirk implies, such awareness should not make sex any less pleasurable – 'Obviously you enjoy it – that is what sex is about.'

After the bad experiences that she recounted earlier in this chapter, Sue Vickermann has 'reservations about sex that has no positive emotional or spiritual context. My Christian ethics inform me that the love in all relationships is of God, and any relationships or encounters that don't involve love, care and trust are a terrible shame and waste of two people. Use and abuse of another person is likely to result in a kind of spiritual erosion, isn't it? An encounter where it would be possible to feel something but actually one feels nothing – doesn't that give definition to the term "soul-destroying"?'

'I try not to treat people badly because I know those actions will affect me,' says Roberta Wedge, who as a Pagan subscribes to the view that 'what goes around comes around – what you do comes back to you threefold'. What this philosophy acknowledges is that none of us is isolated even if we try to isolate ourselves; and that our behaviour should be guided by acknowledging the quality of the experience that it leads to. 'Instead of having a fear of punishment or sin, my understanding is that things come back to me. It's a direct law from nature – nature doesn't have right and wrong, it has consequences.'

Adam Sutcliffe's religion affects his behaviour not because it tells him what to do but because it helps keep him in touch with the humanity of himself and others, and their connectedness. 'Judaism offers me no specific guidelines that I could ever imagine applying directly to my sex life: which is a relief, because I certainly don't want a rule-book to discipline my desires. I do find, though, that going to services, and pondering generally on the myriad aspects of Jewish practice that connect everyday life with a sense of the eternal and the ethical, does contribute something to the way I think about sex. After a good Friday evening service, I have a strong sense of joyous rest and release, and of direct connection with the world around me. If I move on from synagogue to a Soho sex-den, I do so with a strengthened awareness that both sex itself, and anybody I might have sex with, are also part of these connections between the particular and the eternal. The act is special, and the person is too. Does this make any actual difference to the quality of the sex? Not in any obvious way, and certainly not in terms of prescribing certain kinds of sexual activity and proscribing others. In a subtle, silent way, though, the way I try to think about sex does make a big difference to me: it means that sex is real, and part of a real communication both with another person and with something beyond that. Lots of faces and bodies on the gay scene project invitations of detached unreality – "you can enjoy my body", they suggest, "without engaging with *me*". I try to refuse such severance, and, on a good night, when I'm really feeling integrated with myself and with the world, I feel I'm more likely to attract to me people who also are.'

DIFFICULT CASES

'I think if you are going to try to lead an ethical life, at some stage you have to start looking at the difficult cases, otherwise it isn't a real ethic', says Mike Fox, a Catholic. 'Real ethics is involved in the everyday lives of everyday people – who get up to all sorts of things in the bedroom. Any sexual ethics has got to include sadomasochism, sexual fantasies, celibacy, chastity, abusive relationships – you have to, at some stage, say what is right and wrong.' In an act-based ethics S/M might well be considered 'wrong'; but Mike argues the intention is what matters. 'If you take a riding crop to someone's backside with the intention of *hurting* them, then I would say the psychology is wrong – that isn't sadomasochism, that's abuse. If however you are intending to *inflict pain* as part of a sexual game or as part of love-making, then the psychology is different. What *appears* to be happening may be punishment or torture, but the desire and intention is not abusive; the psychology behind the acts is not one of victim and persecutor. The intention is not to hurt or put the person on the receiving end in the role of victim – the intention is to alter their awareness of their own physicality, to demonstrate your care and your affection for them by stimulating them.'

Mike's sadomasochism falls within his fundamental ethic: 'any sexual behaviour should be safe, sane and consensual. It should be safe because that minimizes harm and preserves autonomy and security. It should be sane because that respects both persons, maintains esteem and worth, and accepts that humans are limited. It should be consensual because that allows a meaningful relationship to develop, if desired; it is loving, gives a sense of purpose to both parties, and leaves both parties with autonomy and security.' Within these parameters Mike would argue that sado-masochism, far from being a dehumanizing 'punishment' of the body, actually pays more attention to its spiritual potential. An S/M encounter 'is designed to bring two people closer together through mutual exploring of potentialities, of who they are. The aim of sex is not just the moment of orgasm – the aim is to involve the entire person in an act. That means that you stimulate the entire body in various ways – you are not just concentrating on the genital area. I am relating as a whole person – my feelings, my thoughts, all parts of my body are involved. Sadomasochism is the high church of sex.'

Vieta believes that 'in sex, anything goes'. Her Tantric sessions can go on for eight hours: she makes love with women and men. As a Nichiren Buddhist she chants to feel randy. But the sex she chants for has to be 'respectful sex. Perhaps I enjoy abuse during sex, I'd like my partner to say "come on you whore, fuck me now, fuck me you bitch" – I might like that. It can still be done with love: that would still mean for me respectful sex.' There are no acts that are fundamentally respectful and others that are disrespectful. 'It's to do with the relationship and how respectful *that* is.'

MONOGAMY AND PROMISCUITY

It should be obvious that this approach to sexual ethics does not require the sexual partners to be 'in love', or even, necessarily, to know each other. An ethical approach does emphasize the need for human *relationship*; but there is not necessarily an ideal form which that relationship will take.

Anonymity might make it more difficult for people to relate in an truthful way – and give them an excuse not to respect the other person's humanity; but then being in a long-term relationship could just as easily be the cause of the same problems. 'In the past I've had quite spiritual sex on a quite casual basis,' says Steve Hope. These occasions were with men who were 'capable of having sex in an emotionally open way, even though it was not someone they were in love with at that time. They behaved as though they were aware this was a human being.' What matters, once again, is the intention, 'the spirit in which it's done'. Steve cautions, however, that it is difficult for many people to manage the requisite openness. He now avoids casual sex 'because of what a profound experience sex is for me. I'm not moral about it – my objection is practical, experiential.' He now has a partnership where faithfulness is a crucial element in realizing the full potential of the sexual experience.

There is no consensus amongst spiritually identified queers about whether monogamy should be an ideal. Adam Sutcliffe does not believe 'that "commitment" or "fidelity" should remotely be the key principles of sexual ethics, but rather honesty and respect. And just as a lifelong relationship can be deeply dishonest and disrespectful, so an anonymous grope in a dark corner of a backroom can be both honest and respectful.' 'You can't actually lay down guidelines that are right for every person,' agrees the Reverend Diana Reynolds. 'Some people thrive in relationships with more than one partner. But I would find that very difficult, having been caught up in a relationship where someone else became involved with my partner. I know how painful that was. Personally I could only survive in monogamous relationships. Although people say 'I'm quite happy for them to screw around, it doesn't hurt me', I think at the deepest level of humanity we all have a need to belong somewhere, and part of belonging is about making a commitment. The way you give yourself to somebody in a sexual relationship, and through that giving become aware of that sense of belonging: I don't know if it's possible to manage *that* with more than one person. Sure you can have sex with lots of people, but if it's really self-giving rather than self-gratifying, I don't know if that's possible without someone being hurt. And wherever people are hurt, something's not right.'

It is often difficult enough to relate honestly and respectfully to one individual: can we manage to do so with more? Free love may an ideal, but are we mature enough to manage it? On the other hand, 'love your neighbour as yourself' is an aim we inevitably fall short of in all sorts of ways. Why should it apply more to sexual intercourse than it does to social intercourse? We don't limit our non-physically sexual relationships to a small number in order to ensure their quality. Nagaraja takes a typically pragmatic Buddhist approach to the difficulty of knowing precisely what is right: 'You do have to accept that some things you may do are unethical. Until you're a very integrated person, you have to accept that you'll be based in greed, hatred and delusion' (all actions are, according to Buddhists). 'Accepting that doesn't immediately classify things into good and bad. All you can do is refine.'

Again, it must be stressed that there are no universally applicable answers. We can assess what is right for us only in the light of our experience, and by paying attention to whether our sexual choices bring us into a deeper relationship with each other. Engaging with a spiritual tradition can be one way to discover what works best for us as individuals. For David, this has meant going against the prevailing sexual orthodoxy among gay men: 'Buddhism involves not having fixed ideas about things. So I looked at what my attitudes were towards sex and sexuality. I've always been inclined to want more involvement from someone than having sex with them just once. In the seventies gay groups, the politics of liberation had this imperative not to ape the heterosexual model – so I thought, was I doing that? But I realised that in *not* getting involved with people I wasn't being genuine to myself – it didn't really matter whether there was a heterosexual ideal of monogamy and gay opposition to that, what *I* feel most comfortable with is a monogamous relationship. Obviously you could just use the Buddhist idea of non-attachment as an excuse to have lots of casual sex – and say "that proves I'm not attached". But if you look a bit deeper, you find it could be selfishness. If you have sex with a lot of people, it really amounts to you having sex with yourself all the time. You never have very much contact with the other person, there's never a real exchange, you want to separate yourself off and are not open to anyone.'

Sue Vickermann and her partner value monogamy because they grew up 'in families where that relationship worked – due to the religious commitment of our parents. We've witnessed the obvious benefits. For me the benefits are peace of mind and security, providing the firm ground from which to step out into the world each day re-charged.' Another lesbian found that 'when I returned to Judaism, I stopped having one-night stands and group sex. I have sex less now, but it's better sex. There is no specific commandment that says "Thou shalt not shag strangers". But it no longer seemed the right thing to do, and it was not fulfilling in any way.'

By contrast, Maitreyabandhu now has a non-monogamous relationship, his reasoning likewise based on his understanding of the ethical principles of his faith. 'I don't own him do I? I don't have sole rights to his body. I could say to him "are you sleeping with somebody?", and he could say "yes" – that would be painful. But what causes me pain is my attachment to him, and within that my assumption that I've got a right to his body. Him sleeping with other people isn't unethical, he's not doing it to hurt me.'

An intention-based ethics is not easy. We have a lot of freedom; there is nothing, bar social disapproval and occasional legal intervention, to prevent us from doing whatever we like (unless you believe in a punitive God with interventionary powers). It requires taking full responsibility for oneself, which is in keeping with the contention of part one of this book: authority for queer people is internal (based on personal experience), rather than external (in rules or institutions). A list of rules would be quicker to learn, but probably harder to stick to. It is possible to say what good sex ideally should be – equal, mutual, open, free, honest, affirming, respectful and so on – but coming up with lists of agreeable adjectives for us to aspire to is no substitute for being fully aware of what we are doing. The great advantage of moving away from an act-based ethics, however, is that it we are freed to discern the real value of our sexual relationships, and worry less about their conformity with religious or social orthodoxies. This has liberated evangelical Christian Ewan Wilson from years of doubt, when having sexual desires at all, let alone acting on them, could be fraught and tormenting. These days 'I try to use my sexuality with care, with caution and with a sense of responsibility. For me, this eradicates the concepts of sin and guilt regarding sexuality.' Similarly, Pam Mears says 'I've lost all that guilt – there isn't someone saying you've been a bad girl. But on the other side, I've also taken on responsibility for my actions. It's all about responsibility.'

CONSTANT CRAVING

If sexual acts have no objective meaning, then it follows that they are not always an expression of sexuality. The desire to have sex may have nothing to do with feeling horny; nor will it necessary be accompanied by the desire to relate to another person, even on a limited basis. Sexual ethics should alert us to when other needs are leading us towards a sexual act. Once aware of this, we can decide whether it is appropriate to go ahead and shag – or whether that could ultimately be harmful. This is the chief concern of Buddhist ethics, according to Catherine Hopper. 'Buddhism makes no judgement about sex itself. It's concern is the reason you want all that sex – or the reason you don't want any.'

Roberta Wedge finds that the 'the need for sex-for-something-else (for affection, for reassurance, for brief oblivion)' is less frequent and less strong as a result of her Pagan practice – instead, those needs are met by 'my connection with the earth in Her changing cycles and seasons, and from my deepening connection with myself through ritual and meditation'. Fernando Guasch knows from experience that sex can have many motivations. 'There are ways in which gay men can have sex in which they are punishing one another, or punishing what other men have done to them. I've gone cruising feeling incomplete, and looked for someone else to make me feel validated.' Lev enjoys cruising sometimes. 'But I definitely don't go when I'm feeling needy and vulnerable. It's the easiest time to go, because if I'm feeling vulnerable what I need is intimacy. But the last thing I need to do is have sex with a stranger! If I have the choice between going to the Ashram or going cruising, what I'm doing by going to the Ashram is exercising discipline and doing something that might not feel like what I want that moment, but which is nurturing my deeper self.'

Nagaraja still cruises occasionally, 'for excitement and experience. I'm not going to give that up until I find something else to replace it that gives me such an intense experience of self, a better experience of self. Which is bizarre, because most of the time I cruise, I don't enjoy it. I reflect on the fact that this actually causes me more suffering. But it's an old habit, and it takes a long time to change behaviour. It's been a catapult out of present experience, a kind of drug; not wanting to be in my experience of desolation. It's to do with my background and history: I couldn't cope with all the things that happened to me, being gay, my mother's suicide. I wanted to go unconscious, I didn't want to experience my loneliness, my anger. I was trying to satisfy things that sex wasn't appropriate to deal with, which now Buddhism is helping me make sense of. For me sex has been about avoiding reality; and the spiritual life is about bringing me more into relationship with reality, and having a context with which to support it.'

The intensity of experience that Nagaraja talks of, and that sex appears to offer, is one reason why it can be so very appealing – and may make it harder to maintain the awareness that is a hallmark of a spiritual approach to life. 'Sex is one of the most immediate pleasures and very powerful,' counsels Lionel Blue. 'I don't say, like some of the Eastern European rabbis did, that you have to throw a bucket of iced water over yourself, but at the same time you've got to think. Just because it feels overwhelming doesn't mean to say you do it.' Gay men live in a culture where, if a desire is overwhelming, you can act on it; where desires can be managed by satiating them. On the surface this is the most satisfactory and enjoyable way of responding to our impulses.

The problem, some faiths would suggest, is that there is no way our desires will ever be wholly satisfied. 'Sexual need will never really be fulfilled. I don't know anybody who doesn't wish he could have more sex,' admits Maitreyabandhu. 'The Buddha said craving was like drinking salty water: the more you have the more you want.' The classical Buddhist 'Wheel of Life' divides the world into six realms which represent the ways human beings can approach life. The Hungry Ghost Realm is occupied by insatiable compulsives, described by Maitreyabandhu 'always wanting something from outside, and feeling more and more empty within.' Fernando Guasch suggests that the Hungry Ghost Realm is actually located on Hampstead Heath. Maitreyabandhu agrees: 'I can end up feeling like a hungry ghost when I'm cruising. My cottaging used to get very obsessional. One shouldn't become moralistic about casual sex – I don't think necessarily it's a bad thing. But it can be bad when it creates a whole atmosphere of sex where you can never be content.'

The foundation of Buddhism is the notion that 'craving causes suffering': because our desires can never be truly satisfied, we will always experience life as unsatisfactory. 'If you want something and you don't get it, it hurts you. If you do get it, there's always the potential that you're going to lose it', explains Nagaraja. 'So you get the boyfriend, and you spend all your time worrying if he's off screwing in the bushes, or what happens when he dies, or what happens when I die? Then you get possessive and try to hold on to things. The Buddha says everything is impermanent.' The insatiability of our craving relates to the idea that we seek to meet more than our sexual needs through sex. 'We approach a sexual relationship with expectations it can't meet – that's why it causes so much suffering,' suggests Maitreyabandhu. 'It can give you a measure of happiness, but it can't meet existential needs.' Sex can sometimes *appear* to meet our needs, briefly – it is intense enough to distract our attention from almost anything – but, if there is something wrong, it can at best only cover up the symptoms, not offer a cure.

For some people, then, sexual ethics will include the acknowledgement that, although our desires may be strong, our well-being cannot be made dependent on them being satisfied (because total satisfaction is impossible). 'If we were more sensible about sex and realized its place, it would be much less of an issue and we'd probably be happier,' reckons Maitreyabandhu. 'You've only got a limited amount of time and energy,' suggests Lionel Blue. 'Sex is not a full-time activity, only a part-time one.'[8] 'I learnt by trial and error that sex is like eating and breathing, but it is not the purpose of our life on earth, and if it becomes so, it trivializes life. You need your soul as well as your body to enjoy it without being enslaved by it.'[9] 'Unless sexual desire is seen in a wider perspective it can lead to the numbers game, or manipulation, or the reduction of people to flesh, which does not do them justice. It is not a universal panacea.' For Rabbi Blue, the value of monogamy is that 'it puts sex in its place. The aim of life is not sex.' Adam James remembers the words of the Indian guru who inspires him, Sai Baba: 'you need a ceiling on desire'. Gay Sikh Kauldip Singh agrees with this point: 'How many hours can you stay in bed and have sex? You've got a life to lead.' 'There's got to be something between shags,' declares Pagan Gordon Hunt. 'Sex is not enough to base my whole life round', Nagaraja concurs. A potential problem with sexual identity – and, particularly, the marketing of that identity that was discussed in chapter 6 – is that it does base the whole of life around sex, and encourages us to do so.

'Sex is like two paper bags trying to get inside one another' is a remark I have heard attributed to both the founder of the Friends of the Western Buddhist Order, Sangharakshita, and the Maharishi (proponent of Transcendental Meditation). It suggests that total intimacy is impossible. (This is not the same as saying, as pathological religion might, that all of life – and all sexual desire – is a 'temptation' which should be resisted: some intimacy is possible, and good.) In chapter 5 some people argued that personal relationships were no substitute for a relationship with God, although partly *because* of their inevitable limitations, they do provide some sort of signpost. Christian liturgist and author Jim Cotter thinks the same is true of sexual desire itself: 'My sexuality seems to evoke not only my need for another human being, but also my need for The Other. There is always a beyondness that seems to beckon in and through our sexuality and sexual relationships, and sex never yields all that it promises of creativity and communion. It can give much more than we usually anticipate or experience, but the desire always remains for something less broken, less partial, less temporary.'[10] Lionel Blue suggests that finding something more whole and permanent may even require some reduction in sexual activity: 'if you want to be a religious person you have to have some sort of love affair going on with God too, so you can't fix all your feelings just in the body. You have to give some time and energy to your spirituality.'

CELIBACY

Perhaps the ultimate act of putting sexual acts 'in their place', the most unequivocal dedication of time and energy to spirituality rather than sex, is to become celibate. The idea of giving up sex is, for many lesbian, gay and bisexual people, bizarre, mad, frightening, and proof of self-hatred.

'For so many people sex is their main pleasure,' explains Maitreyabandhu. 'So gay people think, take that away and we'd be left with nothing!' Catherine Hopper recalls hearing a thirtysomething lesbian Buddhist explain that, while still loving her partner very much, she had decided to become celibate. 'I was particularly shocked by this notion that I could give up my sex life voluntarily. I suddenly realized that deep down I believed that there was nothing worth giving up one's sex life for, having fought for it so hard.'

Partly this horror is based on a misunderstanding of what celibacy is; as the Reverend Niall Johnston explains, Christians talking about celibacy are often referring to 'enforced abstinence, a life-denying force, an imposition', whereas queers who have chosen celibacy are adamant that it is not rooted in a fear or hatred of sexuality, and is not the same as repression. 'With repression you squash sexuality flat – and it pops up somewhere else,' says the Venerable K-N, who as a Buddhist monk has vowed not to have sex. 'With celibacy you're *transmuting* this enormous biological imperative and all this energy, using it to control your mind. It does not remove you from desire.' 'To suppress sexuality would be to try to say that it doesn't exist,' says Dirk de Klerk, who when on retreat at the Samyé Ling Buddhist monastery in Scotland undertook vows of 'complete celibacy, not even masturbating'. Far from denying that sexual desire exists, he says celibacy involves paying very close attention to every detail of desire.

'Celibacy involves refraining from genital sexual activity, but that (in my understanding) does not close access to other broad avenues where a person may explore and celebrate the giftedness of human sexuality,' says Damian Entwhistle, who took the vow when training to be a Franciscan friar. 'Celibacy is not emasculation. There is a world of difference between being sexually (genitally) inactive and being asexual.' The idea that celibacy is not sexual 'is grounded in the same paradigm occupied by mainstream Christian denominations, the paradigm that commonly supposes "sexuality" to be synonymous with "genital activity"'. Moira has been celibate for four years, since joining a twelve-step group to recover from drug addiction. 'I do feel sexual, often in a very positive way, and I am exploring this in ways that are more subtle than making love with a sexual partner. When I first started to live without alcohol and drugs, I did not feel sexual at all, except in a hurt and violated way. Now I am taking time to heal, I feel I am strengthening that part of myself that can be true, and trusting, and loving, and fully aware. At the moment I feel fulfilled by learning to love and be loved by my friends, my higher power and my self. I feel that my spirituality will help me to love women with more tenderness and awe, and I want to stay connected to this. I don't want to love a woman if I am coming from a feeling of emptiness and need.'

The queer horror of celibacy is rooted in the fear that someone might force us to give up sex. Celibacy, properly understood, is a voluntary choice. The queer celibates (or former celibates) who contributed to this book were well aware of what they were choosing to give up – as well as what they were hoping to gain. Whereas the celibate of popular imagination is a young man who enters the priesthood still a confused and frustrated virgin – and who doesn't know what it is he's vowing never to do – the Venerable K-N claims to have been 'a positive slut' before taking refuge. Another man, who was in a long-term relationship for many years and had also had many casual sexual partners, has joined a Christian order which requires celibacy: 'having lived the life that I have lived,' he says, 'I know precisely what I've done in giving up sex'.

Even when celibacy is voluntary – and is not motivated by denial or erotophobia – why bother? One answer is that celibacy can shift the focus of relationship in people's lives: from one other person to a number of people. 'Sex and sexual relationships use up time and energy we could be using in a far less narrow and exclusive way – to develop friendships, and compassion for all beings,' says Catherine Hopper. When Damian Entwistle joined the Franciscans, he promised 'to forgo the possibility of forming an exclusive one-to-one relationship so as to live a flourishing life in the context of a fraternity'.

According to the Venerable K-N, celibacy 'gives you distance' from your desires; 'you can examine the whole experience much more objectively. The discipline is a very good learning experience – I can watch the devious way my mind tries to find some way in which sex might just be possible. You get to know your mind better, you begin to control it, which means you can start to use it properly.' Dirk de Klerk explains further: 'For many people, their mind states – emotions – are more solid than the chairs they are sitting on. They are completely manipulated by their conditioning, emotions, fears, desires. One of the main things you can learn from the practice of celibacy is emancipation from this emotional conditioning. You experience your emotions, but you don't need to be controlled by them.' It's not about punishing or denigrating yourself: feeling good for giving something up, or rejoicing in how miserable you can make yourself. 'Freedom from the compelling force of craving is accompanied not by a sense of sacrifice or "lack", but one of relief and satisfaction.' Nagaraja – not, himself, a celibate as yet – summarizes why gay Buddhists may aspire to the state: 'they just don't want to be dragged about by their penis all the time'.

Damian maintains that 'the question of keeping vows seems a much bigger deal to those who haven't experienced it, than to those who have. Like most human experiences, it is not burdensome when you have the love and support of those around you, however demanding it may appear.

Difficult? It depended on a large measure to the degree to which I felt valued, loved and supported by the brothers. When I was feeling depressed or ill, aloof from my support network (those friars – not necessarily gay – with whom I could be vulnerable), then the undoubted pleasures of a consolatory wank were considerable!' Nagaraja believes that 'to become celibate, you have to have very strong and intimate friendships, lots of support and love. If you don't have that, you'd frustrate yourself.' Buddhist vows of celibacy can be dissolved when appropriate – for instance, at a time of great stress. 'It takes a lot of effort. Celibacy has to be about a deep inner contentment. Yes, there will be a certain amount of tension, it won't be easy – but you know the pay-off is worth the effort.'

The suspicion remains – among Westerners, and particularly among queers who have made sexuality, and sex, so very central to our identity – that celibacy is somehow 'unnatural', that it cannot be good for you. Having experienced four years without even bashing the bishop, Dirk disagrees. 'One certainly realizes that sex is only a desire, it's not like food that you need. It's something I *know* from my own experience. It's like fire: if you feed a small fire it becomes a big fire and becomes uncontrollable very quickly. So what you learn to do eventually is not to feed the fire. There's no physical imperative.' Surely there is a biological imperative? Isn't it bad for a man's health not to ejaculate once in a while? 'In my life I'd never had wet dreams before – I had a few on retreat, but towards the end they completely disappeared. You can decide not to have them. Sex is the most pleasurable thing that you can conceive of if you're celibate. But it's not a need: it's just like anything else, you can let it go.'

So why is Dirk no longer celibate? His answer is that his vows were taken only as a discipline for the time when he was a monk: celibacy was appropriate for the intensive 'training' of the retreat, but it is no longer required. He currently has a boyfriend. What matters, once again, is not the external act or form but the intention. 'Celibacy isn't laudable in *itself*,' stresses Catherine Hopper, 'but for the space and the insight it affords you. If it becomes more of a hindrance than a help, the vow can be formally dissolved.' It cannot be stressed too often: in a healthy spirituality celibacy is not forced upon people. Just as the Venerable K-N chose to be celibate, so Dirk is currently choosing not to be. Celibacy has been rejected by all of the Catholic and Anglican priests who have contributed to this book – all of whom, if they obeyed their churches' rulings, should not be having sexual relationships. Freedom to choose what is right for us, according to our individual experience, is one of the key attributes of queer spirituality.

REMEMBERING TO LOVE YOURSELF

For the lesbian and gay community to all become celibate would be as pointless as it is implausible. It is only one possible manifestation of a concern to use our sexuality as wisely and well as we can, and only one possible approach to making the best use of sexual and spiritual energy. An alternative way may, like some understandings of Tantra, intensify physical sexual practice in the pursuit of spiritual connection. Since we are all children of a sex-negative culture, any desire to give sex up has to be looked at very carefully. The limitations of sex need to be balanced by a reassertion of its strengths. As Carter Heyward cautions, though sexual compulsion exists and it is possible to feel 'driven to have sex with people whether or not we know them, enjoy them, or even experience much pleasure with them . . . we ought not to confuse sex-addiction . . . with a strong desire for sexual pleasure, and lots of it, with a lover – or lovers.'[11]

The qualities that have been highlighted in previous chapters as readily available to queer people – awareness, realism, honesty and the challenging of orthodoxies which don't relate to our experience – can all be of use in the pursuit of a better, more joyous sex life. But Damian Entwhistle adds a necessary qualification to this ideal. 'Mature and balanced sexuality is not crafted in ten weeks or even ten years. It is a lifetime's work. Keep a sense of proportion about the good gift of human sexuality. If you find that you have behaved in ways that you feel inappropriate, it's not the end of the world. So you think that you are incorrigible? Laugh about it and then try anew in earnest. Be patient with yourself and others. Try to focus and refocus on the values you feel are important.' Above all, 'it is essential not to get on a guilt trip about sex. Occasionally, we louse it up. Shame, but it's not the end of the world.'

Notes
1. Lionel Blue, *A Backdoor to Heaven* (London: Fount Paperbacks, 1994), p. 145.
2. The fact that the researcher is a gay male no doubt had an effect on this.
3. Such as the way our critics fail to mention it is also pretty harsh about sea food, lending money for interest, textiles of more than one thread, being rude to your parents, and menstruating women; the difficulty of understanding the word commonly translated as 'abomination'; and whether the prohibition against lying with a man 'as with a woman' can be taken to refer to gay relationships as understood today.
4. Rabbi Sarah presents her reading of Leviticus 18–20 in more detail in her essay 'Towards a New Jewish Sexual Ethic' in Johnathan A. Roman, *Renewing the Vision* (London: SCM Press, 1996).

5. John Pierce, *Sex and Spirit* (Drewsteignton: Charisma Books, 1992), pp. 50, 56.

6. Norman Pittenger, *Time for Consent: A Christian's Approach to Homosexuality* (London: SCM Press, 1976), p. 104.

7. A word for having sex, from the old gay slanguage of 'polari'.

8. Rabbi Lionel Blue, *Godly and Gay* (London: Gay Christian Movement, 1981), p. 9.

9. Blue, *A Backdoor to Heaven*, p. 145.

10. Jim Cotter, *Pleasure Pain and Passion: Some Perspectives on Sexuality and Spirituality* (Sheffield: Cairns Publications, 1993), pp. 3–4.

11. Carter Heyward, *Touching Our Strength: The Erotic as Power and the Love of God* (San Francisco: HarperCollins, 1989), p. 136.

8

Suffering and Healing

I think healing and spirituality are the same thing.
For me, all the world's religions and scriptures are
empty, unless they're aimed at healing the world,
and healing ourselves. That's the purpose of the
whole caboodle.

(Lev)

If Lev is right in identifying healing as the purpose of religion, it would be easy to argue that religion has failed: lesbian, gay and bisexual people are among the many who have realized how religion can cause far more pain than it attempts to relieve. And yet, again, a distinction can be drawn between unhelpful and healthy religion. Healthy religion, as Lev says, aims to heal; it also acknowledges that we all need healing.

EVERYBODY HURTS

'To be human is to hurt,' said the late Simon Bailey, an Anglican priest. 'In both senses: we hurt, feel permanently sore, ache inside *and* we take it out on others, hurt them. We all do it. Gay people looking into the well of their own spirit will find what all other oppressed people find, that we are part of the mess . . . The *essence* may be good, may even be restorable, but it is unbelievably twisted in all of us.' 'Life hurts – and that's all right, it has its place,' says Nagaraja, from the perspective of Buddhism. 'I find life difficult. I don't have all the answers. I'm trying, it's hard, it's painful – as long as I stay in touch with that, I'm all right. If I try to kid myself it's not like that, I just get lost. I lose touch with some depth.' 'For me the spiritual is a way of acknowledging how desperate the human condition really is, how truly vulnerable people really are,' says another Buddhist, Fernando Guasch. 'Just paying attention to what is really going on. It's what I find profound in Catholicism – the mystery of pain. Everybody feels scared and alone. I think that is a fundamental experience of what it is to be human. Everybody has shit to deal with. You cannot run away from this mess, but you are forever trying to, by daydreaming of things out there that can make it better. We invent strategies that only land us into even greater confusion. Gay people ought to be able to understand some of these things, in as much as gay people at some point of their lives have had to deal with constant turmoil. What you're living through is disturbing – even if we don't talk about it in the gay press or the gay clubs.'

Life involves suffering, to paraphrase the Buddha. Although central to our queer identity is the fact that we are, to varying degrees and in various ways, oppressed – that is, other people cause us unnecessary suffering – there is sometimes pressure not to admit the human consequences this has for us. 'Gay "pride" can mask a lot of self-hatred which isn't experienced enough, because we are busy being out and proud – it's not allowed to be a problem any more,' suggests Maitreyabandhu. It is our duty to have fun. Our label says what we should be – 'gay' – happy by definition. We've fought so hard to say we're all right; which, as Fernando reasons, leads to the belief that 'if you complain you give weapons to your enemies.' And 'if you dare criticize the non-stop party, you are homophobic, you loathe yourself.' What such defensiveness ignores is that life isn't always a party (which is not to say it sometimes can't be); and because, in our collective forms, we don't always admit this (except when we are arguing for our political rights), individuals can end up feeling the odd one out if they experience difficulty, dissatisfaction, and pain. Worse still, they can blame themselves for these feelings. 'It always looks as if everyone else is having a good time and you're not,' as Nagaraja puts it.

Mature spirituality requires us continually to confront reality. Unhealthy religion does not do this. Fundamentalists virtually believe that you cannot be unhappy if you are a Christian – it would be blasphemous. Drew Payne has left that attitude behind: he no longer has 'the painted smile of happiness, the happiness that graces the mouth but never reaches the eyes, that I tried so hard to keep as an evangelical Christian.' Modern lesbian and gay lifestyle sometimes puts pressure on queers to wear painted smiles of happiness. To deal with pain, we need to do more than provide opportunities for pleasure; as the Reverend Dennis Fraser puts it, 'caring isn't just about having a good time, come on, cheer up, have another lager'. David is a gay Buddhist who sees a lot of the gay scene as offering 'distraction, particularly from emotions. If you've had a painful experience in a relationship with someone, the most common remedy would be to go out and get shagged as soon as possible afterwards, getting back on the horse as it were – you distract yourself from the painful, it will all be all right – you buy into that dream again. But however defensive one is in terms of protecting yourself from being hurt, there's always a chink in the armour.'

GETTING OFF IT

But do we really have to confront pain? Of course it exists – but can't we just ignore it, or dull it, until it goes away? The use of drugs (including, above all, alcohol) in bars and clubs is often blamed on the pressures of the outside – straight – world. Drugs offer temporary escape and relief – as well as confidence to people likely to be low on self-esteem. With their use, however, comes the risk of serious addiction – a problem found disproportionately among lesbians and gay men, compared with the general population.[1]

'I was definitely searching for something,' says Moira of her teenage years, a time of permanent depression; although she had not fully realized her sexual orientation, she knew that she had to 'keep a check on my feelings and not disclose them'. She attended her father's church for a time, in an attempt to meet her needs. 'I had heard that religion helped people, and made them feel transformed, and loved and happy. I went for about a year, never feeling like I belonged, never meeting a passion or a yearning in these people like I felt in myself. I could not say I believed in God – I did not know what it was – and I felt these people would be rather shocked if they knew that. I was also afraid to shock or disturb them with my neediness and emptiness, my desperate searching, as I couldn't see this gaping hole in them. Eventually I realized I would not find "it" there, and looked to alcohol and drugs to fill the hole.'

'For many years, drugs were my "religion" – I believed in them. They were the most important thing in my life, and they provided my life with meaning. I felt they transformed my way of looking at the world, and I felt "enlightened". I looked down on people who did not use drugs as I did as spiritually less than me – bound by convention, with no depth to their lives. Drugs also gave me ceremonies and rituals – the ritual of rolling a joint and smoking it was performed before and after almost every event, from having a bath to eating a meal to going to the shops. It was my talisman, my protection. Dope was the one thing that was always there for me unconditionally. I believed everything would be OK as long as I had dope.'

Moira's high level of drug use continued for many years, 'until the dope no longer took away the uneasy, gnawing discomfort inside me. I wanted something else, I wanted joy, and truth, and connection to people, but at the same time I did not want to even spend time with people, I just wanted to be by myself and smoke dope and drink. I could not maintain a sexual relationship, as I felt so trapped I just wanted to get shitfaced, and I found even a one-night stand too intimate for comfort.' Eventually Moira started attending meetings of Narcotics Anonymous. 'This is a spiritual programme and suggests that a belief in a loving power greater than ourselves is essential. I did not have a problem with this intellectually – particularly when someone said "coincidence is God's way of protecting his anonymity". The word "his" put me off, but so many occurrences and little events had nudged and drawn me to getting clean and finding a new way of living and being, that I could not ignore it, and it opened my mind to the possibility of something greater than myself. Another thing that helped me keep my mind open and explore spirituality was the constant assurance that I could believe what I like, it needn't be a male entity in the sky that likes people to go to church and be respectable.' Moira now feels that 'life is a gift, and I want to honour it by being aware and alive'.

Seamus knew he was gay at an early age 'and picked up it was not acceptable. And in early childhood things went on that left me desperate and disillusioned.' In his early teens he started hanging around with some hippies who were interested in Tibetan Buddhism – and LSD. 'At that stage my life took on two significant dimensions that have been with me ever since – taking drugs, and actively searching spiritually. It was basically a way of trying to find some understanding and relief from the pain I was in.' Over the years he explored Neo-Paganism as well as Buddhism; and indulged in 'massive orgies of drink and drugs'. Like Moira he finally joined the 'twelve-step' programmes of Alcoholics Anonymous and Narcotics Anonymous. 'For me now, the spiritual path is undoubtedly the effective way of dealing with the pain. The drugs didn't deal with it, they diverted it; and you still accumulate interest on the pain, you're just not aware that you're accumulating it. You have to take more and more drugs simply to deal with the interest – it gets to the point where you are literally brought to your knees. I had to finally admit that I was powerless over my addictions and powerless over my life, and I've been a control freak all my life, trying to keep people away from me. Despite the fact that I rejected Christianity at the age of twelve, I realize that what underlies all of my searching is that somewhere I've taken on board the idea that God is a punitive God. What's happening now is I'm beginning to be aware on a day-to-day level that there's a power greater than myself, a loving power; I believe in that and I'm working on trusting that. Since I've been in the fellowship I feel I've got far more understanding in a very real sense about myself and my spirituality. I'm not hiding behind anything. I'd like to get to the place where I trust myself and my connection with my higher power strongly enough that I don't feel that

I'll get swept away and engulfed by religion or a drug or sex, which tends to be what's happened to me in the past.'

The stories of Moira and Seamus demonstrate that drugs are sometimes used to address 'spiritual' needs, but cannot ultimately meet them – and in the end can actually intensify the original needs. This is not to say that all drug use is intended as pain relief – many of us consume alcohol, dope or ecstasy for relaxation and pleasure. Nagaraja, however, would argue that, even so, taking drugs is of limited use. 'It doesn't bring you into deeper relationship with people,' he says: and real relationship, in Buddhism and other faiths, is necessary for spiritual growth. Just as in chapter 7 it was argued that sex becomes problematic when it is motivated not by sexual desires but by a need for something else – like oblivion or security – so drugs cannot be seen as solutions to existential difficulties.

Moira and Seamus both feel that their fears and problems could be solved only by spiritual means. Their understanding of life, and themselves – their whole sense of being – is greater because of what they have been through. An orthodox religion might see them as 'sinners', because they 'got it wrong', they did not live by the rules. In defiance of that concept of faith, Moira quotes a saying she heard at her twelve-step group: 'Religion is for people who are afraid of going to hell. Spirituality is for people who have been there.'

'We're frightened of being lonely, of being rejected, of looking beyond, of all sorts of things,' says the Reverend Jean White. 'Therefore we'll do anything to stop ourselves looking at those issues. Instead of taking care of ourselves we harm ourselves.' Misuse of drugs is not the only way in which queer people harm themselves. Eating disorders, self-mutilation, and attempted suicide – all of which some lesbian and gay people have to struggle with – are motivated by a horror of looking inside, and so can all be seen to be spiritual problems as well as physical or psychological.

GETTING REAL: WE'RE OUT OF CONTROL

Admitting that life can be painful does not prove that 'spirituality' can be of any help. To the contrary: the existence of suffering is one of the major intellectual objections atheists have to religion. How can a loving God allow pain to exist? If God is just, then surely pain must be some sort of punishment – which, given the amount of pain in the world, means God must also be cruel. And why doesn't God protect people who believe? Religion peddles false hope – 'put up with things for now because everything will be all right in heaven'; or 'keep believing and you might be cured'.

Spiritually identified queers do not fall for these facile promises. Their faith is not a crutch. Someone once suggested to Glenn Palmer that his muscular dystrophy would heal if he 'found Jesus'. 'That made me really angry. It suggests that God magically makes things get better. I don't think for a moment that God's going to make it go away. That's ludicrous, that's a fairy tale. The sort of God I hope is there is not a God of "making things right" but a God of understanding.' Understanding is not the same as explanation or solution. 'There *is* something arbitrary and unfair about the nature of life. Christianity's not (necessarily) about denying that. It's saying that certainty is not found in the body; certainty is found within the self. A materialist world says we are in control – of our destiny, our health – and it's patently not our experience.' Glenn is suggesting that religion can actually have a more complex understanding of life's difficulty than materialist philosophies. Father Bernard Lynch likewise feels that religion's role is not to provide answers; certainty is the enemy of spirituality. 'We fear that which to my mind is the absolute *sine qua non* of spiritual integrity – we fear being out of control. All of life, in its most empirical reality, is inescapable – and everything we do is a way of coping with the truth that we are not in control, that we are not masters of our own destiny. People who believe that they are the masters of their destiny can only believe this by becoming specialists in self-deception. Their decisions are really not decisions at all. A real decision makes one humble: one knows that it is at the mercy of more things than can be named. The great difficulty is to say yes to life: to love life, to love it even when one suffers. But life is all. Life is God. And to love life is to love God.'

'Life is always out of control,' agrees Fernando Guasch. 'Yet we live in a culture where we are given the myth that if you work hard, or improve yourself, your life will eventually become under control. And then we feel guilty for not having it under control. Life is a maelstrom. The Buddhist approach is to ride it.' Chris Ferguson has been forced to confront the limits of his own control over life by his HIV-positive diagnosis. At one stage meningitis caused involuntary muscle spasms and fits. 'It's a sobering experience when your body's moving involuntarily. We're so used to our arm bending if we want it to bend; but once it's doing it without your control, and you realize you're not in control of your own body, that can be quite frightening. What Buddhism teaches becomes really alive – everything is impermanent, everything is suffering, and what we see as our permanent self isn't really, it's in flux, it will disappear.' HIV made Chris much more aware of how 'this entity called "you" is falling apart'; the virus speeds up this natural process. Learning of the death of a former partner made impermanence hit home even more; 'it was like a part of me suddenly just didn't exist any more. I don't think many people come to spirituality when life is normal. People come through trauma and difficulties – whenever you realize you're not in control. You think you've got your problems, but you can still win. A major trauma makes you realize just how little in control you are. I've made much more spiritual progress since my own illness – it's too easy to accept things intellectually and think you understand it; it's only when you experience things personally in your life that you really make the connection between your spirituality and systems of teaching.'

Johnathon Andrew has come to a similar conclusion. For him, 'AIDS was the wake up call'. But the call can come in various ways – 'Cancer is the wake up call. Your mum dying is the wake up call. Anything that causes you to doubt is the wake up call.' Johnathon suggests that spirituality comes through doubt, and through difficulty. Unless it acknowledges these qualities, it is of no use. 'If your spirituality doesn't work on the ward at the Lighthouse – on "death row" – it's not worth it. There's no room for sentimentality. It's got to be tough stuff – compassionate, yes, but there's no room for floppy Christians or New Age wimps.'

Atheists sometimes attack religious believers as people who cannot cope with reality, and instead escape into superstition. But the spirituality that queer people are talking about here is not escapist: instead, it embraces the real difficulties of living and suffering – and emerges out of those difficulties. People with 'pathological' religious beliefs, who see religion as magical – about getting rewards for getting it right – hope that by following their faith they can control their lives, and keep away from pain. For queer people spirituality is not about trying to control, but about coping with being out of control.

Michael Seán Paterson works with the spiritual needs of people with HIV and AIDS. 'I think coming out of AIDS for the rest of us is an invitation to let our spirituality start from powerlessness, to start from not being in control. That's what the Christian Church has always resisted. It's not without significance that what we did to God was pin him down, literally. And he gets up again, if you follow the story (never mind whether it's true).' A few years ago, when Michael was still a student for the Jesuit priesthood, he was invited to give a talk to some nuns. 'When I arrived at the convent there was graffiti on the outside wall which said "Your order is meaningless: my chaos is significant." Whether that is a comment about the religious order, or the order of society, it really threw me. I came to HIV and AIDS as somebody who, although very liberal in terms of theology, still would have held on to all those categories as interpretative schemes. Very little of that is relevant any more. Everything that I used to keep control, my framework to understand the world, God – all the schemes I'd have used – are at least under question, because there has been so much in the utter chaos of the pandemic, the mess of so many people crying, so many candles in Trafalgar Square, so many coffins, sitting so many times in the clinic when people have been diagnosed. If three years ago I would say there's something in the Gospel which is about life, I would now say there's something in AIDS which is about life – there's something in the chaos which is so signifi- cant that you've got to admit the possibility that your order might be totally irrelevant.'

One of the organizations Michael works for – CARA – began as 'an Anglican organization trying to be ecumenical', but over the years Michael reckons that it has 'lost more and more of that Christian baggage. We would be more inclined towards spirituality than religion. The issues are deeper than ecclesial identity. You can't survive very long here without being aware of your own mortality, shadow stuff, messy stuff, mixed up stuff – and when you are in touch with that, you no longer hide behind the fig leaves of so many other things. All the certainties that we would have had, both personally and as a group, have gone.'

'You can't get away with the platitudes,' agrees Rabbi Lionel Blue, who has led retreats for gay men with HIV and other terminal illnesses, and also worked extensively with addicts. At a time when prayer was empty and liturgy had died on him, it was people on these retreats who 'conducted me back to belief, and goodness. Their devastating honesty gave me courage to be angry and use four-letter words about whomever and whatever organises the cosmos (it could have been organised better). They led me back to spirituality and love of life beyond the body and what grows out of disintegration.'[2] Rabbi Blue's concept of what religion can achieve has changed in response. 'My God has grown smaller', he confesses, no longer the 'mighty, macho father figure' he once prayed to; and no longer does his prayer 'ask God to reveal to me the mysteries of his cosmos. I now ask for much less, some knowledge of my next small step ahead, and a little courage to take it – no more'.[3] Father Bill is another religious professional who, in his work alongside hundreds of people with AIDS, has found that confronting the reality of the situation is more valuable than clinging to theology. 'I've had great talks with many men on a spiritual level, talking about God in the way they wanted to talk about God, talking about death in the way that meant something to them, in the language they wanted to use, not the language I was used to. I find myself becoming more and more honest about who I am as a result'.[4]

A CONTEXT FOR SUFFERING

This pattern should, by now, be a familiar one: religious orthodoxy is abandoned if it fails to correspond to queer people's experience, or if it does not help us live fuller lives. Spiritually identified queers freely acknowledge that their traditions cannot magic pain away, and may not even suggest any 'purpose' for suffering. But at the very least, Rabbi Sheila Shulman suggests, religion can give 'a context in which to think it through'. 'In our society we're not given much space to be aware of suffering and impermanence,' argues Chris Ferguson, whereas 'Buddhist philosophy has suggested for two and a half thousand years that it is a common aspect of life'. 'All through my life I have seen people be able to express fears about pain, illness, death, and caring, through the discourse of religion,' says Sister Latex, who spent much of his youth with relatives and family friends who were clergy. As a member of the Order of Perpetual Indulgence he aims to 'use the discourse of religion for its most positive purposes, purged of its negative ideological power.'[5]

Though we live in a culture that tends to deny the full reality of pain (or persuades us that any problem can be solved with enough money), suffering is taken very seriously by the world's religions. Neil Whitehouse sees this in the story of Christ. 'What is going on in the death of Jesus is an integration at some level of the positive and the negative of life. It is of great importance and comfort that the Christian story suggests the shit of life is taken up into God. That's not to deny that people can get on very well without formal notions of God, but to say that I and others have stumbled across a story which seems to encourage and enable us to face reality. I think the Christian story offers an understanding of human wholeness which is truthful – which does accept mortality, and is able to live with death and dying. That's not done cheaply.' 'I have great difficulty with the traditional Christian concepts of Christ taking all our sin upon him and paying the price for it all – that leaves me cold,' says Jacqueline, an Anglican priest. 'But the underlying pattern of being brought face to face with ourselves, our failure, and our deepest needs – and knowing that, in spite of and because of who we are, we are acceptable and loveable (accepted and loved by God, in Christian terms), and learning to forgive and accept ourselves (and others likewise) – are important values and concepts, all found at the heart of Christianity.'

Jacqueline sees acceptance as a crucial value embodied in the story of Christ. Accepting suffering does not mean approving of it, nor saying that its causes should not be removed where possible. It does, however, allow it to exist, and, by doing so, allow the possibility of a wider perspective. Seeing the wider picture is more than an abstract exercise: it can be the start of healing mental and physical pain. 'Meditation, because it intensifies your awareness, can re-open old memories,' says Varabhadri. 'Maybe what's been happening is that one has been living sealed off from your emotions. We find bits of us which aren't integrated. For some people that might mean rediscovering emotional damage – we devise all sorts of strategies to survive, and with all the new input those strategies start to get threatened a bit. One day, in the middle of a retreat, I saw in my mind's eye the man who raped me when I was eight. It's not something I'd ever forgotten, but for the first time in my life I felt anger – that nobody had ever caught him, for the conditions that had kept me in silence. If that had arisen years previously I might have wanted to track him down or get some kind of revenge going, it would have eaten at me. But I discovered I can let go of things – I can acknowledge the feeling, but let go. It doesn't amount to forgiveness in the Christian sense; but I've understood that everybody is a product of particular conditionings, everybody has things happen to them which makes them behave in a certain way. We can apply to that moral or emotional judgements; but the basic realization is that this isn't a unique thing, I haven't been singled out as a particular victim. It was good to feel anger; the energy helped free me from the past. That experience doesn't have to dictate how I am for the rest of my life.'

Chris Ferguson, who has meditated through bouts of AIDS-related illness, suggests that meditation can put physical pain into some sort of perspective as well: 'It puts all the suffering into context. It's not the whole of who you are. Meditation is insight into reality. It's not thinking about things, it's an awareness of the reality of things. What is this thing called pain? What is this thing called a body? It's a basic Buddhist practice, to know who you are, trying to find a permanent self, and realizing *everything* is in constant flux.' Suffering is transient and impermanent too.

HEALING

In the acceptance of suffering, there is the potential for healing. Healing does not make pain go away; the best it can hope for is to transform it. 'Use our wounds,' is Father Bill's advice. 'Our wounds can either be co-creative or co-destructive. We need the empathy of compassion, to go where it hurts, to enter into places of pain and to share in the anguish of an unknown path.'[6] Father Bernard Lynch suggests that 'there are places in the heart that cannot be born except through human suffering, and science will never touch them. That's not an explanation or a justification. But it's an attempt to maybe understand a little more, and so accept, that I myself am a mystery.' In the 1980s, after taking a very high profile in campaigns in support of people with HIV, and against the homophobia of the Roman Catholic Church, Lynch was falsely accused of molesting a young man. His name was dragged through the mud by the world's media. In court the FBI's case collapsed – it had been fabricated, apparently in order to silence Father Lynch.[7] Bernard was fully exonerated. The trauma it caused him could not be cleared as easily as his name, however. 'I wouldn't wish it on anybody, even my worst enemies. But the life I got, and am still getting, because of that death, no one could have taught me. Suffering for me is about humanization of my own humanity. There is more of me as a result of that.' Glenn Palmer, although angry at his deteriorating physical condition, also feels that 'I am who I am because of this'.

To say that in accepting pain it is possible to partially transform it – and that we grow as a result – is to say that it is possible to learn from pain; and some queer people (but by no means all) deduce from this some sort of 'purpose' in suffering. Steve Graham suggests that 'we're here for a reason. There's lessons to be learned. Some lessons are quite easy; some lessons will bother us all our lifetime.' Father Bill believes that 'life is a school'. 'Everything I do has a reason, and everything I do helps me grow spiritually,' reckons Jason Oliver, a Pagan. 'I may not recognize it at the time. If you stop seeing bad things as bad, and see them as things that are happening which may have some good coming out of them – if you *learn* from them – good things can come. But if you ignore the good, these things will happen over and over again, as if life's trying to teach you a lesson. It's not like you're being punished. All that shit that's happened to me' – including being homeless, rejection by his parents, the death of his best friend from AIDS and his own HIV diagnosis – 'it's made me have more strength in myself, and more trust in what's around me.'

The Buddhism of Nichiren Daishonin takes this to an extreme with a very literal view of karma, the 'law' of cause and effect. 'Every effect that we experience comes from a cause that we have made at some point,' is how Robert Bristow explains it – although the cause may lie in a previous life. 'When you understand that you've chosen to be where you are, then you can also choose to get to be where you want to be – and to make where you are the best possible place in the world.' Nichiren Buddhists believe that by chanting *nam myoho renge kyo* they are 'bringing into play the mystic law, which is your inner life state and also that of the universe' – and can affect the pattern of cause and effect. 'Up until shortly before I discovered the practice I had subjected myself to not having a choice. Whatever the problems we have, most people find through this practice they turn to being of great use. If it's part of the world, then it's useful to the practice. If something does make us suffer, then, as long as we're practising, we'll turn that round. Putting suffering in that context is reassuring.'

A belief in the individual's total power to change everything about their life is not entirely compatible with the argument that, at some level, we have to accept our lack of control. Some New Age philosophies contradict Christianity and Buddhism, believing, for instance, like Louise Hay does, that you are completely in control of every action, and things happen because you allow them to. Different spiritual practitioners take different stances on this, as on every other issue. What is important is that spirituality is addressing the *need* to be healed – when so much of the culture around us suggests we shouldn't need healing.

SHAMELESS

Psychology, as well as spirituality, teaches that genuine acceptance of anything can occur only if there has been real acceptance of yourself. The famous Judeo-Christian ethic, 'Love your neighbour as yourself', is often truncated to just 'love your neighbour'. It is interpreted as meaning love other people more than yourself, or instead of yourself: rather than, 'you have to feel compassion for yourself before you can manage any for other people'. 'Spirituality (rather than religion) is about self-loving,' according to former priest Mike Way, now director of CARA. 'And it's much harder to love who you are when you've learned to hate who you are before you know who you are.' Fernando makes the same point; he says Buddhist meditation gives one 'a chance of being able to live with oneself', which is necessary because 'gay people have been infected with a form of mental illness – they have been made to be at war with themselves all the time. I think we are deeply fucked-up individuals.'

Coming out, and being out, is rarely enough to banish all the self-hatred, guilt and shame that growing up in a homophobic culture can cause. For many people – especially those who had religious childhoods, regardless of sexual orientation – shame and self-hatred are the pillars of religion anyhow. Catholicism and Orthodox Judaism are almost synonymous with guilt for some of their followers; queer kids get double the dose. But, as Mike Way said, spirituality is about self-loving, not self-hating. This book asserts that queer faith is chosen: it would make no sense to choose something that made you feel worse about yourself. Queer spiritual 'professionals' dispute that guilt has any place in a mature faith life. When Dennis Fraser preaches in his kirk on Sunday, 'I try my utmost not to make people feel guilty – my intention is to remove guilt. I try to avoid the use of the word "should" at all times.' Tibetan Buddhist and former monk Dirk de Klerk asserts that 'acknowledgement of having done something wrong is important. But guilt is always wrong – assuming that there is some part of your mind that has the right to judge the other part of your mind'. Spiritual healer Steve Graham is convinced that shame and guilt 'stunt growth. It's so restricting. It effects our ability to become conscious spiritual beings.' 'Anything that makes you feel less than divine is a hindrance to our spiritual progress,' agrees Transcendental Meditator Henry Giles.

This is why the Sisters of Perpetual Indulgence have made 'no more guilt' their mantra. Among the many things the Sisters do, they deliberately confront the possibility that people's internalized homophobia has religious origins, which have not been addressed because, on coming out, religion is made taboo, as if simply by rejecting it we can also purge the guilt it has caused. 'People come into the gay community without being deprogrammed – "right, you're with us now, just forget about it",' explains Sister Mary-Anna Lingus (formerly Sister Ethyl Dreads-A-Flashback, and founder of the current British Order of the Sisters of Perpetual Indulgence). 'All that moral indoctrination has been so powerful you can't just decide to put it all behind you – snap your fingers, it's all gone. That doesn't give permission to acknowledge the influence that it's had over you.' We need the space, Sister Mary-Anna argues, 'to calmly say, it was terrible – but it's made me, it's part of who I am, and if I want to change it I have to work out how it has had such a powerful hold on me before I can let it go.' When the Sisters manifest themselves in public, some queer people treat them with contempt, others admire them, and still others confide in them. They provoke queer people into talking about religion: 'the habit scratches the surface, and you get to the guilt'. As well as indulging all pleasure-seeking desires, the Sisters give out 'indulgences'. Indulgences granted (or, more usually, sold) by the Church purported to let people off their punishments in purgatory; the Sisters' indulgences 'absolve queers of stigmatizing guilt'. Whereas Catholic indulgences constantly had to be topped up, the Sisters' indulgences are perpetual: 'people should take responsibility for themselves. There's a direct relationship between you and your understanding of morality – no institution has that authority. It's about being true to yourself, and using that as a basis to decide what's good and bad behaviour.'

While the Sisters graciously bring down the religious (as well as political) barriers that prevent queer people from accepting themselves fully, some people are fortunate enough to learn this from religion itself. Most lesbian and gay Christians and Jews will affirm that God made them in His/Her own image, and loves them 'just as they are': 'God loves one for *who* one is, not in spite of who one is', as Bernard Lynch puts it. Despite the fact that this message rings clearly throughout the scriptures, it is a struggle for many lesbian and gay believers to embrace the idea – most come to do so gradually, thanks to the work of religious support groups. Mike Fox was unusual in hearing it from his Church. 'The first time I said in the confessional I was gay, the priest said, "O God, not another Friend of Dorothy". I didn't know what he meant at the time, so I was thinking, who's Dorothy? He looked at me and he said, "does God love you?" And I said "yes, God loves every human being". He said "no, I didn't ask you that – does God love *you*?" "Yes, Father." "Does God love you as you are?" Pause. "Yes, Father." "Are you just saying that or do you really know it?" And that's what got me thinking – realizing that no matter what I did, even if I didn't believe in God, God would still love me. And it made me think well if God can do that, I can love myself – and I can love anybody. God makes gays in God's own image, and loves them just as they are.' When given more than lip-service, this insight can have a revolutionary effect. 'When I caught religion, I was told God loved me as I was, without conditions,' remembers Rabbi Lionel Blue. 'This mind-blowing fact helped me to like myself, and this helped me to like other people, not as I wanted them to be, but as they were.'[8]

Buddhists believe the idea of a God who can accept and love them – or reject them – is a delusion. This makes self-acceptance even more crucial. 'You can't make anyone approve of you or accept you – those things will always be beyond your control.' says Catherine Hopper. 'If you truly accept yourself you can put up with just about anything anyone else does to you. But you can have all the approval in the world, and if you hate yourself, it's worth nothing. I can try to educate straight people about gay issues, but what really frees me is the fact that I have changed my view towards myself, and therefore I'm less oppressible.' 'The practice is to learn to be with yourself, and find a home there. You've got nowhere else to be in any case,' states Fernando Guasch, who experienced such vicious homophobia from his family and native Spanish Catholic culture that he suffered two nervous breakdowns when younger. 'When we were younger in the closet, we had to be with ourselves because we were locked in. Then we dared step out and we tried to run a mile from ourselves. To say "if I only stopped doing this, became more like him" is a huge act of violence against oneself. You're absolutely all right as you are.' Coming out can be a start to this self-acceptance: 'the hurt transforms itself – when you feel it, it is followed by a sense of compassion for oneself – not self-pity, but a real sense that "I'm not such a bad person". Then the anger comes, with any notion of dignity there has to be anger, because what's been done to us is really unfair. You cannot bypass the anger – if you refuse to get in touch with the anger, you're losing access to the rest of yourself. The only way to grow is to stay there – not to sanitize it. Start making friends with yourself as early as possible, whether there's support out there or not. You have to look after yourself. You can't get there by trying to subsume your interests in some large party called the lesbian and gay community.'

Varabhadri is another Buddhist who makes the point that self-acceptance can give us strength even if we are not able to rely on the support of a community. 'Whether there is a culture that's supportive or not, you still can't get away from knowing that you are in a minority – that outside of your supportive network, or outside of a large city, things might be different in terms of discrimination. One thing Buddhism does for everybody is help us to accept ourselves – not simply as we are (we could always be better), although that's a place to start – but realizing it is not external conditions that makes us lesser or better beings. Our attitude to ourselves is what really counts: we don't have to act defensively or be self-effacing. In the *Metta Bhauana* meditation [which helps in the "development of loving kindness"] we start with ourselves. People say I can't generate good will towards myself, that's selfish – I should be more concerned about others, their feelings and wishes are more important. But you can say, "I'm as important as anyone else, and need to cultivate respect and care for myself, otherwise how can I be genuine with other people, really respect and care about them?"' Carol follows Nichiren Daishonin's Buddhism, sometimes caricatured as selfish because it encourages you to chant for what you want. 'Most important for me is not chanting for Porsches, but the inconspicuous gains: how it changes you inside, how you get more self-worth and see yourself as OK. Particularly in the young women's division, low self-esteem is one of the main problems that comes up. If I hadn't been practising, I don't know whether I would have had the strength to come out – I've always been very shy. Now I think if someone doesn't like me for it, it's their problem, not mine.'

The crucial importance of self-acceptance is not a message propagated by only the major religions. Ted is a clairvoyant. To get to talk to spirits, he says, is 'a long slow process, the main criteria being that you are happy with yourself in all respects. That takes a lot of doing, as you have to pull all those skeletons out of the cupboard and face up to them.' For Ted this meant 'being happy being gay'. For most of his adult life he avoided religion because of its attitudes towards his sexual orientation. It was in his fifties that he first attended a clairvoyant evening. 'The fact that I was gay had to be addressed at some time. So, in a meditation I told a spirit I was gay. There were no bad reactions whatsoever. It was only me that had those doubts.' New Age paths place great emphasis on 'loving yourself', sometimes to the extent of claiming this is the only thing necessary for happiness and success. 'You have to accept yourself unconditionally,' says Rupi who follows Louise Hay's methods. 'I always used to feel I wasn't good enough. One of the ways to build your self-esteem is to say affirmations. I find them very strong and very useful. She says your subconscious is always listening, so if you're saying your affirmations, they will become true. One of my favourites is "I am loved, loving and loveable". The first few times you giggle, but when you mean it, it creates very strong emotions. The first time I did it properly with the mirror I broke down. Its purpose is to make you feel more self-aware, more self-confident, more centred and whole – and it has succeeded for me, I feel more relaxed and safe, and it has removed a lot of the tension I felt around sexual orientation – similarly with race.' Rupi began by saying affirmations hundreds of times a day, as Louise suggested; he now does them at the gym, on a running machine. 'I say them internally. I'm not shouting "I approve of myself"; they'd probably section me.'

'When you can say "I'm OK as I am", that's when the real inner bliss begins to come,' claims another New-Ager, Adam James. He found that this internal acceptance affected his external appearance. 'I'd done drag in the past, which at the time was very exciting: but even with that, you get to the point where you're only happy when you're done up and getting the adulation. Drag queens are lovely people but they tend to want a hell of a lot of attention, they're saying "look at me, aren't I beautiful?" When I realized that's what I was doing, I thought, my God, do I have to dress up in lipstick and wigs – magnificent though they were – do I have to do this to be loved? Away they went in the drawer: I'm good enough as I am.' Adam had also experimented with S/M; but again 'my aim in life was to be content as myself – not to have to dress up this way or that. I'd found I felt very good in leather but not so good out of it – that began to ring alarm bells.' Adam does not see sadomasochism and a spiritual life as incompatible 'so long as it's done from inner comfort and love, rather than an inner need to dominate someone or be dominated. If it's a game, that's fine, many people play a game sexually. But if it's a *need* to be dragged round a club on your knees and act like a dog, I think one has to question, am I really hating myself and wanting to be treated like dirt?' Adam felt he had to confront his own levels of self-hatred if he was to be effective as a complementary therapist, his current occupation. As fellow New Age healer Pam Mears puts it, 'all healing is about self-healing – the more whole you are, the better you are for someone else.'

MAKING WHOLE

Father Bernard Lynch is convinced he could not have survived seeing so many hundreds of people die, nor the accusations that were made against him, without 'a belief that somehow out of this dirt good could, should, would be made. One can only be oneself in God – by in God, I mean in the safety of an environment that is predisposed to life as good. Without that basic trust – that attitude that life not death has the last word, that time is on the side of love, or as Julian of Norwich would have it that "all shall be well and all manner of things shall be well" – without that I don't believe that we can go forward in our search for freedom, which is why I would submit that secular humanism has failed.' Bernard is talking about faith: about trust in something greater than himself. To have this trust is not to deny the reality of suffering. Faith is, however, a commitment to looking for what good can be born from that reality. 'I am courting something that is totally beyond me, and absolutely incomprehensible, incalculable and inestimable; but a positive force; the force of life.'

Different traditions have developed various techniques in their attempts to access the power of this positive force of life. Prayer can be one. 'I have always prayed, reflected, listened with joy to sacred music in the presence of God,' says Bernard. 'I have done this not from any sense of duty or obligation, but out of that inner space in me that sought to be in touch with the mystery of life. The real purpose of my prayer was that through it I came to understand the questions I was asking of God; I learned to live with my lack of answers, always receiving a greater sense of my centredness.'[9] The Reverend Jean White also draws strength from prayer. 'Without prayer I don't know where I'd be. Prayer for me is communication; being in contact with that spiritual energy outside of yourself. God is a good therapist – a wise counsellor, that's what the Bible says. Prayer is the lifeline that opens me up to that supreme power. Some people would say they open up their chakras – it's all the same. When you're caring for a lot of people you can get drained: the spiritual energy that God gives to me enables me to go on when sometimes I don't feel like it, or I think "I've had enough of all these men dying, I don't want to know any more". When I'm at my lowest and can't, something else can, and does. God takes over. The situation hasn't changed, but I have gained strength to go on.'

Other traditions have other techniques. Buddhism, Paganism, occultism and various New Age philosophies use visualization meditations (which are also widely used by people who would not wish to identify as spiritual, and see them simply as complementary therapies). Chris Ferguson describes one, known in Tibetan Buddhism as the *tonglen* practice: 'you breathe in negativity, and breathe out positive emotions and feelings. You visualize smoke going in and light going out; and inside you, a wish-fulfilling jewel, which transforms this black gunk you're breathing in.' You visualize various people who this will help: yourself, friends, people you find problematic – 'you can go through the whole universe!' While Chris concedes it sounds unlikely, 'I've found it very helpful to deal with difficult situations, and when friends are ill'.

Pam Mears is a professional aromatherapist, and healer, who uses crystals and works with the chakras. 'You're getting rid of blockages in their aura – the energy field that surrounds you.' While her understanding of how this works is obviously linked to her New Age beliefs, she is adamant that to heal 'you don't have to have a faith'. Her teacher was a Christian, 'but she believed everybody could heal – it's tapping into the energy that's already there, all around us. If you want to do it, you *can* do it.' Steve Graham draws on Christianity as well as spiritualism and esoteric traditions in his healing and massage work; he uses essential oils and Bach flower remedies as well. He works as a healer because 'it's difficult out there. We all need help in this world. Mary Magdalene massaged Jesus. He needed comfort. Sometimes we think we can do it alone; I don't think we can.'

Steve makes the point that we heal each other. Some people may be able to draw strength from a transcendent source; but this strength is of use only when shared with other people. 'It is the mystery of *our shared pain* that releases the mutuality of our compassion,' says Father Bill, who describes one consequence of AIDS as being 'an epidemic of compassionate empathy, a reaching out to others by those infected and affected, with hope and a non-judgemental acceptance of each other'. Compassion, literally 'to suffer together', emphasizes equality of relationship – something same-sex couples sometimes find easier than heterosexuals. Suffering together is what defines an oppressed minority. Compassion acknowledges that everybody hurts, instead of dividing people into the sinners who have problems, and the pious who have the answers. 'A lot of traditional models of ministry are actually very abusive; they start from, "You're needy, and I come with power, I can lift you up",' argues Michael Seán Paterson. The name of the organization he works for – CARA – is an acronym for Care and Resources for people affected by AIDS and HIV, but is also the Gaelic word for 'friendship', a crucial quality in its work. CARA's motto is an aboriginal saying: '"If you've come to help me, then you're wasting your time. But if you've come because your liberation is bound up with mine, then we can walk together." At the heart of this work is relationship.' As Father Bill reiterates, 'In the brokenness of our wounds we are profoundly and indissolubly interconnected.'

'This is what Jesus said it was all about: being broken and being made whole,' says the Reverend Jean White. 'It's a wonderful thing to watch people who have perhaps been very broken receive Communion and go back in strength thinking I'm accepted, I'm part of a whole; I'm not just a little fragment.' Being made whole, and being made to feel part of the whole: whether the Christian finds this in the Eucharist, or the Buddhist through meditation, or the New-Ager through oils and crystals, this is the healing that spirituality aspires to. 'It is holy work, making people whole,' Rabbi

Lionel Blue said when he addressed the Lesbian and Gay Christian Movement; as Jim Cotter, among others, has pointed out, *whole, holy*, and *heal* all have the same linguistic root – suggesting that, ultimately, they refer to the same thing, and we should aspire to a state of well-being.

Religion needs queer people if it is to see the whole picture, to understand the whole story. Many lesbian, gay and bisexual people have been integrating their sexuality and spirituality, bringing the pieces together into a more coherent whole. All of this is an extension of an impulse which is fundamental to being queer: to come out. We refuse to keep important parts of our lives hidden, and insist on telling the truth – the whole truth, the holy truth – about who we are, about life as we see it, and how we want to live it. We do this even though others may not want to hear. We become more integrated when we come out – we don't split the secret self from the public persona – and, so, we become more whole. When we come out we find others who have had the same experiences and want the same things; there is scope for compassion.

If we are to keep becoming more whole – and so to keep healing, and to be more holy – we must tell the truth about our pain as well as our pleasure. In the words of Nagaraja, 'you've got to bring more than your sexuality out of the closet.'

Notes

1. Cf. Dominic Davies and Charles Neal (eds), *Pink Therapy: A Guide for Counsellors and Therapists Working with Lesbian, Gay and Bisexual Clients* (Buckingham: Open University Press, 1996); chapter 11, 'Alcohol and Substance Misuse'.

2. Lionel Blue and Jonathan Magonet, *How To Get Up When Life Gets You Down* (London: HarperCollins, 1992), p. 127.

3. Blue and Magonet, *How To Get Up*, p. 74.

4. This comment was taken from an interview with Bill in Mary Loudon's excellent *Revelations – The Clergy Question* (London: Hamish Hamilton, 1994), pp. 341–2.

5. The negative power of religion around these issues is, of course, considerable. The absence of discussion of it from this book is not an underestimation of its destructive effects on my part. Both Michael Seán Paterson and Bernard Lynch pointed out to me that religion has made it considerably harder for many people with HIV and AIDS to live with their illness – and to face death.

6. Bill explores this idea in more detail in *AIDS Sharing the Pain: A Guide for Carers* (London: Darton, Longman & Todd, 1993).

7. The details of this sensational trial – including the judge's furious berating of the prosecution for bringing the case – can be found in Bernard's compelling book, *A Priest on Trial* (London: Bloomsbury, 1993).

8. Blue and Magonet, *How To Get Up*, p. 102.

9. Lynch, *A Priest on Trial*, p. 62.

Mortality

*One of the most striking things being with people
dying is the difference when . . . whatever it is . . .
leaves them. The life goes out of people. It's
radical. They may be warm, their eyes may be
open, they may still hold your hand, but they're
not there any more. I suppose since the beginning
of time people have asked, what has happened?*

(Bernard Lynch)

Father Bernard Lynch has been with hundreds of people as they died. Such work has always been part of a priest's job; as an openly gay priest in New York, when AIDS began to claim so many lives during the early and mid 1980s, Bernard was 'pitched into a continuous encounter with death'. Other lesbian and gay clergy tell similar stories from those grim years. The Reverend Jean White from MCC in London was burying 'as many as fourteen gay men in a week; in those days undertakers wouldn't touch them, and I'd lay people on dining tables and triple bag their bodies because nobody else would do it.'

Religion has always been associated with death: the ultimate cross-cultural phenomenon for human beings, a truly universal experience, and one of the defining facts of our existence. Spiritual traditions inevitably reflect its importance in creating our 'sense of being'. Many people look to religion to help them cope with death (their own, or the consequences of other people dying), and have an expectation that religion might know whether there is anything after their current existence. Many religions control their followers by exploiting their fear of death, and by holding out fantastic visions of future reward that can be collected in the next life.

The pattern that I have suggested in previous chapters holds true for the ways in which lesbian, gay and bisexual people think about the spiritual implications of mortality. Queer people are not religious through fear; they turn to spiritual traditions in order to confront rather than escape the

185

realities of existence. Before he came out, Peter Ashby-Saracen had a fearful attitude to mortality, and an immature understanding of religion. 'While I drifted in and out of evangelical Christianity I was obsessed with death; it's "finality", its uncertain route (up there or down below), the feeling that you had to constantly be on your best behaviour because if you weren't you'd blow your chance in Eternity, and the whole taboo nature of death.' After coming out, and discovering Nichiren Daishonin's Buddhism with its emphasis on the practice serving the individual rather than the individual serving the religion, 'death has become a thing I can talk about and contemplate without icy fingers clutching my heart; it's become more of a staging post or a doorway than a cul-de-sac'. He talks of 'a growing ability within me to allow the past and the future to look after themselves, and to live in the present, and delight in the wonders of the moment'.

Peter refers to the taboo around death. Queer people know, from their experience of the taboo around sexuality, that to censor the expression of feelings is damaging, and that the desire to do so is usually rooted in fear. This seems as true of necrophobia as it is of homophobia; the unique revulsion with which AIDS can be greeted is often attributed to its violation of both taboos. Queer people have an obvious incentive to break the taboo around sexuality; the gay ex-Jesuit John McNeill suggests that we likewise have an incentive to challenge the taboo around death. Lesbian and gay people cannot take 'the normal escapes from mortality – disembodiment and procreation'.[1] Most queers do not chase perpetuity through children; and, as chapter 4 argued, we are more aware than many heterosexuals of the importance of the body – which should lead to an awareness of its limitations and inevitable decay. 'Our fear of death,' McNeill argues, 'should be understood not primarily as a need for an indefinite future' – a need which heterosexuals attempt to meet by producing children and disconnecting from their bodies – 'but as a need to live fully in the present moment.'[2] (This is exactly the shift that Peter Ashby-Saracen described in his life.) McNeill asserts that 'it is the reality of death that gives every moment of our lives a meaning and urgency that are essential to the quality of human life.'[3]

In denying death we deny life, whereas by accepting it we can live more fully. This paradox is present in the statement that used to puzzle Chris Ferguson: 'I heard people who are HIV-positive say, it's the best thing that ever happened to me. Since I've had my own diagnosis, I can understand much better what they mean.' Chris doesn't deny the horror of losing friends, or the physical pain. However, 'it puts a lot of things into perspective; you question what the important things in your life are. There was this assumption that I would always be here, no problem; I'm going to die, but not yet. Since my diagnosis, a couple of times I've fallen asleep and suddenly realized: I'm just not going to exist any more.' 'An awareness of death is central to the spiritual life,' argues another Buddhist, Maitreyabandhu. 'The founder of the Friends of the Western Buddhist Order has said that Buddhism can ultimately be reduced to one word: impermanence. The Buddhist becomes more and more aware of impermanence. The most extreme impermanence being that you will die. What are you going to do with that? Are you going to try to be really alive?'

This is not a perspective unique to Buddhism. 'I have always believed that dying is the ultimate spiritual experience – a constant activity at the very centre of life,' says Father Bill, another priest who has been working in the midst of the HIV pandemic since it's beginning. 'I have had the humbling privilege to be alongside many as they were making their transition into the mystery labelled death. The confrontation with one's own mortality can create an awareness and perception of another dimension, as we prepare to move into the greater, unknown future; and this awareness can inspire and enrich one's spiritual journey. While the mystery prepares us for the other world, it does not make us other-worldly; it prepares the pathway for us away from the superficial in our lives, and, at the same time, releases us into greater awareness of how our lives are being nurtured.'

Bill calls death 'the journey that we are all born to travel, hopefully in the presence of significant others'. No one can get out of making the journey – if you're alive, you've got to die – but spiritual traditions can offer some support on the way. Bernard Lynch regards death as 'the most powerless of all human conditions. I can understand medieval monasticism having such an apparent over-emphasis on preparation for death. Unfortunately in present times there is no preparation for death; and one would question then, what preparation is there for life? I don't mean that philosophically. I don't think one can have one's joy until one has faced death. It's the yin and the yang again, the thorn in the rose. And very often people who are the most Churched are the most ill-prepared; the whole Church culture militates against it.' This is true not just of religious culture; as Dr Elizabeth Stuart observes, 'discussion of death and dying in everyday life is discouraged and labelled as "morbid", and when death occurs everything is done to sanitise it and remove it from view.'[4]

One consequence of AIDS is that this is much less true for many gay men, and the many lesbians who have cared alongside them, than it is of the broader culture. The countless candlelight vigils and memorial events have kept death – at least from HIV – in the forefront of our consciousness, and many queer people have been fighting 'to bridge the gap between what's going on in our lives and what's going on in our deaths' (in Bernard's words). 'Queer people are talking about things that the Church used to talk about but doesn't any more: dying, death, afterlife, and resurrection', says Elizabeth Stuart. 'If I'm teaching my students about the theology of the after life, I show them a video of a group of men living with AIDS discussing these issues. I also play them the Pet Shop Boys' version of *Go West*: and show them the final scenes of the film *Longtime Companion*, which contains (to my mind) one of the most vivid modern resurrection scenes. When did you last hear the Church talk about resurrection? They are too busy talking about us, so we have been left to do theology for ourselves (often totally unconsciously) in the midst of the horror of AIDS.'

Evangelical Christian Michael Vasey thinks that 'gay skills in art, in celebration, and in the voicing of anger, love and pain mean that the gay movement is well placed to play some part in articulating death's new voice' – a voice that isn't stifled by embarrassment and fear.[5] David Randall, the priest who founded CARA as a Christian response to AIDS (and who died in 1996), wrote that 'for many people living with AIDS, death is now natural – it happens all the time, and we are deeply involved in it. As a dear friend of mine put it, we walk through the valley of the shadow of death as the person with AIDS points out the scenery.' This raises questions for all of us: 'How do we go on living, and going for life, with our health often deteriorating, and our friends dying? How do we celebrate our living, and go on being realistic about death?'

LIVING WITH DYING

'It's almost like in the darkness, that's when the light shines the brightest,' says the Reverend Diana Reynolds, of her experience with people who are dying. Accepting death, she says, can bring strength to those who survive, as well as those who die. 'There's something about approaching death that puts a kind of dignity into people. I know that's hard to understand – you see a skeletal body on the bed, that may be covered in sores or writhing in pain, how can there be any dignity in that? But it's when the body is so broken that you really see the soul, and the wholeness of that. That gives hope to other people, because it then helps them to recognize that there's something within themselves. That's not to deny pain; but there is something that transcends the pain. Being with a dying person can sometimes be like holding a mirror up to yourself: you actually see so much more about you, it makes you think about what really matters to you and examine your quality of life. It's in doing that that you then have hope of new growth.' Whether the dying is our own or other people's, queers who follow spiritual traditions claim that, in the words of one Buddhist, 'death gives an edge to life'. Or, as Tantric practitioner Amneon puts it, 'death is driving people to become more conscious. In a way, AIDS is part of the spiritual evolution of the gay community.'

'As a Pagan living with HIV, I try to make every second the best I could have – so my life is more fulfilled and I'm more spiritually aware.' Jason Oliver is in his mid-twenties. 'I try to turn everything negative into something positive. I think my life's more focused now on what I have to do. I think I've come to terms with my death earlier because I am HIV-positive. My spirituality helped me do that – knowing that when I die it isn't the end at all. I try to get on with living rather than worrying about dying all the time.' As Jason makes clear, people's spiritual beliefs help them confront mortality, giving a support and context that can otherwise be lacking. 'Very few of us are so assured in our practice or beliefs that we're not scared of death,' admits Chris Ferguson. 'But hopefully my practice and beliefs make me more able to face it. I know people who are positive who are quite threatened by it, because they don't have a belief system; they've never questioned things before, and they have nothing to support them.'

When Robert Crossman received his cancer diagnosis, he was told he could have six weeks to live. He lived for nearly three years longer. Before he died, he told me that 'being a Quaker has helped me face the fear of dying, and express it.' This is in spite of the fact that Quakerism, being non-credal, gives no doctrinal reassurance about an afterlife; for Robert, it was 'about trying to live a good life now, and recognizing that we are one with another.' Father Bill has observed that, at some stage in terminal illness, many patients reach some sort of acceptance, and 'then something takes over, something inside that is helping them through – and I would say that's their emerging spirituality.' For Robert this 'something' was very palpable. 'It wasn't till Christmas day I realized how ill I was. That night I had an out-of-body experience: it was like I was looking down on myself. I saw a lot of the episodes of my life and I realized the pain that had been there, but also the great joy and the achievement that had come with that pain. And that was the first occasion when I encountered my personal angel, who has stayed with me all the way through this, and has actually stepped in at times and taken over when it's been too hard for me. There's this golden light that comes from it and fires me up. I think it's a spirit that has decided to come and be my companion whilst I've been going through this very difficult time, so I knew I wasn't doing it all on my own – the rest of my life up till that point felt like a very tough struggle. I don't struggle any more. Things happen and I come through them. Perhaps it's my unconscious self looking after me, now I realize that I can care for myself. But it certainly feels like an angel.'

'Being assured spiritually that I have a life that is acceptable to God is one thing that takes the fear of death away,' says Jean White. 'That doesn't take the fear of the process of dying away – nobody wants pain – but it gives me inner strength.' A few years ago, Jean was treated for breast cancer with chemotherapy, and was frightened that she would die. 'There came an inner peace within me that said, it's OK, because *you* are not going to die, although your body might go.' As Elizabeth Stuart points out, 'Christianity should be able to help here, holding up as it does a God who experienced what it means to be human and who has known the terror of death, the despair of grief and the feelings of apparent meaninglessness that death induces. Christianity also offers the hope that death is not the last word, that beyond death is the possibility of new life, new relationship, new being – a foretaste of which can be experienced in this life, if we let go of the fear of chaos, lack of control and meaninglessness which underlies our fear of death.'[6]

'We let go into the mystery beyond our comprehension,' is how Father Bill describes dying. For Bernard Lynch too, dying is 'the ultimate letting go'; but he sees accepting a lack of control as fundamental in living as well. 'I think if one has learned to let go as one goes through one's life – in all of our experiences, including the sexual – then the letting go at death is easier. Every time I've lost myself in life I have become more – who is to say that when I lose myself in death I may not become more? We're learning that in love all the time I think; one's heart is broken, in order that it may become more.' Harold Rurlander suggests that coming out marks a death: the death of a false identity. We let go of trying to live the life that others expect, and find something better. Harold is confident that, having gained so much from letting go of heterosexual conditioning, his physical death will be a similar liberation: another 'pivotal trigger to a new state'. His vision of life after coming out – and life after death – is of moving from 'a world of darkness and thick fog' to a place pervaded by 'the most wonderful light', a light ('all the colours of the rainbow') that contains 'an all pervading sense of wonder, peace, joy, laughter, friendship, love, comfort, protection, safety and fulfilment'.

SEXUALITY AND DEATH

Bernard referred to 'letting go' in our sexual experiences as somehow a preparation for death; he likes to point out that the French call orgasm 'le petit mort', the little death. According to Amneon, various occult traditions refer to it using the same term. 'When you ejaculate,' he explains, 'you're given a taste of the ultimate orgasm, and the ultimate release: death. Before you can feel the eternal life you have to let go of your body, you have to let it die. Orgasm is the letting go of the body: you go up into the sheer feeling of the soul.' For Bernard, 'sexual orgasm (ecstasy) points to a total sharing that cannot be realized, at least in this time called life.'

Our sexuality can tell us something about our mortality, just as it gives us insights into our spirituality. These three profound aspects of human life are intimately connected. Sex has the potential for self-transcendence, which is essential to spirituality: death is the ultimate in going beyond self (whereas the sexual and spiritual are momentary glimpses of what this can be like). Sexual, spiritual and mortal longings can be experienced as a great yearning for release, for oblivion of the self. Death – like the sexual and spiritual – involves confronting the mystery of 'otherness'; it is the most altered state of consciousness we can imagine. Chief among the earliest concerns of religion, archaeological and anthropological speculation would suggest, were mortality and fertility: death and sex. The same combination can still be found today – not least in the spirituality of people living with HIV. As Jim Cotter writes, 'the hint of death in sexual orgasm' is now, with AIDS, 'shouting'.[7]

Michael Seán Paterson has found people looking for sex in a place where his religion commemorates death. After visiting a dying man in hospital, he was seeking somewhere to sit in peace. He walked a short distance to a cemetery. 'It was full of gay men – cruising among the dead, when we couldn't be more clear that some of our sex could be life-threatening, death-dealing. Maybe people living with the virus, maybe people who'd crossed the road from one of the main HIV clinics. The only place to have sex there, because they've cut all the bushes down, is where the graves are at their closest, you actually have to be between two tombstones. What does this say about our spirituality? I wonder if for some of us, because we're gay, and because we're sexual, death is so familiar that we don't even run away from the grave. Are we saying it doesn't matter? Or are we defeating it: are we saying fuck off death? One or two of the graves are covered in spunk, caked in it. Semen, the life force, entering into the death space. That really brought together what I call the trinity of AIDS – Sex, Death, and God.'

AFTER DEATH, FOR THOSE WHO LIVE

Religion has traditionally been involved in the practicalities of death; burial, mourning, commemoration. How necessary these are when a loved one dies can be measured by the distress caused to gay and lesbian people when religions exclude them from these rituals: when the family prevents lesbian or gay partners and friends from attending the funeral, or when the priest prays for forgiveness for the deceased's sexual 'sins'. The Sisters of Perpetual Indulgence have held 'funerals after funerals, ceremonies over burial plots, because they've been buried in a completely fake ritual. We gather together the friends to say goodbye properly, and have the true ritual. The heterosexualized funeral can be the most awful torture,' explains Sister Latex.

The Sisters' act here recognizes the importance of burying the whole person. In life, queer people struggle to be more of who they are – which is the spiritual quest as well. At death, good ritual strives to respect this wholeness. 'You can't put people back into the closet on their deathbed,' says MCC's Neil Thomas. 'It makes a nonsense of their lives.' Michael Seán Paterson, who for the last few years has been burying an average of six people per month who have died from AIDS-related illnesses, emphasizes that gay funerals do more than dispose of a body – 'that might account for three funerals I've done in the last few years' – and are rarely motivated by conventional religious belief (or by a superstitious fear that, at the last moment, bets ought to be hedged) – 'I have come across plenty of baptized and confirmed Christians, but have only once been asked to arrange a religious funeral.' More fundamental is 'the need for some form of communal expression, the need for ritual, the need to do publicly what we can't cope with doing privately'. Michael thinks the funerals he has led are 'a statement about: we're here and we're not going away'. This could be taken as a metaphysical idea – people die but the group goes on – but Michael is thinking in more specific terms, of sexual identity, 'moving out of the closet in a public way, at a crucial moment in somebody's existence, where the grief's up but the defences are down'.

He cites a vivid example: a funeral for a sadomasochist, where the congregation were all dressed in leather, many of them joined together by a chain through their nipple rings. The central wreath was a round of flowers with a trussed-up doll in the middle, legs spread. 'It was very *real*. It had no hint of insurance-policy funerals, where the person suddenly becomes religious just in case, and the life becomes tidied up. It was his partner and his friends doing what they'd have done if he'd have been there. It's saying as in life, so in death. It's also putting two fingers up, it's defiant, like a demo. "I'm going to go out the way I came in – I will really be myself, no compromise." Pastorally what it did was allow those people to grieve in the most natural way to them. The eulogies said how many people he had given pleasure to. They were actually saying, it's a pity he's not here to shag any more, they were naming exactly that which they will miss now he's gone, which I think is crucial for their own grief. As the officiant, I was asked to say the God word. I didn't superimpose something from outside, I took up the threads and said, "this is the reality of what I would call God, the experience of life: love, loss, pleasure, fun, play. If God ain't there, I don't know where God is." They could go with that. I don't know what they'd have done if I'd have given them assurance about the resurrection.' The reality of the deceased's death, and the experience of his life, were confronted head on, instead of dressing him up in a suit and talking about when he was a sweet little boy. Spirituality depends upon reality and experience; religion sometimes prefers to avoid both. Michael warns that at 'a lot of traditional funerals the real person is not being sent off, whether that's to the crematorium or heaven'.

Earlier it was argued that death makes us more aware of what it means to be alive; memorial services do the same. Dudley Cave is a Unitarian, and a founder member of the Lesbian and Gay Bereavement Project. He has conducted many funerals; the words he uses affirm life as well as mourning death. 'We come with grief because one we love is no longer among us. We come also in gratitude, in praise, in tribute to the life of [the deceased] . . . The need that is upon us is the need to accept both the glory and the tragedy of life, its holiness and limits. The love of the human heart is the most real and the most beautiful of all the realities we know. It is the richest gift we have . . . . Whatever the length of time may be, to have known something of this is to have experienced the supreme privilege of being human. The anguish of parting cannot destroy this most real of all realities . . . as real, as strong as anything in life. The love that was once born can never die, for it has become part of our life woven into every texture of our being.'[8]

'The funeral should be a springboard for good grief', Dudley asserts.[9] Because spiritual traditions take death so seriously, they give more priority and respect to mourning than our secular culture is able to. 'On mourning, Judaism is very realistic in insisting that people need time to grieve,' contends Rabbi Mark Solomon. 'It sets out, traditionally, a graduated mourning process with well-defined stages through which people can move without feeling rushed. Jewish mourning rituals take a lot more time than many people are prepared to take in the bustle of twentieth-century life – and with the denial of death in our culture.' The laws for mourning set down in the Talmud rely upon everyone in the community sharing the same understanding of, and respect for, death. Although the grief of the mourner is not diminished, the sense of isolation and meaninglessness is relieved: the individual isn't left to make sense of it all on their own.

The Sikh faith also brings grief out of the closet, according to Kauldip Singh. 'To be grieving in public when someone dies is very important. The grieving systems and supports that have been set up in our communities are very strong – there is a space for you to grieve, a forty-day period when nothing is required of you. The community acknowledges that you've lost someone dear.' Sikhs will gather and weep publicly. 'Because everyone else around you is crying there's no fear of crying – you've just got to get on with it.' Both Judaism and Sikhism have formalized grief – there are rules to follow, procedures to observe – which makes it less strange and unusual: grief is connected to the rest of life, and crucially, to the spiritual sources of life. It is seen as part of the spiritual journey. The Reverend Dennis

Fraser, who meets more mourners than most of us, has noticed that people who have faith cope with bereavement better than those who do not: 'that's an empirical observation'. Gay men – while largely lacking a set of common beliefs that unites them – have rediscovered something of the importance of mourning in the context of a wider community, with the candelight vigils and other rituals that have come in the wake of so many deaths from AIDS.

AFTER DEATH, FOR THOSE WHO DIE

The idea that there could be life after death is one that attracts many people to religion, to New Age thought and to all sorts of superstition as well. The unlikeliness of life after death is a common reason why atheists reject spirituality. Since this book has maintained throughout that queers are likely to reject religious orthodoxy, it should come as no surprise that on the subject of an afterlife no one is prepared to make definitive statements. 'I don't know what happens after death, that's the truth,' confesses Christian Jean White. 'I know what the scriptures say but they don't tell us exactly – they just say that we will go on, that there is life after death.' 'What happens to us at death I don't know,' admits Buddhist Chris Ferguson, although he has, like Jean, some hope: 'I genuinely feel there's much more to our existence than we're experiencing now.' Pagan Jason Oliver similarly combines frank realism with a degree of trust. 'I think it's one of the only things, as humans, we can never understand. But I think it's only your physical body that dies.'

Queer people's concern to limit what they believe to what they can measure by their experience means they are unlikely to have simplistic beliefs about the afterlife; obviously, no one can talk with the authority of experience about death. On the other hand, people's spiritual experience in this world – whether that's a feeling of oneness with the universe, or the belief that they can communicate with the spirits of the dead – may create a conviction that life continues in some form, even if they cannot speak with certainty as to what that form may be. 'I've had an experience, realized quite often in my retreats, that I do not finish when my body dies,' says Aziz. Nichiren Buddhist Robert Bristow has found that 'over the years I've been chanting, my faith in the eternity of life has become very solid and very definite'; Peter Ashby-Saracen finds in Nichiren Buddhism 'a way of looking at life that fits in with my ideas about the constancy and indestructibility of all things (they change their nature but can't be destroyed)'. Neither of them could say exactly what this will mean when they reach the point of death.

Bernard Lynch recalls being asked a question by an HIV-positive Catholic. 'He said "Bernard, do you really believe in the resurrection?", which is a very ordinary question for a Catholic student – especially one aged twenty-three, facing death – to ask of a priest theologian. I didn't know what to say. It was so clear there was going to be no nonsense here – he wasn't looking for a theological discourse or a hermeneutical exegesis of the resurrection narratives, that I could give with such eloquence. I said, "I don't know", and it hurt me to know that I didn't know because I'd never really faced the fact, I'd been brought up with this.' He retains some trust in life after death, but in very general terms: 'that from which we came is that to which we desire to return, that force of our life. The ineluctable loneliness at the heart of all human striving is to my mind not simply significant of an incurable absence, but also of a one-time presence. I believe that which is and "once was full" can be and will be filled again – in God – over the rainbow.'

Michael Seán Paterson is uncomfortable with ideas of literal resurrection. He recounts a visit to the chapel in a London hospital, after visiting someone who was facing imminent death from an AIDS-related illness. 'Normally there is this huge, incongruous, horrible fifteenth-century painting of the resurrection. That day the painting was missing. I sat down and looked at a blank wall; there were the holes where the painting hangs, and the wall behind that hadn't been repainted – so it was screaming at me, "there's nothing here". It felt so uncomfortably appropriate. I couldn't have found anything more trivial than the resurrection image at that moment – it would have been blasphemous for me to have identified with that. It captures the dilemma I have if I am asked to give a funeral by a Christian believer – what can I say that doesn't trivialize the reality?'[10] MCC minister Neil Thomas does talk about heaven at funerals. 'To *me* heaven is in the presence of God – the people I love and have loved will be there with me'; but at funerals he emphasizes that 'heaven is whatever *you* can imagine it to be. You can't force images on people. That's a barrier to God, to spirituality, and the barriers are already up.'

It would be wrong to suggest that, beyond a commitment to open-mindedness, there is any consensus among queer people about life after death – or that there is much consensus among different faiths – or that sexual orientation makes any difference to what position people arrive at. Spiritual traditions can be helpful in addressing the issue; and, whatever theory you subscribe to, there's no reason to think that you are excluded on the grounds of your sexual orientation. Both heaven and reincarnation seem to operate a policy of equal opportunities.

And while for some queer people life beyond this life is central to spirituality, for others it is not of much interest. Niall Johnston says: 'My spiritual beliefs mean that, for me, death is largely irrelevant.' Fellow-priest Diana Reynolds agrees: 'I don't think you have to believe in life after death to be a Christian. I would never say that it doesn't exist, because I don't know; but I think eternal life is much more about quality. When we lose somebody they're always with us. I think about friends I've lost over the years; what really matters is they are still inside me. That's where, for me, they live on, and where their lives make a difference. Maybe they are in a heaven somewhere – I don't know. I don't need to believe that.'

Johnathon Andrew feels that, for a time, his belief in an afterlife actually impeded his spirituality. Two-and-a-half years ago he was given just forty-eight hours to live. 'I didn't die, but I totally lost my faith. I think that the faith I then had needed to be destroyed. I was defining my faith by a belief in the afterlife, I was totally dependent on it – I'd read all these New Age books about rushing down tunnels or coming back as a seagull. We've all had dark little thoughts and held them down, then one day when we're not feeling very strong, up it comes, there's no escaping it any more. Lying in hospital, my dark little thought was: "All this mystical spooky stuff is bunkum. Because they can't cope with the darkness, the abyss, they've invented this astonishing fairy tale – it's crap." With that my whole faith imploded. I couldn't say my prayers, I couldn't perform any of the ritualistic stuff. I came to the conclusion that there was probably no afterlife, and I really wasn't sure about God. At one point I turned round to a friend and said, if there's no God, then the only thing that there is is Love. That's all there is. I stayed with that.' Gradually some faith returned: 'but it's changed totally; it's basically a complete belief in God rather than in the afterlife. The afterlife is none of my bloody business. When the time comes, I will go across. I hope that it might be something better, but the best I can do is hope – I'm allowed no proof. I trust totally, implicitly in this being, this other, the whatever. It is the thing that will receive me when I die.'

Whatever view they take on a life to come, queer believers are agreed that it cannot be used as an excuse to avoid life in the present. 'The only thing you can work on is your own mind at the moment,' says Chris Ferguson. 'I don't think spirituality is all about death. That's a very negative approach. It's about life, and death is part of life.' Or as a gay man training for the Anglican priesthood put it to me: 'Eternity is now. We don't have to wait to die.'

Notes

1. John J. McNeill, *Taking a Chance on God: Liberating Theology for Gays, Lesbians and Their Lovers, Families and Friends* (Boston: Beacon Press, 1988), p. 156.
2. McNeill, *Taking a Chance on God,* p. 152.
3. McNeill, *Taking a Chance on God,* p. 151.
4. Dr Elizabeth Stuart, *Daring to Speak Love's Name: A Gay and Lesbian Prayer Book* (London: Hamish Hamilton, 1992), p. 128.
5. Michael Vasey, *Strangers and Friends: A New Exploration of Homosexuality and the Bible* (London: Hodder & Stoughton, 1995), p. 243.
6. McNeill, *Taking a Chance on God,* p. 128.
7. From Jim Cotter's poem 'Letting Go in Love and Death', included in Sebastian Sandys (ed.), *Embracing the Mystery: Prayerful Responses to AIDS* (London: SPCK, 1992).
8. Stuart, *Daring to Speak Love's Name,* pp. 131–2.
9. Stuart, *Daring to Speak Love's Name,* p. 143.
10. Michael reflects more full on this and other issues he has touched upon here in his book *Singing For Our Lives: Positively Gay and Christian* (Sheffield: Cairns Publications, 1997).

Politics

For all that has been said in defence of spirituality, the suspicion may remain that it is fundamentally escapist – a distraction from the real issues, a luxury that we cannot afford while we're fighting the political battle for our lives. While the political activist might agree with the believer that life is a serious matter, and there's more to being queer than a 'lifestyle', they disagree about what that 'more' is. How will 'spiritual' navel-gazing win equal rights for our queer sisters and brothers?

Arguments like these depend on a false opposition. There is no reason why a sense of spirituality should make you any less politically active than a non-believer: on the contrary, there may be reasons why it makes you more radical. Moreover, taking political action does not require the condemnation of spirituality: real political commitment can actually lead people to think spirituality is a necessity.

SPIRITUALITY DEMANDS POLITICAL ACTION

'I'm not willing to let spirituality be my private domain,' says Michael Seán Paterson. 'It's beyond self – it's to do with how we relate to each other. It's a societal issue.' Spirituality, as a number of people in this book have said, is about our relatedness and relationships: so is politics. In so far as politics is about how we live and what we live for, as opposed to simply how we effect change, then there is significant common ground. 'Politics and spirituality are not separate, they can go hand in hand – they're different faces of the same thing, like Janus the two-faced god,' argues Roberta Wedge, a feminist as well as a Pagan. 'Spiritual practice is sneered on by some as a hobby – but if it helps me ground and centre and be real, and go out into the world better equipped to face it, then that in itself is political. I don't want to see spirituality as a running away from things, or a sense that things will be better in the afterlife or the next incarnation; I want to see it as a way of giving me more strength, and access to my power to do what I know is right – which is not always easy. I have to be in touch with the better side of myself before I can go forward.'

Queer spirituality distrusts external claims to authority, if they clash with the inner truth of our experience. Having come to this understanding of where real power lies, we are more likely, not less, to challenge whoever tries to deny our hard-won sense of self. 'Quakerism drives us to inner mysticism, but also to practical action,' says Peter Wyles. 'The inner light also, somehow, makes us more outwardly concerned. Is the purpose of religion to console, or to challenge? to be easy or to encourage a moral life? It has to be more than simply an hour feeling restful in some public building – you can get that in an art gallery.' Being a Quaker challenges Peter 'not by finger wagging and strict rules, but by forcing me to examine my life honestly and reach my own conclusions'.

Far from being an alternative to political action, a sense of spirituality can mean that there is no alternative but to act politically. It makes the Reverend Diana Reynolds aware of her responsibility: 'It's all very well to see injustice and say, dear God please help this situation get better. But it doesn't work like that. It's us that has to make it better: God only works through people. As long as I have been a fighter within the Church, my motivation has always come from my prayer life, which is why, I think, I am a contemplative. We can only hear what God's calling us to do, to challenge and to change, if we actually take the time to listen. You look around you, you see the injustice, you sit in silence and you reflect on it, and you know what you have to do.'

Spiritual practice – whether prayer or meditation – may motivate political action. Scripture and other religious texts may also be a source of inspiration. The Torah includes the commandment 'You shall surely pursue Justice'. 'That understanding of God as a God of Justice is very primary, to me that's unquestionable,' says Rabbi Sheila Shulman. 'In the traditional texts, the objects of said justice and righteousness were the stranger, the orphan, the widow – the Other – and if we're not the Other, I don't know who is. Even before I was engaged with Judaism religiously, what I knew about being a Jew was that you were against oppression of any description. The most central chunk of our narrative is slavery and the exodus – it says everywhere in the service, remember you were a slave. The only way I can read that is: you know about it, so you know nobody else should be ever. Whatever form slavery takes, it is an outrage, a blight on creation. We are utterly, absolutely justified in struggling against it.' Jews are also supposed to work towards *tikkun olam*, 'which means "mending the world". There's a mystical cosmological dimension of that, but there's also a very practical dimension: the world is not perfect – it is not finished, in a way. It is our responsibility, in partnership with God, to work towards that. That's why we have to seek justice – creation is by no means sorted out yet.'

'It gives you that sense of your task and what to strive towards,' says Rabbi Elizabeth Sarah, who like Sheila Shulman, was involved in radical politics long before she trained for the rabbinate. 'There's a phrase in the Mishnah, the first code of law: it's not our task to complete the work, but neither may we desist from it. The work is continuing – the prophetic vision, of a future world where swords are beaten into ploughshares, is a future that you've got continually to work for. You never really arrive. That doesn't mean you don't do it. The critical lesson is rooted in another rabbinic saying: every individual action matters, each individual action for good tips the scales in the direction for good – and the bad does the same for evil. It gives you a sense that you have potential to change things: it's not predetermined.' The story of the people of Israel, and the Jewish religion, is of a continual struggle for freedom against oppression. Thus Rabbi Mark Solomon interprets the festival of Chanukah as 'a celebration of the rights of minorities to be themselves'. It commemorates a successful Jewish revolt in 160 BCE against the Greeks, who were trying to make the Jews conform to their customs and beliefs. At the darkest time of the year, eight candles are lit, one a night. 'In the darkness of prejudice, it takes one person to make a start; after a while, others join in. We think we're all alone – gradually we discover more and more people who are like us. If we all shine together we can create a much greater light.'

Father Bernard Lynch has been campaigning ever since he was ordained, twenty-five years ago: for peace in his native Ireland, against racial discrimination in Zambia (where his Church first posted him) and for the civil rights of lesbians, gays and people living with AIDS in New York, and now Britain. 'Anything that leads to the freedom of people is profoundly spiritual work and has to be. I took the Gospel serious. The hallmark of Christian faith is "love one another", and "as often as you do it to the least of these, you do it to me". For the Christian the personal is political: there are no two ways about it. I do whatever I do for my queer brothers and sisters because I believe not in the Church, or religion, but in the Christ – God – in all of us. We follow a man who spared no price and counted no cost for the sake of the freedom and liberation of his people.'

'Jesus was an astonishing radical,' agrees Johnathon Andrew. 'The guy didn't get done in for being nice to little old ladies.' Dennis Fraser, a Scottish minister, explains how Jesus is a model of political action for many Christians: 'Christ was a campaigner and a political animal, who fought for the rights of those who society at that time marginalized, and showed compassion to many folk on the fringes who had no power, and no voice – that's what I perceive happening in the Gospel. The Gospel contains the powerful imperatives to love, forgive, act with justice, and to welcome and embrace the outcast.' The resurrection is reassurance that 'ultimately, what Christ stood for and fought for was not beaten. There is some solace there for what we try to do in terms of rights, equality and combating prejudice – it's a battle worth fighting. At the end of the day we're going to win.'

'We can't as individuals be happy without everyone else being happy,' asserts Robert Bristow, who belongs to Sokka Gakkai International – which describes itself as 'the Buddhist Society for the Creation of Value through Peace, Education, and Culture'. To work for a society in which everyone can be happy, or for peace, is a political objective. Buddhists are sometimes portrayed as passive and self-obsessed. But Fernando Guasch, for many years a campaigner with the direct action group OutRage!, contends that 'whatever Buddhism might be, it's not about suffering fools gladly. I understand spirituality is fundamentally about human beings, and their pain. And for me that's political, it means you have a duty. If you encounter homophobia, you don't hurt the person, but you let them know what they're saying is ignorant and dangerous.' Catherine Hopper notes that 'the paintings of the Bodhisattva Manjusri show a great archetypal being slashing a flaming sword through ignorance and delusion. He expresses wrath in pursuit of the good', although she stresses it is 'a wrath rooted in wisdom, compassion and awareness, not anger and hatred. Bodhisattvas speak firmly, but always kindly, in terms appropriate to the listener.'

SPIRITUALITY, POLITICS AND RELIGION

A real sense of spirituality doesn't force you to be a collaborator with the enemy: instead it may bring you into political conflict with religion. When Fernando Guasch was involved in OutRage!, he invaded Westminster Cathedral on several occasions, to protest against the harm caused by the Catholic stance on homosexuality. 'People were going through something I knew consisted of a set of very lofty ideals – words like "love", "compassion", "kindness", "community", "fellow man" were going to be bandied about, like every Sunday for the last two thousand years. We surrounded the altar, stood there with placards, and delivered a sermon, which said we are human beings too. We suggested the congregation watch out for potential hypocrisy, and question how the Vatican can say love your fellow human being, while at the same time sending queer people to an inner hell. Some people shook hands with us and told us what we were doing was important and moving. Some people cried – we had disrupted the Sunday mass. I'm prepared to see that as part of the complication of politics, of what it is to be human – sometimes, if you dare speak the truth, you do things that clash with other people's interests.' The action generated much debate among Catholics, and Fernando hopes it demonstrated solidarity with closeted people within the Church. 'But even if it hadn't, for me personally, it was spiritual. I felt I was perfectly justified to problematize their faith at that moment where their emotions would be soaring up into the heights of a perfect world.' He does not think anyone should insult another person's faith, but he does think he has the right to confront it with the reality of queer people's experience, 'especially if that faith persists in trying to make people feel less than human'.

OutRage!'s action had a precedent in the religion they were protesting against. 'The charges of blasphemy, sacred contempt and sacrilege were also levelled at Jesus for his "Stop the Temple" disturbance . . . he violated sacred space just prior to a religious festival', according to Robert Goss, a former Jesuit priest in America who now takes part in zaps against churches. Jesus's destruction of the temple (Mark 14:53–65) is 'a staged political action that challenged social practices controlled by the Temple aristocracy and manipulated to their own financial and political advantage . . . Ecclesial tradition has domesticated the Jesus tradition; it spiritualizes the dangerous elements of the Jesus narrative to legitimize its own social practices . . . ACT UP and Queer Nation are more faithful to the gospel of justice than most churches . . . Often [queer] irreverence for sacred space manifests a deeper reverence for God's justice.'[1]

'Jesus taught us to pray for the Realm of God to be manifest "on earth as it is in heaven",' wrote another American gay priest who became an angry radical, Robert Williams. 'The Christian response [to the world] is to feel dissatisfied with the reality precisely because we have a vision of how it could be, should be, in the realm of God. The Christian stance toward the world is to confront the evil and imperfection, and to live our lives as though the Realm of God had in fact come on earth.'[2] 'The love of God is something to be expressed and experienced in the here and now, not in some never never land,' asserts Father Bernard Lynch. 'In a Christology that teaches the first shall be last and the last first, it is imperative for any queen worthy of the name to be out – and out there – for his/her people.' Bernard's participation in successful political campaigns in New York make him impatient with British queer politics, and campaigns for change within Britain's religious institutions. 'I believe we are backward politically because we have not owned our spiritualities. From a Christian perspective, identifying with the queer Christ can and does empower us to go after our freedoms under the law, even though, like him, we may be crucified. It is no accident that some of the most effective and successful political leadership in New York came from queer Catholics. Women and men disillusioned with Church politics, and feeling betrayed by Church leadership, took back the gospel and made it their own for the liberation of their people. These people – not unlike Martin Luther King and Gandhi – were unquestionably and unequivocally empowered by drinking from their own wells of deepened spiritual awareness, resulting in heightened consciousness of the truth of their religious traditions. The consequence was a truth that set us free.'

In these examples the boundaries between the political, the spiritual and the religious become blurred. Fernando is aware that his political zeal could be seen as some sort of replacement for the Catholic faith of his youth, 'in the sense that OutRage! at least gave you the feeling of some larger scheme, that was worthwhile sacrificing things for; and some kind of code for what was acceptable and not acceptable.' He also thinks that 'most people who go to activism go to it for good reasons, because of a fundamental spiritual intuition that what's been done to them is wrong. Activism can allow people to connect with tremendous forces of anger and hurt, and in as much as you begin to achieve a greater well being about yourself, you then begin to be able to make space for the larger issues, for spirituality.' Rabbi Elizabeth Sarah is also struck by 'the spirituality in political struggle. When I was younger I would have just seen it in political terms'; now, 'there's an appreciation of the depth beneath it'.

'TUNE IN, DROP OUT' – COP OUT?

So religion prizes justice (at least in theory), and working for freedom can be seen as spiritual. But you don't need to believe in religion to believe in equality and liberty. With such worthy aims, who needs anything else? Why do some queer people, who start out with political beliefs, end up professing spiritual ones?

'My sense of justice was so strong that I really believed that you couldn't talk about spirituality: spirituality was a luxury that people who were hungry did not have,' says Aziz, now a Sufi but for many years a communist. 'My belief then was that the purpose of life was to be happy, and feeding empty stomachs was the first step.' He became worn out by the 'interminable internal ideological strife' among the various communist groups; and was kept in the closet by their homophobia. On a visit to India Aziz was struck by how people smiled much more than in Europe. 'Could it be that you didn't have to have a full stomach to be happy, as my belief system decreed? I had to accept it was true, I could see it around me. So I had to let go of my belief system, of communism.'

Varabhadri, before she was a Buddhist, was involved in the women's movement and lived in feminist households for several years. 'There was a feeling I'd slept with everybody, got drunk with everybody, lived with everybody – now what? The women's movement was divided. I got weary of it all; weary of the way that quite often it seemed to be people's relationships that held things up. We never had a policy that everyone agreed on – there were often disagreements, competitiveness and power struggles, and sometimes they came down to who was currently in a relationship with whom. There was always a tension and sexual rivalry, as if that was the most important issue. We may have had other ideals, but the ideals foundered if the relationships were in trouble.' She came into contact with the Friends of the Western Buddhist Order at a festival – where she was too broke to afford any food, and they were offering free sandwiches. 'Somehow I got chatting and I got the feeling, for the first time in decades, I was being spoken to as an individual. I wasn't being spoken to as someone who must hold a political stance. I wasn't being spoken down to, or being convinced of anything. They spoke from a very disinterested point of view, and didn't particularly want anything from me.' Discovering that the movement's meditation centre was in the working-class East End of London rather than the bourgeois groves of Hampstead further convinced her that these people were all right. 'Objectively there were all kinds of things to be anxious about. But I knew that I'd reconnected with something very precious inside.'

Her relationship of the time broke up – her partner 'got hung up on the fact that the Buddha was a male' – but Varabhadri is still with the Western Buddhist Order nearly twenty years later. 'The task of creating harmony' remains a preoccupation. 'There's a multiplicity of lifestyles going on', but there is 'a basic trust in one another, because we're committed to a set of ideals.' The feminism of the 1970s was also committed to a set of ideals of course, 'but there was so much muddle about how to set out to achieve them'. With the FWBO 'I could see some people were capable of embodying the ideal more than others, but there was something very strong going on. Somewhere in my life I had the notion that there was something called truth, a spiritual vision worth aspiring to. I see the Order as my companions on the way to truth.' Because the FWBO is split into men's and women's divisions, Varabhadri still spends most of her time living with and working for women; and, just as she did in the women's movement, she is raising consciousness and is committed to a better world.

When Catherine Hopper went on her first Buddhist retreat, she met some 'radical lesbian feminists of the kind you don't find any more; they were warning "it's patriarchal, don't have the wool pulled over your eyes again, don't bow to male statues". I felt I had a duty not to be tricked. There are a lot of things about Buddhism that sound really right off at first.' One woman Catherine met had, before she was a Buddhist, given up having anything to do with men; now she belonged to a movement headed by a man. 'So I said, given all your reservations about this patriarchal stuff, why are you here? And she said, quite frankly, I decided it was much too good a chance to pass up.' Catherine came to the same conclusion. At the puja (worship) ceremony on the last evening, she found herself bowing:

'Regardless of the ideological problems my head was putting in, my heart said "give in, this is an amazing experience". I was tired of resisting. I found myself feeling profoundly grateful for being there, and I found myself walking to the shrine and lighting some incense. I turned round to the woman leading the retreat, who I'd found difficult, because she'd said she was not a feminist, and I found myself bowing to her. And I discovered that far from losing something, I received; in bowing, I felt bigger afterwards – it was such a relief to be able to express admiration and gratitude to someone, instead of going through life saying you've done me wrong, you're letting the cause down. I've found that again and again since.'

Catherine was, for a couple of years, one of the few lesbian members of OutRage! 'I wanted to be part of a community of people who had shared ideals, wanted to change the world and wanted to look after each other. And those are exactly the same things I have found in the FWBO. The difference was that when people fell out in OutRage! there didn't seem to be any way of sorting it out, people just left, that was the end of their allegiance to the group.' Political ideals alone are not enough to hold people together. Although the ideals may be admirable, political discourse sometimes fails to accommodate the complex reality of human experience. In the words of a gay man who flirted with Marxism but became a Quaker: 'political theory couldn't explain the world; it couldn't explain the purpose of life'.

SPIRITUALITY IS MORE RADICAL THAN HOMOSEXUALITY

Catherine Hopper wrote for Britain's weekly *Pink Paper* for several years. She and three other ex-employees, including one of the founders, are now Buddhists. She suggests this is a natural progression from their original impulse to be politically radical. 'The Buddha taught that our only task in life was to become truly ourselves, and transcend all our limitations. That's subversive. It's revolutionary. We should seek to get over conditioning and conventionality: what could be more in tune with lesbian and gay thinking?' Certainly, the feminist and gay lib message that the personal is political is nothing new to religion: early Christianity is a story of people living out their private beliefs in a way that was at first so political as to be fatal, but which eventually transformed whole societies. Faiths have a vision of how life can and should be lived, just as the Gay Liberation Front and other political visionaries did; except the spiritual vision is more all-encompassing. 'To be ordained into the Western Buddhist Order is a statement of absolute commitment to the teachings of the Buddha, and to the Order as a community of friends who are endeavouring to practise that teaching with the whole of their lives. It's putting that at the heart of your life: everything else becomes secondary. You have absolutely re-oriented your life,' says Catherine.

'I was attracted to politics because I wanted to do something with my life,' says Maitreyabandhu, 'something that was radical, something that was a genuine response to the conditions I found around me. As I got into Buddhism I began to feel the most revolutionary thing I could do would be to change myself and the world. Politics can be the beginning of a spiritual life – it asks what is the cause of suffering? But Buddhism offers gay men and lesbians incomparably more scope for personal development than gay politics or the gay scene possibly can.' Maitreyabandhu's long-standing boyfriend is a communist. 'He wants to change the world and I want to change the world – we've just got very different ways of thinking how that's done. To me his communism seems like mumbo jumbo. I think it is incredibly conventional.'

In the past Maitreyabandhu was more sympathetic to his lover's ideology. 'At first I thought class was the cause of suffering – that if you got rid of that and had a socialist state, you wouldn't have suffering. Then I thought it was patriarchy – if you got rid of that, you'd have no suffering. Now I believe suffering is in the human heart. Suffering in the political arena is caused by power. I think people will always resort to power if they haven't got some sort of commitment to a spiritual life. Even if you take up an apparently right-on political perspective, you'll end up wielding power. A political way of changing the world is inherently foiled by human nature: the human being will move to power if it can. You will avoid that only if you're committed to something which can unify all people. Homophobia is an expression of hatred: hatred is the issue. Any expression of hatred will cause you pain, and will cause other people pain. So, to change yourself and to change the world, you need to change hatred. You can't change the world organizationally and think that will resolve hatred. You can change some of it – it's very important that the law treats people equally – but you won't change basic human tendencies. You can't, by changing the State, change people's minds. It can't do your work for you.'

EXTERNAL CHANGE THROUGH INTERNAL CHANGE

So, although spirituality is not an escape from politics for queer people, it may lead to a different emphasis: on internal change as well as external reform. 'I still want to change the world, but I now want to change it person by person' explains Catherine Hopper. 'Running around blowing whistles in front of people who don't know me,' – which Catherine did during protests with OutRage! – 'I don't think is that effective. You cannot force people to be fair. I came to the conclusion that the best thing was to help run another meditation class. I can help individuals who come along to the meditation centre become more loving, less defensive and less interested in people's sexual orientation. Having seen how my life has been absolutely radically changed – I just suffer so much less now just as a human being, never mind as a lesbian – I think the most constructive thing I can do is to give other people the opportunities with which to become happier. It's far more constructive than any number of hours spent on the street screaming. Feminism tries to change women themselves, through consciousness raising – but it's not as radical as what spiritual paths can do.'

'It is only to the extent that you've changed yourself, and really looked at what your own motivations are and what your conditioning is, that you can do anything effective to change the world around you,' Catherine continues. 'People often accuse Buddhists of being self-centred, but the goal of all this meditation and self-examination is to develop perfect wisdom and compassion "for the benefit of *all* sentient beings". Genuine change in me, through practice of the Buddha's teaching, can only be good for other people – and animals, and even the planet – as well as myself: for the degree of wisdom and compassion in my actions depends upon my practice, and the consequences of my actions affect others.' Catherine points out that 'you could go round campaigning until you're blue in the face, but if you're completely obnoxious to be with, nothing immediately around you is changed.' The common problem of people whose public behaviour is politically right on, but who are shits in private, is one that is difficult to address by means of political discourse alone: most ideologies tend not to demand much self-scrutiny from their followers, instead focusing all criticism on their opponents.

Glenn Palmer has been active in radical and gay politics for many years, in both Britain and Australia: he has recently been confirmed as a Christian. His understanding is that 'I'm not moving from being political to being spiritual, I think I'm moving from being activist to introspective. What informs my politics is justice, and right and wrong. Spirituality to me is about that quest for truth and knowledge – it's not just about acknowledging a supernatural aspect to identity. The movement to introspection is not a political cop-out, it's a political act. It's not about "fuck the world, I don't care about you any more"; it's saying, "well actually I'm part of this world, and, until I get my head round what I am, I'm part of the problem".'

Glenn and Catherine are both aware that this could sound like a cop-out (although, as long-serving campaigners, they have worked harder for lesbian, gay and bisexual people than the majority of the current consumer-queer generation). But the political strategies which they now deem insufficient are ones they have attempted to work with, long before they took up their spiritual paths; they are religious partly *because* of their political experience – not because they are trying to avoid the hard, political realities of life. Adam Sutcliffe is someone else who has carefully scrutinized his motives: 'I still sometimes feel a sense of disquiet when I realize that going on demos and signing petitions has effectively been replaced in my life by going to synagogue services and writing subscription renewal reminder letters. The pleasure of being part of a religious community brings with it the danger of insularity. I'm still very angry about many things in this world, and sometimes worry that my increased spiritual commitment over the last couple of years has perhaps diffused this anger rather than helping to focus it into practical commitment to radical reform. But we live in confusing times, in which perhaps the most radical changes happen not through angry struggle but through the personal development of lots of individuals.'

There is a risk that spiritual introspection will leave you less clear about what form of political action is most appropriate. 'We must help relieve suffering, and speak out against injustice,' Catherine still maintains; but she now qualifies this emphatically, 'when we can do so effectively, being well-informed and taking full responsibility for the consequences'. The reason for being so cautious, she claims, is that 'we unenlightened people lack the wisdom to know what the really appropriate response to suffering is'. As Glenn puts it, if we do not accept that we're part of the problem, the danger is we say 'I'm the solution. Which leads you down the path of "I know all about this: if only you lot would just do what I reckon you should do, everything would be fine". And even Christ's message isn't that simplistic.'

Rabbi Lionel Blue warns that 'we should not fall into the trap which has ensnared many followers of festivals of light. They forgot that both light and darkness dwelt within them. They spoke as if they were the light and the darkness was outside them, in others. Being right should not make us self-righteous, and may God keep us from that suspect emotion, righteous indignation. Many people have suffered injustice. It does not justify them in blowing up the world or even in blowing up society. Some of the injustice has to be absorbed – I can say this as a Jew – and with God's help it can be used.'[3]

POLITICAL/SPIRITUAL VISION

This chapter has established that there is nothing mutually exclusive about politics and spirituality. I wouldn't want to imply, however, that there is a direct causal link between a sense of spirituality and a single kind of political strategy. Not all spiritually identified queers will be politically involved; those who are will not all act in the same way.

One thing held in common by all spiritually identified queers, however, is that their politics are founded on a wide-ranging vision of how *all* people can live – rather than being simply the pursuit of equal rights legislation. People in this chapter have told of how their ideological models of the world eventually had to be surrendered in the face of the more complex reality of their lived experience. Spiritually identified queers generally reject simplistic and restrictive political orthodoxies, just as they reject religious and sexual ones. This includes the assumption that since queers are right about one thing (the evil of homophobia) we are right about everything else; and the notion that we are fundamentally different from our political opponents – or from our oppressors.

'One of the things which being a Quaker, or being spiritual, does oblige one to do – which I'm not very good at, I have to keep trying – is this attempt to put yourself in another person's shoes; no matter how hateful they are, to try and imagine what the world must look like to them,' says Steve Hope. 'If you try to do that even a little bit, it does make the desire for revenge harder. It's essential to understanding one's own humanity. I have very deep rage and anger about homophobia in general, but I find it quite hard to feel bitter or angry about individuals who are homophobic.' Steve cites Maya Angelou. 'Her basic philosophy of life is that even the most apparently different people actually have more that unites them than separates them, and acting on that is the only hope the world has got. I feel that she's profoundly right.' The quality Maya and Steve feel is so crucial – imagination – is central to the work of another spiritually identified gay man, best-selling author and artist Clive Barker. 'One of the things that imagination does is allow you access to other people's lives. In imagining another person's thoughts and feelings, you better understand them. It's the only way to fight the phobias that are in everyone, the only way to fight the animal impulse to view the world tribally, making everyone unlike us the enemy.' He does not believe 'there are any true solutions to the world's various ills without spiritual solutions.'[4]

Sue Vickermann, who has become involved in the Methodist Church again after many years of angry opposition to Christianity, says 'I've come to realize only recently that our respect for each other has to be mutual (not only them respecting me!) and that our discussion of our differences, however painful, has to be ongoing until we come to the fullest realization of the justice taught in the Gospels. (I think I know what that justice entails, but as long as there are people in my faith community who disagree with me, I'm under obligation to engage in tolerant discussion with them.)'

'We suffer because the world doesn't like us: this is the main spiritual lesson, understanding what it is to be persecuted,' says New-Ager Adam

James. 'That can make you go two ways: it can make you think, "well I must be worthless because I'm persecuted", or you can say "I know I'm worth loving, so how am I going to deal with it?" Again there are two ways: loving the people who are hating you, or hating them back. So much of the gay world is geared towards fighting hate with hate. This is where the spirituality comes in. Gay spirituality, if there is such a thing, should be about honouring our own culture, our own history, our own sexuality; but also being loving in adversity, having compassion and forgiveness for our persecutors, fighting hate with love, and engaging ourselves in useful work, in intelligent support networks, and worthwhile service and humanitarian endeavours – so that we set an example in human living.' Rabbi Sheila Shulman, coming from a very different perspective to Adam, none the less argued, in a sermon to lesbian and gay Jews, that the best strategy for fighting homophobia is not '"talking to the walls", which I've always felt is a waste of energy,' but 'being more and more ourselves, more energetically, more vibrantly, more Jewishly ourselves, so that no one will be able to ignore or reject either our presence'. Spirituality, it was argued earlier, is about being 'the whole of who I am'. Adam and Sheila both assert that being yourself is political, and may even be more politically productive than fighting homophobes in the same antagonistic way that homophobes attack us.

To see our political task as simply reacting to homophobia, and trying to defeat it, is to accept a definition of our existence that has been dictated by the homophobes themselves. The approach advocated by some of the people in this chapter is, where possible, to break out of the antagonistic binary opposition between straight and queer, and see all people as having the same spiritual potential. Varabhadri quotes one of the Buddha's teachings: 'He insulted me, he hurt me, he defeated me, he robbed me. Those who think such thoughts will not be free from hate.' Even though we oppose what it says about us, it is homophobia that makes us most aware of our difference and identity: as the Buddha makes clear, we conceive of ourselves in terms of what other people have done to us – and, consequently, cannot be free. The Queer politics of the early 1990s styled themselves as transgressive: they were thus dependent on there being something to transgress. 'I'm not into transgressing the rules,' says Buddhist Dirk de Klerk. 'I'm saying, do you have the right to make those rules? I don't need to break your rules: I am at ease within my own moral code. You have no authority over me. Gays need to grow beyond the adolescent phase of being the bad school kids who are fighting the teachers. To come truly of age, you have to say, to society at large, to institutions like the Church, "I do not need you to play the judgemental parent any more".'

A more challenging politics – one that arises out of a sustained reflection on our situation – is one that truly offers an alternative vision, rather than simply a reactive vision. 'Did we think the solution to life's problems was merely the solution to homophobia?' asks Fernando Guasch. 'We need to invent a new kind of agenda, political with a small p, political in terms of how we understand ourselves. Maybe this is the connection, this is how politics could be made more spiritual and spirituality more political: you need to start with a fundamental act of honesty, which is, we don't know what the fuck is going on, and we're not particularly satisfied. To merely hear that would be a highly humanizing experience. If I encounter models of the world' – whether political or religious – 'which are not connected to this fundamental fact, I sense the phoney.'

The lesbian, gay and bisexual political struggle is ultimately seeking the right for us to live our lives: only rarely does it concern itself with how we live, or why we do so. A healthy spirituality will still inspire us to seek the right to live our lives: but it presents a more all-encompassing vision, of how the whole of life can be lived, both by us and by the people who currently oppress us. If we are to sustain ourselves during the battle for our rights – and if we are to determine what it is we are fighting for – we need that vision. If seeking justice becomes the whole of our life – our raison d'être – then what are we going to do when that justice has been won? Or does our sense of purpose – and righteousness – depend on there always being something to fight against? I am not naively suggesting that we are within sight of an end to all oppression – as Jesus apparently said, the 'poor' are always with us. But, even if the whole of one's life is dedicated to building a better world, the issues raised in other chapters of this book – our existential nature, our embodiment, our mortality, or our place in the universe – still need to be addressed: the fact that you're doing something politically worthwhile doesn't make them go away. Politics can *sometimes* be used as an excuse to avoid these concerns – a siege mentality is developed, 'there just isn't yet time to deal with anything other than our oppression' – which is no better than using spirituality to hide from political realities.

Queer politics focus on freedoms: the crucial freedoms to live without fear, without violence and without discrimination. But freedom, while necessary, is a limited ambition. Chogyam Trungpa, one of the most influential Tibetan Buddhists to come to the West, entitled his most famous work *The Myth of Freedom*. David, a Buddhist who has received the teachings of the same tradition and greatly respects Trungpa's work, explains, 'we think of freedom as the ability to do whatever we want to do, have the money to buy what we want to buy, have sex with the people we want to have sex with, as much as possible – the Buddhist perspective is that that's not true freedom. You are imprisoning yourself; you have all these preconceptions – chasing after comfort that we never reach, or when we do, doesn't give us what we were hoping for.' In the 1990s, queer people have the freedom flag, available on a wide range of merchandise from key-rings to beach towels; London's gay ghetto even has a café called Freedom, where we are free to buy designer beer and wear the same clothes as everybody else. A more spiritual concept, perhaps – and the one that was embraced by the lesbian and gay political visionaries of the early 1970s – is liberation. Liberation is more revolutionary. According to Rabbi Sheila Shulman, it is an accurate translation of the Hebrew word usually rendered as 'salvation'. Liberation is more than having rights; it is more than being unimpeded. Liberation is breaking through to different reality. 'Usually the vibrancy and boundlessness of the world scares us into accepting far less than our birthright as humans offers us,' says David. 'We choose edited "video highlights" rather than real life.'[5]

Fernando Guasch spent years of his life fighting for the freedom of queer people – sometimes going without food and sleep for days. He has a ruthless analytical mind, a fiery contempt for both homophobia and sentimentality about gay people, and a pessimistic analysis of the political situation. And yet these days he joins with other Buddhists to chant for liberation – for everyone. 'You find yourself saying such extraordinarily powerful and beautiful things. You commit yourself to try to help all beings achieve some end to self-torture. I become struck to the point of tears sometimes when chanting, by realizing how powerful and how rare it is to find yourself saying out loud – "may all beings without exception on this earth enjoy peace, happiness, and profound, brilliant glory".'

Notes

1. Robert Goss, *Jesus Acted Up: A Gay and Lesbian Manifesto* (San Francisco: HarperSanFrancisco, 1994), pp. 148–9; 177; 179.
2. The Rev. Robert Williams, *Just as I Am: A Practical Guide to Being Out, Proud, and Christian* (New York: Crown Publishers, 1992), pp. 223–4.
3. Rabbi Lionel Blue, *Godly and Gay* (London: Gay Christian Movement, 1981), p. 5.
4. *Gay Times*, July 1995, p. 51.
5. Lest I misrepresent the complexity of Buddhist philosophy here, David explains: 'In Buddhist thought, the world is enormously rich *as it is* and as it changes. By shifting our perspective we can realize this and feel completely fulfilled by our journey through life, including *all* the ups and downs. In that sense, the real richness of life is free – and ours for the taking – if we only realize this. We are intrinsically free and always have been – but are scared of the implications and intensity that offers.'

Conclusion: From Queer to Eternity

What we are today comes from
our thoughts of yesterday, and our present
thoughts build our life of tomorrow:
our life is the creation of our mind.

(The Buddha)[1]

Adam Sutcliffe came out at university. 'Almost immediately I hurled myself
into a manic whirl of campus gay politics. The painful confusion and
isolation that had intermittently blighted my teenage years abruptly
evaporated; and defining myself loudly and proudly as a gay man, here,
queer, and not going shopping, helped me to flush away those already semi-
repressed memories, and to forge a new, confident, positive personality. I
slipped easily into the off-the-peg identity of an upfront Gay Man,
impatiently crusading for his love rights against the complacency of
bourgeois breeders, bigots, and – especially – Christians.

'During my gay infancy I needed the certainty of a strong, clear, gay
identity. Within a couple of years, though, and particularly once I
confronted the realities of life beyond the student ghetto, I began to realize
how much of myself I'd pushed into the background in my enthusiastic
adoption of a mono-dimensional gay identity. My sense of antagonism with
the "straight world" was displaced by a growing awareness of how much
I had in common with many of my non-gay friends. I found myself
considering my sexuality as a relatively straightforward and even banal
aspect of myself, and began to explore questions of my ethnic, religious
and spiritual identity which I had sidelined for many years. As I de-gayed,
I re-Jewed. In Beit Klal Yisrael, a predominantly – though not exclusively –
gay synagogue I have found a space in which I can simultaneously explore
my ethnicity and spirituality and feel part of a queer community. I used
to deride religion as an easy escape for the insecure into package-deal
thinking – and undoubtedly, for many gay people damaged by homophobia
and prejudice, religious belief does serve as such a sanctuary. But now I
realize both that I also chose a kind of package-deal thinking to help me

to overcome the initial insecurities of gay life, and that gay people can bring a very different, positive dimension to spiritual life.'

Many of the people in this book have discovered, like Adam, that religion does not have to be escapist, and that queer people bring to it crucial perspective and experience. Others have, like him, suggested that modern gay life can also involve little more than 'package-deal thinking', and that their spirituality has challenged them to overcome this. As Richard Woods puts it, 'uncritically identifying yourself with the whole gamut of experiences, institutions, and lifestyles in the gay world is just as much a capitulation of moral discernment and autonomy as is the sad and mindless conformity still so characteristic of our life in society'.[2] The spiritual value of being queer is that we resist stifling social and religious orthodoxies, and are more open to direct experience of our inner lives; the danger is that we replace one orthodoxy with another of our own invention, which again blinds us to the greater whole – of all that we feel, all that we are, and all that we can be.

According to John J. McNeill, 'pathological' religion will discourage individuality, ensure obedience through fear of rejection, repress feeling, and encourage a hopeless quest for perfection.[3] Queer culture – particularly the gay scene – has been found guilty of all these traits by contributors to this book. 'If we are not careful, we will move from one set of constricting assumptions to another; our gay liberation will become a gay limitation,' warns Maitreyabandhu, who is particularly concerned about the social norms that gay men adopt. 'The self-awareness we started to develop in coming out will be borne down in a torrent of recreational drugs, deadening music and sexual compulsion. Either that or smothered with the pink duvet of banal consumerism and hetero aping. One of the things that attracted me to being gay intellectually was its radical potential, in the sense of not accepting the world as it is, not accepting the conventional ethical, moral, psychological and spiritual assumptions. We challenge so many assumptions. The lack of family responsibilities means we can commit ourselves wholeheartedly to what is most important in life – the development of universal loving kindness and true individuality. If this is to happen we need to rediscover our radical roots and reconnect with the urge to change ourselves and our world.' Gay liberation was fired by this sense of radical potential; but the experience of near-thirty years since Stonewall has proved that radicalism does not automatically follow on from being queer. 'Now people talk about radical sex. S/M – is it radical? Or is it just more consumer durables? Somebody said to me at Pride a few years ago, "Don't all these gay men make you proud?" I said "It depends on what they are doing".' Nagaraja, another gay Buddhist, argues 'if you really want to be different, don't just settle for being homosexual – it's not special any more. If you really want to come out of the closet, go beyond just being another man wearing Calvin Klein underwear – there's more to you than that. I don't think we're individuals any more – the gay culture is so cloned. We can't hold, as a generalization, that we're any more creative than heterosexual culture. Tragic but true. They've created their stereotypes of what masculinity is, we've created our stereotypes of what a gay man is – and we're sticking to them.'

What is being criticized here is not so much the state of contemporary queer culture as the near-consensus (found in the gay media, and lesbian/gay studies) that where we are is where we want to be – or if it isn't, that heterosexuals are to blame. To be proud of the progress that we have made, and to acknowledge all the reasons why we're like this, must not exclude us from wanting more. 'At the moment we're peddling a fiction that this the best of all possible worlds,' argues Fernando Guasch. 'People are deeply uneasy about it all, but it's a conspiracy of silence. The only bad news we're allowed to hear is about homophobia, which is true enough, but by now we should be an adult enough community to realize there are some home-grown problems of our own. The source of them may be that people tell us we're shit. But if, in the space that we have gained, we do not begin to investigate our problems – and try to create structures to at least be able to air these feelings, and really grow through them – all we're doing is a huge bypass of the whole issue. The increased visibility of queers in society must give hope to people who are still in closeted hell; but for those of us beyond that, we can't pretend it's good enough. Gay is good? Gay is not good enough. Is this all we want?'

THE LIMITATIONS OF SEXUAL IDENTITY

The question that is forced upon us when we realize we are not straight is: who am I? To this question we can answer lesbian, gay or bisexual, and in so doing we tell the truth. But only part of the truth. As Jim Cotter says, 'who am I? can never be completely answered in sexual or personal or societal terms. There is a spiritual quest too, bound up with sexuality and society, yes, but having its own uniqueness.'[4] And spirituality perhaps expresses more about us than our sexual identity. There is more to life, and more to us, than our sexuality, however central that might be. 'We cannot be defined and limited by definitions of our sexuality,' argues Jim Cotter.[5] 'Your sexuality is only a part of you,' asserts Maitreyabandhu. 'It doesn't have to be that big a part of your life even. It's not a problem, but neither is it a status – or a career.' Fernando offers one explanation of why we can be reluctant to believe this: 'As Foucault observes, because sex has been repressed, and because we have been made to feel alienated from our sexuality, there is an almost irresistible temptation to want to locate in sex and sexuality the true self, the real me. "Up until now I have been denied access to this aspect of my life, and my life has felt like shit: well, it seems to follow, if I allow myself access to this area of my life, things might improve – I'll have found out what I really am, who I really am." It's bollocks.' The idea that 'the self is fundamentally a sexual self' is just another delusion to distract us from the often painful nature of reality. 'Buddhism would be suspicious of absolutely anything that's going to be an escape mechanism from certain facts about who you are – your inescapable mortality, and the mental tricks you are playing on yourself all the time.' Someone once told Maitreyabandhu that their sexuality was the foundation of their life, like a chair that they sit on. 'I said, well it will break: it's not big enough. To try to understand life from the basis of being gay is absurd – it's not big enough to contain what life is about, and therefore drastically restricts human potential. You limit yourself by over-identification first of all with your own sexuality, and secondly with the group of people that you belong to.'

When I was coming out, I went through that familiar stage of saying 'I'm not A Gay Man, I'm just a man who happens to be gay. It's not a big deal.' What I was actually saying, at that time, was that I didn't really want to deal with it and of course I wasn't like those other gay people who 'flaunted' themselves and whom I found rather embarrassing. As my understanding of my sexuality matured, I came to see how very central it is. The way I relate to the world is partially determined by my sexuality; the same is true for heterosexuals as well, but as a gay man I'm more likely to realize this. The experience of being different to the majority, and part of a minority which experiences prejudice simply on the basis of this difference, obviously influences how I understand the world and my place in it. Acknowledging the importance of my sexuality is important politically, as well as psychologically and socially – and I'm now quite happy to flaunt it.

So to say, as Catherine Hopper now does, that 'Buddhism has freed me from my sense of Being A Lesbian' may set alarm bells ringing. And yet, repeatedly when researching this book, people have made similar statements to me: queers have been emphatic that there is more to them than their sexuality, however all-encompassing a force they understand sexuality to be. 'Because we're gay doesn't mean we've got to deny the rest of our life; we're not just sexual people, we're spiritual people,' says the Reverend Jean White. Ewan Wilson, a Christian, argues 'for me being gay is only a part of my life – a big part certainly – but still only part. There are lots of other interests I have and roles I play which need have no connection with being gay, or in which being gay or not does not feature.' Statements like these may, for some readers, finally confirm the ever-lurking suspicion that spirituality is just a refuge for those who don't want to accept the reality of their lives.

The people making them, however, have experienced the misery of repression, and oppression, and have no intention of returning to the closet. Although they may appear to diminish the importance of sexual orientation, what they propose is not a retreat *back* from sexual identity; it's a move *forward, and beyond*. Peter Ashby-Saracen, a Nichiren Buddhist, makes clear both how much he values his sexuality, and his need for something more: 'For me finding freedom within my sexuality and finding spiritual fulfilment are very closely linked; being gay is one manifestation of being human, and being human is, among other things, to be aware of our place in the "scheme of things". Being openly gay, and being part of the gay community and gay activities, gives me a great sense of belonging, but it doesn't satisfy everything in life – being gay isn't my whole life, though it's probably the thing that affects it most. I need some kind of expression for my feeling of the infinite and where I fit into it, and my spirituality does this for me.'

Sexuality may be a large part of Peter's life; but infinity, obviously, is larger. In the first chapter Rabbi Elizabeth Sarah said her spirituality was about 'me as a whole . . . and myself as part of the whole . . . about what it is to be human, what it is to be alive, what it is to be a part of creation.' Sexuality partially determines our experience of what it is to be human; but, again, that experience is larger. Spirituality is about the whole of life. Our sexual identity is not, and cannot be. At the start of this book I drew attention to the fact that 'queer identity' (or queer identities) does not (do not) acknowledge the large number of lesbian, gay and bisexual people who also identify with spirituality in some way. One could just as readily argue, by the same criterion – the image we hold of ourselves – that 'queer identities' rarely refer to the number of us who ride bicycles. The reason, I guess, is that cycling doesn't seem to have very much to do with sexuality, except in the broadest understanding of the term. That example throws into pointed contrast the things that *are* acknowledged to unite us. Our identity focuses on sex, politics, some art, clothes, the scene, health and a few organizations because these are the only things that we visibly have in common, or at least have in common exclusively with other queers. This may be naively simplistic, but to me this implies that our queer identity (whichever one we choose from the catalogue) is limited. There is more to us than it can include, unless we make the identity so non-specific that it no longer serves to identify us.

Being queer, while it may give us insights, does not offer many answers to the Big Questions that, chapter 1 suggested, are fundamentally spiritual ones – the how-do-I-live and what's-life-all-about questions. Spiritual traditions make some guesses – guesses honed over thousands of years –

as to how those can best be approached. Being queer does not guarantee any particular ideals, integrity or moral worth. 'In the Friends of the Western Buddhist Order we have a shared set of ideals,' says Catherine Hopper. 'No one could believe that lesbian and gay people have a shared set of ideals. Lesbians and gay men are both socialists and Tories. Just being a lesbian or gay man doesn't make you compassionate; rich gay people don't help poverty-stricken gay people. Most of the time we're just like the mass of the population, we just live slightly differently. Having embraced ourselves fully as lesbians and gay men, we need to move on with the process, which is to stop identifying as lesbians and gay men and become human beings. It's all a matter of stages: newly out lesbians or gay men often need to spend all their time with gay people in order to gain that sense of acceptance and strength, but they then need to move out into the rest of the world. In the FWBO sexual orientation is of so little consequence, it's no good saying "I'm a lesbian, I'm special". This used to infuriate me when I started – I'd ask, why isn't there a lesbian or gay group? People, including gay people, said "you don't need one, you're a human being." Which has allowed me to see myself as a human being. I clearly am a lesbian, I'm in a relationship with a woman. But I've stopped categorizing myself; categories are incredibly limiting. It is foolish to go around saying I'm gay so I know what I'm talking about and you've got to be nice to me. It's much more to the point to say – listen, I'm a human being, and you're not treating me like a human being. Out of my friends, the people who are suffering most are not the gay ones; they're the straight ones, who are stuck on the tramlines. As Buddhists we're even trying to transcend our sex; we want to abandon over-identification with being a woman or a man, let alone lesbian or gay.'

Politically, Catherine says she still thinks it 'important to stand up against homophobia wherever advisable'. But 'if you want to really belong to this minority, for a lot of people that means that you've got to follow the crowd. Buddhism says that we must become individuals: the man who founded the FWBO says that at our most highly developed, each person could be a species of his or her own. I think the function of a spiritual movement is to help people become who they truly are, and make themselves naked. It's only through that that you dissolve all barriers. It's what everybody needs really – I don't want to be defined by my sexuality all of my life.'

'For straights, other aspects of their identity define who they are much more significantly than their sexuality,' Glenn Palmer observes. Buddhist monk the Venerable K-N thinks that is healthier: 'When gay people get round to the situation where they are what they are, and their gayness is not the centre – the absolute focus – then I think the gay community will start to mature. We get things the wrong way round: the emphasis is *I'm gay*, I'm Fred; rather than I'm Fred, and I'm gay.' The Reverend Jean White is sure of where her priorities lie: 'I would say I'm a lesbian Christian, I wouldn't say I'm a Christian lesbian. Being a lesbian is part of my life, but my faith covers the whole of my life. It includes my sexuality, and that's important for me, but Christianity is my belief system, and the most important thing: it touches every part of my life.' Dennis Fraser is aware of a whole host of potential identities: 'I'm not just gay, I'm also Christian, I'm also a man, I'm also Scottish, I'm also the son of my parents.'

Rupi has a minority ethnic identity, as well as belonging to a sexual minority. He has attended groups where he did 'a lot of reading and thinking and talking, with black and Asian friends. But at the end of the day, I didn't want to live my life through that. I'm aware of all the issues around identity, I've dealt with them. But I don't want a label ascribed to me – I'm me.' Adam James still lives his life as an out gay man. But as his sense of spirituality has developed, he feels 'there has been a drawing away not from being gay, but the *idea* of being gay, and the mass gay culture. Any mass culture is to be avoided.' Roberta Wedge's Paganism – and her bisexuality – teach her to value 'fluidity' over rigid categories. 'Just as my love for and understanding of myself has grown beyond my mortal body, so does my love for others reach beyond the pigeonholes of heterosexual and lesbian . . . For me, now, it means the blurring of boundaries, between Nature and human, outer and inner, female and male, self and Other.'

Harvey Gillman is well aware of the potential complications when identities collide: he is a Jew who is gay and has become a Quaker. 'The gift of minority living is that we do not take existing majority norms as truth; we are forced back to our experience to consider what is the truth of our lives. But this would lead to a very partisan vision if the only truth for us was that which emerged from that tiny part of the globe on which we found ourselves. That would be the false view of the sectarian who dismisses all other truths as falsehoods.' Harvey writes of how he never feels *completely* at home in any one group – each is only part of the whole, even though he tries to bring to them the whole of himself. He has tried to avoid 'dividing the world into two camps, the us and them syndrome that confronts all minorities'.[6] Ultimately 'we are all a minority of one'; this does not mean we have to be alone. As another Quaker, Peter Wyles, protests, 'why should I restrict my time and friendship to people of my own gender, sexuality, politics or religion? If I was only interested in bisexual Quaker poets, I would have few friends and nothing to write about.'

'Can we understand each other only to the degree to which we've got things in common?' asks Maitreyabandhu. 'That's just patently not the case. I remember hearing a gay man saying that this straight man couldn't understand him because he was gay. If you use that language, nobody can understand anybody else. Ethics is based on imagination, the fact that you can imagine how other people feel. One of the ways that we really change ourselves is by putting ourselves in close connection with people who have a different set of conditioning. You've then got to work out how to communicate. There's a value for gay men coming together as gay men, particularly earlier on; but increasingly one wants to come together with persons as a person. The gay community can be far too cosy – everybody tends to agree with you, people have got broadly the same ideas as you, assumptions about men and women, about religion, about life, which sometimes don't get adequately talked about because you all agree.' Fellow Buddhist Catherine Hopper takes a similar view. 'You can certainly over-identify too much as a gay or a lesbian person. To live in a ghetto all your life is limiting, given the incredible diversity of people outside.' Rabbi Lionel Blue warns 'it is easy to escape from a ghetto imposed on you, and then to build one of your own because it seems safe and cosy. The aim of gay liberation is to make people whole, not to increase their divisions.'[7]

The Quaker yearly meeting of 1834 made a resolution which Steve Hope thinks is still useful advice. 'It says you must not suffer "a party spirit" to prevail among you, because it's a spirit that makes tribal loyalty more important than the truth; issues of betrayal and loyalty become more important than discerning what is true. It's very insightful – cliquishness makes you treat people as outsiders when there's no need for it. When you are gay I think you are very vulnerable to the dangers of being on a "side". One of the ironies is that you can have straight friends who are far more committed, even passionate, about lesbian and gay equality than some of the barflies you see in gay clubs – you can actually have far less in common with the barflies.'

When Fernando Guasch started to attend a Buddhist centre regularly, the absence of much basic difference between straight and queer people came as a revelation. 'For me it's been truly humanizing after four years of OutRage! where you develop a siege mentality, where straight people are demons and oppressors, to be able to sit down and have genuine and warm communication with these people.' Steve Graham thinks that all people need spiritual healing, regardless of their orientation: 'I don't see much of a difference between gay and straight really. We have different parts of the same story. Everyone needs connection with themselves and to the greater life force.' Homosexuality was illegal for much of Rabbi Lionel Blue's life, and caused him a great deal of personal conflict. And yet he asserts that 'everything that gays go through a straight person goes through too. The scenery is somewhat different, but the same dramas are played out. I shouldn't think because you are gay there are experiences that no other person has ever had. The pressures are different, the emphases are different, some things are felt more deeply – but you've got to keep away from elitist attitudes.' Even the General Secretary of the Lesbian and Gay

Christian Movement, Richard Kirker, who has for twenty years campaigned against a Church that asserts the superiority of heterosexuals, maintains that 'I've got much more in common with a lot of people who aren't gay, personally and spiritually, than I'd have with a congregation that is exclusively gay. I think my worship and spiritual life should not be restricted to devising a method of being Christian which detaches me from all those other people who – through no fault of their own – aren't queer.'

Although Richard Kirker thinks LGCM will have its work cut out for many years to come, he looks forward to a time when sexual identity is not only accepted but inconsequential.[8] 'I suspect that we will find, at some unspecified time in the future, that what unites us is our humanity; and we will identify ourselves by features that are common to other people's experience as much as or even more so than our emotional/erotic object choice. I think there's far more that binds us together with non-judgemental, loving, inclusive-minded people than separates us.' For Kate, breaking the boundaries is part of the Christian vision: 'Christianity, in my opinion, is not about different ghettos of people worshipping in isolation; be they middle-class, black, lesbian, etc. It is about acknowledging that before God *all* people are equally loved and accepted. Utopian? Maybe; but to me it is the heart of the Gospel.' 'Reconciliation begins for me', says Father Bill, 'when I am able to de-label, to go beyond whatever labels others have given me or I have given myself for whatever reasons. In God, the only label (if it is such) is that of Son or Daughter, "This is my son, my daughter, in whom I take delight" . . . Once we start looking behind any label we shall recognize that the peoples of God are beautiful, wearing as they do, however imperceptibly and imperfectly, the multi-coloured rainbow cloak of God.' The late Simon Bailey described religious queers as pioneers, on a 'lonely journey'. And yet, he said, 'the result of the journey is to discover not only what you share within with all gay people, deep in the heart, but also what you share with all people everywhere of every kind'.

ARE QUEER PEOPLE BETTER?

When younger, Adam James thought that 'gays must be on a higher level'. He reasoned, as many of us have at some stage, that queer people are more visionary, creative and sensitive – just look at Alexander the Great, Plato, Sappho, Michelangelo, Whitman (and the rest of the role-model call). In the early decades of the century Edward Carpenter justified his arguments for the acceptance of homosexuality on the same grounds: 'Uranians' are temperamentally likely to be 'students of life and nature, inventors and teachers of arts and crafts . . . diviners and seers or revealers of the gods and religion . . . medicine men and healers, prophets and prophetesses', 'thinkers, dreamers, discoverers'. Our queer ancestors, he claimed, 'ultimately laid the foundation of the priesthood and of science, literature and art'.[9] Many others have taken up this theme since Carpenter. It is still a routine defence of our sexuality to point to how many of us work in the caring professions and the arts. So it was understandable for Adam to conclude that 'the world hates us because we're so wonderful'.

But now he thinks this was 'a defence mechanism. We're hurt, so we become superior. But we are human first, men or women second, gay or lesbian third. Gay spirituality is no different from any other spirituality. Spirituality itself is a universal concept of awakening to the essence within us which is our life force. Gays are different from the mainstream, but cultural difference does not make for spiritual difference. As Sai Baba says, "There is only one religion, the religion of love; there is only one language, the language of the heart." At the root of it all, we are all souls on our journeys back to the infinite soul from which we came.'

If we accept that our sexual identity refers only to some of what we are, and if we can (or, as some religions suggest, must) find common ground with people who do not share that aspect of our being, then Adam's position seems to me the only one tenable. When I started this research, I inclined towards the essentialist view that Carpenter represents. The idea that we're 'special' has an obvious appeal. If Jung reckons I'm more spiritually receptive than other people, well, who am I to argue? Since we've all been fed, to varying degrees, the lie that we're somehow worse than everybody else, then it's especially gratifying to hear the opposite. We're not ugly ducklings after all; and we haven't merely grown into plain old ducks, either; we're actually rare and beautiful swans. Most tempting of all were the arguments assembled in two deeply compassionate and insightful books by Mark Thompson, *Gay Spirit* and *Gay Soul*. Together with his collaborators, including Mattachine Society founder Harry Hay and anthropologist Will Roscoe, Thompson believes 'gay men and lesbians possess the ability to lead society's next phase of cultural revolution – liberation of the soul – if only they realise that potential'. [10] This book concurs with many of Thompson's major arguments; for instance, that a 'way to the soul is through the body', and that queer people 'are on the frontier of understanding how flesh and spirit can be – must be – integrated in a soulful life'.[11]

Many crucial questions are posed by Thompson's books; but the answers he comes up with tend to rely on a deeply essentialist concept of sexual identity. He claims that 'gay men constitute a third gender – and . . . lesbians a fourth . . . Homosexuals are as different from heterosexuals as men are from women. Individuals now categorized as gay and lesbian represent significantly different ways of being, and . . . have a purposeful social function, a function that is not contained by today's emphasis on sexuality alone'.[12] The popularity of this notion in America seems to owe a lot to the Native American tradition of the *berdache* and *shamen*, important tribal figures whose authority, and social and magical powers, were attributed to their gender/sexual nonconformity (i.e. they sometimes cross-dressed and had homosexual relationships).

As I researched this book I became increasingly unconvinced by the notion that queer people are intrinsically, spiritually different. A major factor in my growing scepticism has been the sometimes fierce opposition which has been expressed by the majority of people contributing to this project.[13] 'Every soul is unique in so far as the soul is the essence of the individual,' in the opinion of the Reverend Niall Johnston. 'But as a "species" do homosexuals have a different sort of soul? No.' 'I don't think there's any such thing as a gay spirituality,' asserts Maitreyabandhu. 'There's gay men practising a spiritual path – gay men will have particular issues to work with – but there's no difference in principle. Spirituality, by definition, is universal.' The Reverend Jean White holds that 'each person is created in the image of God whether we're straight or gay.' The experience of oppression, she argues, will lead to a different awareness – whether because of sexuality, gender, race or disability. But 'if we're all part of a divine plan, then we can't be that different.'

Partly my objection is empirical. Thompson says that queer people's 'role is as carriers of soul to a world which prefers to dwell on surfaces'. I know too many queens who like nothing better than to dwell on surfaces – perhaps on how they can be most tastefully redecorated. You only need to listen to the conversation going on in your average gay pub to realize that queers don't, automatically, represent a higher order of consciousness. For the essentialist this is further evidence of how terribly we are suppressing our spiritual potential. But, if our potential is untapped, could we not admit the possibility that this is also true for heterosexuals?

If we believe that a queer tribe will save the world, we write off the vast majority of humanity. A remarkable minority of visionaries, teachers, artists and healers can indeed be identified in our queer heritage and in the present day (Thompson talks to many of those currently at work). Equally, a remarkable minority of visionaries, teachers, artists and healers can also be found amongst heterosexuals. Extraordinary people tend, by definition, to be a minority. I'm unconvinced that this means that they automatically belong to *our* minority, unless we propose that some straight people are actually queers trapped in heterosexual bodies. 'Liberation movements tend to attract visionaries,' Fernando Guasch argues, 'but it doesn't follow that everybody who shares the same predicament will equally be visionary.' In one sense, straight visionaries undoubtedly are 'queer', in as much as they are markedly different from the majority; but this won't necessarily be reflected in their sexual practice. Conversely, the sexual difference of the majority of homosexuals won't make them 'queer' in this visionary sense. The truly queer will always (and by definition) be an elite.

The idea that homos somehow represent the ideal balance of 'masculine' and 'feminine', and are working as modern *berdache* – a necessary bridge between men and women – also strikes me as implausible. 'I can't see how spending my days in Old Compton Street helps straight men and women get on better with each other,' as Glenn Palmer puts it. Obviously I recognize the stereotypes that this fantasy draws on: straight women adore gay men because we are more open to our emotions, and anything a straight man can do a dyke can do better. Like most stereotypes, these have some basis in reality. However, if queers *in their essence* (or souls) are like this, then male and female behaviour and 'role' must also be pre-determined. Such a scheme of the world is favourable to us queers – we get the best (although, strangely, not the worst) of both worlds – but it traps the majority of our fellow human beings in the restrictive gender roles that feminism helps us deconstruct. It also opens the whole Pandora's box of gender essentialism, and ignores the wide spectrum of gender-identification practised by both lesbian and gay people: for instance, gay men can be just as if not more macho, objectifying, emotionally inarticulate and misogynist as the next (straight) man. (And I know many straight men who display none of those characteristics.)[14]

Where do bisexuals fit in to this scheme of queer saviours and straights who need to be saved? Are they a fifth gender? Even if we were to accept that there is some intrinsic link between loving someone of the same gender and having a different gender-identity to the majority, does that mean bisexuals will be a watered-down version of the third and fourth genders, or do they have to switch between male/female and gay/lesbian 'genders' in schizophrenic fashion? What about people who wouldn't call themselves bisexual, but don't score a strict zero or six on the Kinsey scale? If I were to have sex with a woman would my gender-identity change, and would I forfeit my spiritual powers and visionary role?

When people get spiritual about masculinity and femininity, there seems to be a great deal of confusion – not least mixing up sexual orientation with gender, and physical gender with psychological identity. I may be guilty of slightly misrepresenting Thompson's arguments, which rest on the assumption that the 'new' genders are defined by 'social function, a function that is not contained by today's emphasis on sexuality alone'; people currently labelled according to their sexual proclivities actually represent a 'soul type' that has always existed. But my chief objection is not so much theoretical as pragmatic. I have argued that a potential spiritual gift of queerness is our freedom from social and religious norms; our ability to see that these orthodoxies have no authority but have been falsely imposed upon reality. I fear that the idea we should be modern *berdache* and *shamen* could become another expectation that most of us will fall short of; another 'norm' that disguises the full complexity of who any of us is; or another distraction from reality. Just because we've been spiritual pariahs, do we have to go to the other extreme and become triumphalist evangelists?

Being queer does not automatically mean we are 'special', any more than it automatically meant we are evil or sick. It has no intrinsic, objective meaning. It does not predetermine our 'spirituality'; spirituality grows out of our experience. And, although Thompson's work is grounded in the experience of some remarkable men, his overall argument – that we are significantly 'deeper' than most people – does not correspond to the 'overall' experience of lesbian, gay and bisexual people as a whole. That experience is too diverse to make many generalizations about. Even Thompson's opening premise – that all gay men are deeply wounded – is debatable. Woundedness varies – with each new generation there are ever more lesbian and gay people who have escaped much of the torment and conflict that is assumed to surround homosexuality. As an identifying characteristic of queer people, 'woundedness' is dependent on the oppression that we are fighting against. If it is produced by social conditions, it cannot be something which will always be characteristic of queer people – unless we assume that homosexuality will never be accepted by the heterosexual majority. That is not an assumption I am prepared to make, politically or personally.

Fernando Guasch opposes essentialism on both theoretical and spiritual grounds. 'I think the postmodern trip about homosexuality is quite correct, and very exciting; really we don't exist, this is a complete set of words and fictions we've imposed on ourselves and one another. We have tried to invent something common, something essential and fundamental among this enormous variety of experience. What is interesting about it is that the same insight can equally be applied to straights. I think some queers understand that "men" and "women" don't exist: they're just people who have been convinced of a certain set of fictions. I know women who could make better fathers or cowboys than men. I know as many straight men who are as shackled and limited by those traditional roles of what is to be a man. Hopefully "queer" theory might have clarified a bit more that we're just people who have been hypnotized with certain sets of fictions. And that's very Buddhist: there's no essence at all, nothing solid. All equally vanishable. I don't believe in an essence of any kind, so I don't believe in a different [queer] soul.' Because, in our culture, our sexual behaviour is treated as a significant difference, we can potentially perceive these fictions more readily. But, as Fernando and others have already argued, we are in danger of 'beginning to believe another set of myths' – whether those are social fictions, like those the gay scene relies upon, or spiritual ones, as Thompson suggests. I draw hope and inspiration not from how my queerness makes me different but from the ability it gives me to perceive that, as Fernando says, *everyone* is a victim of these fictions.

Harvey Gillman locates the oppression of minorities in dualistic thinking, which inevitably proclaims one is superior to the other – whether that's straight over gay, male over female, spirit over matter, divine over human. This creates 'an inhuman striving, an impossible norm, which denies the gift of being where we are or at least stops us from listening to the Spirit in the here and now of our lives. It makes love conditional on some ideal we can never reach.'[15] Such dualism is not only the prerogative of homophobes. Queer essentialism once again proposes to divide us into Us and Them; it is fundamentally dualistic; it gets in the way of our being here now. For Steve Hope 'that's the problem. We keep saying we're like everybody else, but when we discover it's true, we don't like it.'

RESISTING ASSIMILATION

'Reality is unitary, that is one individual existence in which all things are in relationship.'[16] According to Harvey Gillman, this is the realization that should replace dualistic thought. The Reverend Neil Whitehouse talks of this in more social terms: 'we're not an island. We relate to each other as lesbian and gay people, but that's just a construct: we need to relate to everybody, even if it's painful. The final vision is a hopeful one: despite the Holocaust and the homophobia and violence, there's something that defies that, that says in the end, all shall be well.'

There is no reason why queer people cannot be all the things that Edward Carpenter thought we would be; at this point in history, for some or many of us, there may even be elements of our experience that make it particularly likely. The vision held out by spirituality, however, as Harvey and Neil express it, is one of ultimate *unity*; and, to have any real value, must be inclusive of, and available to, all.

The danger with saying that, underneath it all, we're all basically the same, is that it sounds like either self-hatred (not being able to accept our own 'deviance') or assimilationism (which to some queers is synonymous with self-hatred). Some people may get nervous at anything which smacks of one of the subtler forms of heterosexism: 'you're just like us really, so why do you have to make such a big fuss about it?' When Harvey Gillman says that 'reality is unitary', I think we can assume he is not referring to reality as defined by the majority, a social status quo which we can join in with so long as we behave. This is not an attempt to persuade anyone that we should be allowed 'our place at the table'. In terms of justice, obviously we should, and this is the line that most books on religion and homosexuality take: the Church or whoever should let us join in.

For understandable reasons many queer people do not want to be like The Majority. The dominant ways of living in our culture are deeply problematic, and a lot of us – straight as well as queer – resist any attempt to be assimilated by them. Spiritual growth, however, is not assimilationist. With their emphasis on reality instead of easy answers, depth instead of superficial materialism, and trusting personal experience instead of deferring to external authority, spiritual ideas generally oppose most of the values and expectations of Western society. In gay and lesbian political history the assimilationist view has traditionally been opposed by the liberationist/revolutionary position: instead of campaigning for heterosexuals to accept us, we offer our insights as to how heterosexuals can change. While religious institutions tend to be assimilationist in their relationship with the majority culture, the message that they supposedly propagate is usually liberationist and revolutionary.

So I would argue that the spiritual vision is not tainted by assimilationism. Furthermore, spirituality is more intrinsically revolutionary, and more anti-assimilationist, than sexual orientation. I am not saying that there is not much in society that needs to be challenged. I am saying that we have misinterpreted the basis of the conflict. It is not queers versus straights. It is authentic individuality versus conformist pressures. Or the reality of experience versus whatever orthodoxies seek to deny that reality. Or liberation (for everyone) versus assimilation (into a spiritually dead culture). These battles must be fought within our own community as well as outside it. Queer lifestyles can be orthodoxies masquerading as transgressions; conformity with the pretence of individuality. The rhetorical declarations of how different we queers are sometimes bring to mind that superlative satire of religious orthodoxy, Monty Python's film *Life of Brian*. Brian, mistaken for a messiah, tells the massive crowd gathered outside his window that they have to think for themselves, that they're all individuals, they're all different; and they chant back, as one, 'yes, we're all individuals, yes, we are all different'. One figure in the crowd says 'I'm not', but is quickly hushed by everyone else, as they demand: 'Tell us what to do.'

PARTICULARS AND UNIVERSALS: QUEER AND ETERNITY

Rabbi Elizabeth Sarah describes the Jewish vision as 'a universalism rooted in particularism. Christianity is often seen as universalism. But Christian universalism is rooted in everyone being Christian, which is fine as long as you are a Christian. Jewish universalism is based on everybody being who they are. There's a famous prayer that we recite three times a day, just before the kaddish for the dead – which foresees a world in which there will be no prejudice, where everybody will be united in recognizing God's unity, based on their own experience, their own language and their own ways. So it's a unity rooted in diversity. As lesbian and gay people, that's what we're looking for, that's why we've got a flag of many colours – recognizing that we are part of a rich fabric of what it is to be human. Our humanity is what brings us together and our differences are what we want to celebrate within that.'

Talmudic and Biblical scholars generally accept that the 'purity codes' of Leviticus – which include the famous injunctions against men lying with each other – were motivated by the need for the people of Israel to distance themselves from the cultic tribes that surrounded them, to prove their holiness by not committing the 'deeds of the land of Egypt'. Maintaining the faith's purity has always been a Jewish concern; Rabbi Elizabeth says 'the imperative all those thousands of years ago was forging a separate identity in an alien environment. Just as it was in the early days of the lesbian and gay, and feminist movements. One of the ways in which we expressed ourselves politically in the seventies was gravitating into like-minded groups. Sometimes, like-minded groups, even radical ones, can be just as conservative as the male clubs of old, because they're so dependent on everyone agreeing with one another. The new model is about embracing diversity, and pluralism. I don't want a Jewish haven or a lesbian haven – what I want is to be in a situation where there's a criss-crossing of everything, but I'm constantly aware of being part of the whole, of being human – *and* of all the differences.

'I had a vision, when I went on my journey to the rabbinate, of an airy building on the morning of the Shabbat. Instead of there just being a service, in every room there would be something different going on: different services, dance, movement, silence, a whole range of people expressing what it was for them to be doing Shabbat. All happening in one place, but differently. Then people could come together, share a meal, have a party. It's about having the frame, being part of the whole, having a sense of community; but also all these opportunities to express it your way. There must be space within a group to express your individuality. That's one of the biggest challenges. People would prefer to have certainty and uniformity.' Many Jews prefer 'what they've been brought up in rather than participating creatively.' Likewise, 'an awful lot of us lesbian and gay people are not radical. We want to lead quiet lives, we're bothered that we have this difference to cope with, we would rather be able to get on with it like every other "normal" person.'

This book has been about the ways in which 'we' are different, and the ways in which we are the same. We are both, at the same time, of course. Everyone is an individual minority of one; and everyone is part of the same whole. Universalism does not invalidate our particularism, and cannot be taken as an excuse for us to ignore our particulars, to fall for the lie that there is a 'normality' we are failing to achieve. But our particulars contribute to the universal.

It is only through our particular experience that we can apprehend the universal. We have to start the journey from where we are; we can get to eternity only from *here*. Spirituality is not about turning yourself into somebody else – whether that somebody else is the heterosexual that orthodox religion would like you to be, or a *berdache*. It is about being more of who you are. Being queer can be the catalyst, and part of the fuel, for the journey. This book is full of examples of how people's sexuality has been a source of spiritual growth. The particular experience of being other-than-heterosexual in a heterosexist society has been a source, for these people, of universal insights; they have been led from queer to eternity.

Rabbi Elizabeth Sarah's vision – a universalism rooted in particularism – is shared by lesbian, gay and bisexual people from other traditions. 'The Holy Spirit of which each of us is an incarnation is the basis for community,' explains Harvey Gillman; 'or as the Quaker phrase has it, we "get to know each other in that which is eternal", which means our acceptance of each other is based on a profound acceptance of what we really are.'[17] For Father Bill reconciliation is achieved by 'coming to terms with oneself, so that one may reach out to others and allow them to reach out to us, through the mutuality of our wounds, our own imperfections.' Dylan, training for the Anglican priesthood, balances the fact that everyone has 'the same basic needs, the same basic experiences', with an acknowledgement of our 'individual gifts and insights'. Adam James, at the same time that he argues spirituality is universal and cannot be specific to any social group, says that it is inevitably personal and individual as well: 'we all come from different ways. It's like there are many different languages, but they are all talking about the same thing.' It is the argument propounded in earlier chapters, as the first line of defence against religions that try to deny our experience: in the end we can only be ourselves. And yet, in being ourselves, we are more able to see what we have in common with others.

A still greater paradox is that we begin to realize ourselves only by being different from those around us. As Harvey Gillman puts it, 'I am what I am because you are what you are'.[18] He writes about the strength that minority members can gain from each other; similarly, Niall Johnston thinks that 'a ghetto which we have been put in can be an incredibly creative experience in terms of self-discovery'.[19] Yet Niall also says 'being in a ghetto which we have put ourselves in will limit our potential for growth – it will constrain us and stop us being truly free'. We can and should work with the differences we discover in ourselves – we certainly should not be ashamed of them – but to seek to make them the centre of our lives is to miss the point. Our differences are not all there is to discover. They lead us on to our similarities. Queer leads to eternity.

Up to a point, this debate is merely a question of emphasis. Essentialism emphasizes the ways in which we are different; this conclusion, drawing more on social-construction arguments, emphasizes how much is shared. Except these are not, in the final analysis, equal alternatives; it seems to me that one is a more accurate position than the other, that the particular is ultimately subservient to the universal. This book begins with a quote from Oscar Moore's *A Matter of Life and Sex*. Hugo realizes he has not asked what really matters: 'who the fuck are you, instead of who are you fucking?'[20] The latter is merely a question of sexual identity; what Hugo thinks is 'too dangerous' to ask is the (potentially) spiritual question: who am I? That question has preoccupied some of the human race for a very long time, and the proposed answers gesture beyond time. Sexual identity, as we understand it, is a concept that is historically and culturally highly specific; social constructionism helps us see the ways in which the invention of 'homosexuality' is bound up with the last few centuries of Western culture. 'Queer' won't be around for eternity: what frightens me about essentialism is its assumption that it will be, the deeply conservative and rather arrogant idea that humans have been and will always be basically the same as they are in a few Western cultures in the late twentieth century. The homosexual as a 'type' of human being is temporal, maybe temporary. Spirituality, though it works in the temporal and with the practical, is about infinity – and the timeless.

I could be entirely wrong about this. I am sure some of the contributors to this book would disagree with me. Some would feel that to talk of universalism or transcendence is to indulge in the sort of religious escapism that coming out has saved them from. For others, like Lev, there is no conflict. 'I don't think the notion that queer people are a separate species, and that on the other hand we're all essentially the same, are exclusive notions. There's enough about me because I'm gay that makes me completely different; as gay men we have cultural norms and values which set us apart, they might be very broad, and expressed in different ways, but I feel that we do. Yet at the end of the day, everyone on the planet is part of the same thing.'

At the same time I find some justification for my arguments in something else that Lev said to me. 'When I've felt most spiritually connected is when I've had the strongest and clearest sense of my core being, rather than being a Jew, being a gay man, being a professional, being white, whatever. It's what's underneath that.'

This is a final irony: that the sexual identity we have fought so hard for becomes, in the silence of meditation or prayer, just another part of the psychological baggage that we need to leave behind.

I AM WHAT I AM (AGAIN)

When God is revealed to Moses in the burning bush, Moses suggests that the people of Israel will be curious to know what God is actually called. God replies with words from Harvey Fierstein's libretto for *La Cage Aux Folles*: 'I am what I am.' (Perhaps Yahweh also speaks with the *voice* of Harvey Fierstein – deep-throated, Jewish, and permanently on the verge of exasperation?) We have seen that, spiritually as well as socially, life is not worth a damn until you can say, I am what I am; until we acknowledge the truth of our being. We can say (as, indeed, could the creator God) – that 'it's my world, and it's not a place I have to hide in'. But God's answer, in the story, is curious and (as we might expect from an omniscient being) rather canny. It actually represents a refusal to be named, a refusal to be limited to any single identity. In response to Moses's (perhaps rather presumptuous) question, what matters is not *who* God is but *that* God is. It's like the distinction that gay mystic Ram Dass makes between 'being' (which is what God does) and 'being somebody' (which is what we spend most of our lives trying to do).[21] This is not, one suspects, what the people of Israel wanted to hear. And quickly, God's refusal to give a name becomes God's name: YHWH, Yahweh, means 'I am'. As usual, religion pins down, categorizes – and ultimately limits and misinterprets – the ineffable and inexpressible.

Perhaps we make a similar mistake when we keep identifying ourselves as lesbian, gay or bisexual. Coming out is a glorious insight into our own sense of being. But we think that what we have found is our identity, our name; instead of a signpost that points to the greater truth: the fact that, in many further ways, we are more than the culture around us would lead us to believe. The 'I am what I am' of the song is a statement of certainty and closure: this is the 'me', warts and all, that you can judge (with hook or ovation). God's 'I am what I am' is a statement of a continuing process – some scholars have suggested that 'I will be what I will be' is a closer translation. God is a verb, not a noun; and so are we.[22] We think 'I am what I am' is the conclusion, whereas it may be just the beginning. It doesn't stop at this. Our real identity is beyond identity.

We can never say too often that it's OK to be gay. It will be many generations before we fully, unquestioningly believe this message ourselves, let alone persuade everyone else. Wherever there is a homophobe, or someone in the closet, it is very important to identify as lesbian or gay or bisexual or queer. There is nothing to be gained – politically or spiritually – by 'passing'. But if we are to live our lives to their full potential, then we must not allow ourselves to be limited to an identity that has been formed in reaction to hostility, that defines us in terms of what we are not. For our own sakes, we must find out what we truly are. A single act of honesty – coming out – does not absolve us from the fuller truth that sets us free. We must come out inside; we must bring more and more of ourselves out of the closet. And in doing so, we may find that 'we' cease to be 'us' – at least the us that equals a collective of queers. To get to 'eternity' (or at least that which is eternal within us) we have to move on from here – and move on from queer.

This is a difficult task, perhaps more difficult than fighting the homophobia around us, maybe even more challenging than our first coming out – because the first time, for many of us, there was a ready-made identity to adopt, and a group to come into, but this time there is not – and perhaps, cannot be. Having already disengaged from one set of social programming – when we broke loose from the straight world – we may be daunted by the prospect of having to move on again, this time from the orthodoxies and dogma of queer culture: but this may be necessary, if we are to find true authenticity.

WHAT DO WE WANT?

'Vaishnavism says you get what you want,' says Greg, a follower of the Hindu philosophy. 'That's a very profound statement. If you want sex, you get sex, that's all. If you want a relationship, you get what you're prepared to give to it. And if you want what you truly are – in Vaishnavism, you are within your inner being a part of God – you get that.'

'If the gay community is going to go anywhere,' reckons Maitreya-bandhu, 'the next step is a spiritual one. You can only fully come out if you can integrate being gay into a wider, overarching aim.'

So what do we want? What do we choose? We're here, we're queer – but dare we aim for eternity?

Notes

1. *Buddha's Teachings*, translated by Jan Mascaró (London: Penguin Classics, 1995), p. 1.
2. Richard Woods, *Another Kind of Love: Homosexuality and Spirituality* (Fort Wayne: Knoll Publishing Co., 1988), p. 129.
3. John J. McNeill, *Taking a Chance on God: Liberating Theology for Gays, Lesbians, and Their Lovers, Families*

and Friends (Boston: Beacon Press, 1988), p. 18.

4. Jim Cotter, *Good Fruits: Same Sex Relationships and Christian Faith* (Exeter: Cairns Publications, 1988), p. 16.

5. Cotter, *Good Fruits*, p. 16.

6. Harvey Gillman, *A Minority of One* (London: Quaker Home Service, 1988), p. 105.

7. Rabbi Lionel Blue, *Godly and Gay* (London: Gay Christian Movement, 1981), p. 7.

8. 'You're asking me to look into the crystal ball, which I shouldn't.'

9. Edward Carpenter 'Intermediate Types Amongst Primitive Folk' in *Selected Writings, Volume 1: Sex* (London: Gay Men's Press, 1984), p. 273.

10. Mark Thompson, *Gay Soul* (San Francisco: HarperSanFrancisco, 1995), pp. 178, 3.

11. Thompson, *Gay Soul*, p. 5.

12. Thompson, *Gay Soul*, p. 4.

13. To be fair, I should stress that some contributors to this book would very much agree with Thompson's overall arguments.

14. I have yet to be convinced that any characteristic is 'objectively' male or female, and so I cannot believe that lesbian and gay people are born with a particularly judicious mixture of these masculine and feminine traits. I think it is far more plausible to reason that, because the dominant culture has partially ostracized us due to our sexual difference, it is unable to police gender roles so strictly as it does for people who find themselves nearer the centre of power. Gay men and lesbians are 'allowed' to show emotions and abilities because we've already forfeited hetero-social approval. There is no reason to imagine that exactly the same emotions and abilities are not available to our heterosexual counterparts; they are repressed by social forces, not by evolution. Our freedom from gender roles is, of course, by no means complete – it is curtailed partly by the conditioning we received as children, and partly by the alternative orthodoxies, and consequent policing of identity, that are formed amongst ourselves – and in reaction to the society we have left behind.

15. Gillman, *A Minority Of One*, p. 106.

16. Gillman, *A Minority of One*, p. 106.

17. Gillman, *A Minority of One*, p. 108.

18. Gillman, *A Minority of One*, p. 108.

19. This raises the possibility that in a future where sexual difference is no longer perceived to be significant, people would not have the same catalyst for self-realisation that is presented to modern queers. At least, this is a possibility for those of us who believe that the significance of our difference is socially constructed: essentialists would argue that sexual orientation will always be important. We can hardly argue that homophobes should stay around because they're good for our souls; but without homophobia, Fernando suggests, 'it might well be that we will cease to become interesting as a community.' I suspect that the absence of homophobia is not something that we will have to consider for some time to come.

20. Oscar Moore, *A Matter of Life and Sex* (London: Penguin, 1992) p. 209.

21. Ram Dass is a spiritual teacher based in America. Formerly a psychologist named Richard Alpert, he was kicked out of Harvard for experimenting with LSD. Psychedelic experiences eventually led him to India, where he found his Hindu guru, experienced an extraordinary personal transformation, and gained the name Ram Dass (which means

'Servant of God'). His books include *Grist for the Mill* and *Be Here Now*. He is one of the figures interviewed in Mark Thompson's *Gay Soul*.

22. From Northrop Frye, *The Great Code*, as quoted in Lucinda Vardey (ed.), *God in All Words: An Anthology of Creative Spiritual Writing* (London: Chatto & Windus, 1995), p. 6.

Select Bibliography

Balka, Christie and Rose, Andy (1989) *Twice Blessed: On Being Lesbian or Gay and Jewish*. Boston: Beacon Press.

Blue, Lionel (1994) *A Backdoor to Heaven*. London: Fount Paperbacks.

Boswell, John (1980) *Christianity, Social Tolerance and Homosexuality: Gay People in Western Europe from the Beginning of the Christian Era to the Fourteenth Century*. Chicago: University of Chicago Press.

Boswell, John (1995) *The Marriage of Likeness: Same-Sex Unions in Pre-modern Europe*. London: HarperCollins.

Bouldrey, Brian (ed.) (1995) *Wrestling With the Angel: Faith and Religion in the Lives of Gay Men*. New York: Riverhead Books.

Cabezón, José Ignacio (1992) *Buddhism, Sexuality and Gender*. Albany: SUNY Press.

Carpenter, Edward (1984) *Selected Writings, Volume 1: Sex*. London: Gay Men's Press.

Conner, Randy (1993) *Blossom of Bone: Reclaiming the Connections Between Homoeroticism and the Sacred*. San Francisco: HarperSanFrancisco.

Cotter, Jim (1988) *Good Fruits: Same Sex Relationships and Christian Faith*. Exeter: Cairns Publications.

Cotter, Jim (1993) *Pleasure, Pain and Passion: Some Perspectives on Sexuality and Spirituality*. Sheffield: Cairns Publications.

Evans, Arthur (1978) *Witchcraft and the Gay Counterculture: A Radical View of Western Civilization and Some of the People It Has Tried to Destroy*. Boston: FAG RAG Books.

Gillman, Harvey (1988) *A Minority of One: A Journey With Friends*. London: Quaker Home Service.

Glaser, Chris (1994) *The Word is Out: The Bible Reclaimed for Lesbians and Gay Men*. San Francisco: HarperSanFrancisco.

Goss, Robert (1994) *Jesus Acted Up: A Gay and Lesbian Manifesto*. San Francisco: HarperSanFrancisco.

Herrman, Bert (1990) *Being, Being Happy, Being Gay*. San Francisco: Alamo Square Press.

Heyward, Carter (1989) *Touching Our Strength: The Erotic as Power and the Love of God*. San Francisco: HarperCollins.

Loudon, Mary (1993) *Unveiled*. London: Vintage.

Loudon, Mary (1994) *Revelations – The Clergy Questioned*. London: Hamish Hamilton.

Lynch, Father Bernard (1993) *A Priest on Trial*. London: Bloomsbury.

Magonet, Jonathan (1995) *Jewish Explorations of Sexuality*. Oxford: Berghahn Books.

Mariechild, Diane and Martin, Marcelina (1995) *Lesbian Sacred Sexuality*. Oakland, CA: Wingbow.

McNeill, John J. (1988) *Taking a Chance on God: Liberating Theology for Gays, Lesbians, and their Lovers, Families and Friends*. Boston: Beacon Press.

Nelson, James B. and Longfellow, Sandra P. (eds) (1994) *Sexuality and The Sacred: Sources for Theological Reflection*. London: Mowbray.

Nine Friends (1995) *This We Can Say: Talking Honestly about Sex*. Reading: Nine Friends Press.

O'Neill, Craig and Ritter, Kathleen (1992) *Coming Out Within: Stages of Spiritual Awakening for Lesbians and Gay Men*. San Fransisco: HarperSanFransisco.

Paterson, Michael Seán (1997) *Singing For Our Lives: Positively Gay and Christian*. Sheffield: Cairns Publications.

Pierce, John (1992) *Sex and Spirit*. Drewsteignton: Charisma Books.

Roscoe, Will (1995) *Queer Spirits: A Gay Men's Myth Book*. Boston: Beacon Press.

Simpson, Mark (1996) *Anti-gay*. London: Freedom Editions.

Stevens, John (1990) *Lust for Enlightenment: Buddhism and Sex*. London: Shambhala.

Stuart, Elizabeth (1992) *Daring To Speak Love's Name: A Gay and Lesbian Prayer Book*. London: Hamish Hamilton.

Stuart, Elizabeth (1995) *Just Good Friends: Towards a Lesbian and Gay Theology of Relationships*. London: Mowbray.

Swidler, Arlene (1993) *Homosexuality and the World's Religions*. Valley Forge: Trinity Press International.

Thompson, Mark (1987) *Gay Spirit: Myth and Meaning*. New York: St Martin's Press.

Thompson, Mark (1995) *Gay Soul: Finding the Heart of Gay Spirit and Nature with Sixteen Writers, Healers, Teachers, and Visionaries*. San Francisco: HarperSanFrancisco.

Vasey, Michael (1995) *Strangers and Friends: A New Exploration of Homosexuality and the Bible*. London: Hodder & Stoughton.

Webster, Alison R. (1995) *Found Wanting: Women, Christianity and Sexuality*. London: Cassell.

Williams, The Rev. Robert (1992) *Just as I Am: A Practical Guide to Being Out, Proud, and Christian*. New York: Crown Publishers.

Wilson, Nancy (1995) *Our Tribe: Queer Folks, God, Jesus, and the Bible*. San Francisco: HarperSanFrancisco.

Woods, Richard (1988) *Another Kind of Love: Homosexuality and Spirituality*. Fort Wayne: Knoll Publishing Co.

Woodward, James (ed.) (1991) *Embracing the Chaos: Theological Responses to AIDS*. London: SPCK.

Yearly Meeting of the Religious Society of Friends (Quakers) in Britain (1994) *Quaker Faith and Practice*. London: Quakers.

Young, Ian (1995) *The Stonewall Experiment: A Gay Psychohistory*. London: Cassell.

Index

The spiritual tradition followed by individuals who personally contributed to this book is indicated in brackets. Pseudonyms are given in italics.